D1256260

"ALADDIN"

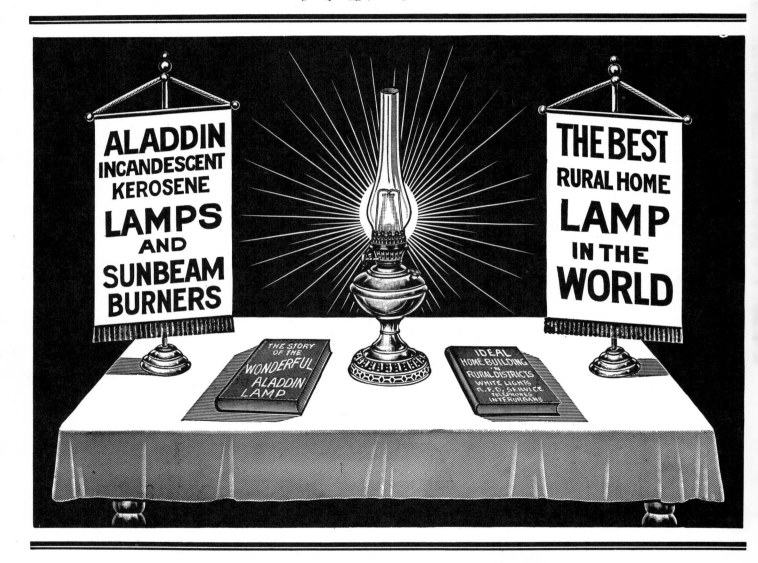

THE MANTLE LAMP COMPANY OF AMERICA

CHICAGO, U. S. A.

Branch Offices:

Waterbury, Conn.   Portland, Ore.   Montreal, Can.   Winnipeg, Can.

THE MAGIC NAME IN LAMPS

Aladdin Kerosene Mantle Lamps,

Aladdin Electric Lamps,

and Alacite by Aladdin

by

J. W. Courter

Printed in the United States of America
by Wallace-Homestead Co.
1912 Grand Ave., Des Moines, Iowa 50305

A NOTE ABOUT THE AUTHOR

John Wilson (Bill) Courter is a collector of Aladdin kerosene and electric lamps. He grew up in Ocean View, New Jersey and while he enjoyed the benefits of electricity, some of his neighbors did not. After moving to southern Illinois the nostalgia of Aladdin light captured his interest. Electric high lines invaded rural areas there in the early 1940's and nearly every household had one or more Aladdin lamps gathering dust in storage.

He is an Associate Professor of Horticulture at the University of Illinois and is the author of numerous publications in his agricultural specialty.

Additional copies of this book may be obtained from the author

J. W. Courter
RR 2
Simpson, Ill. 62985

To Mary, Kathryn and David

CONTENTS

ACKNOWLEDGMENTS

The author wishes to express his sincere thanks and deepest appreciation to the persons who gave him valuable information, assistance, and encouragement in writing this book. Special thanks to V. S. Johnson, Jr., and Aladdin Industries, Inc., for their full cooperation and permission to reprint catalogs, advertising, and photographs. This book could not have been written without their generous help. Compiling information was a labor of love made especially pleasurable by many new friends: Earl Durr, Herman Durr, Andrew C. Elbert, Jr., Frank Field, John Green, Roy W. Hall, Henry T. Hellmers, Ralph High, S. B. Huse, Ed Kriel, Anne Lawrason, Mrs. Ruth McConnell, Wallace Meissner, Ernest O. Phillips, J. L. Piot, A. von Plachecki, Willard Presba, Rollo T. Rexroat, Vesta Rinnman, Marquis M. Smith, Tom Teeter especially for his unbounded interest and enthusiasm for my project, Ken and Aggie Thatcher, and Harold Warp.

Thanks to Margery Suhre and Gladys D. Wilke for their editorial assistance, Jerry Richardson and Ray Evans for photography, and Bob Lyon, printing director.

Thanks are due also to the many collectors who have helped along the way by sharing their collections and their knowledge with the author.

The sources of photographs and illustrative literature that appear in this book follow:

Aladdin Industries, Inc.—Figures 1, 3, 5, 8, 12, 13, 18, 23, 24, 25, 28, 39, 42, 46, 48, 67, 68, 69, 71, 72, 73, 74, 75, advertisements appearing on pages 5, 46, 55, 58, 59, detail drawings on pages 65-79 and catalogs on pages 129-136, 143-154
The Baltimore Sunday Sun—Figures 16, 17
Roy W. Hall—Figures 2, 4, 14, 15
Koopman-Neumer, Inc.—Figures 21, 22, 27, 30, 37, 38, 49-66, and catalogs appearing on pages 155-164
Glenn Leathery—Frontispiece and catalogs on pages 87-97, 118
Ernest O. Phillips—Figure 47
Presba-Muench, Inc.-advertisements appearing on pages 5, 57
E. W. Pyfer—advertisement appearing on page 63. Catalogs appearing on pages 139, 140
Rollo T. Rexroat—Advertisements appearing on page 53, catalogs on pages 85, 86
Jerry Richardson—Figures 3, 12, 13, 39, 42, 67, 68, 76
Ray Evans—Figure 45

The following figures show items from collections courtesy of:
Aladdin Industries—Figures 6, 7, 70
Mrs. Vance Collins—Figures 41, 43
Earl Durr—Figure 13
Mr. and Mrs. Ernest O. Phillips—Figures 39, 42, 43
Pearl Street—Figure 40
Tom Teeter—Figures 39, 42, cover
Ken and Aggie Thatcher—Figure 45

To everyone who has helped, I am grateful.
J. W. Courter
Simpson, Illinois

FOREWORD

by V. S. Johnson, Jr., President
Aladdin Industries, Incorporated

Eighty years ago a very small boy on a Nebraska farm read and reread the Arabian Night's story of Aladdin in a room of darkness but for the flickering yellow light of an open flame "coal oil lamp." Several years later that boy, grown to manhood, found a lamp that erased the darkness with a soft white light and it was only natural that he named the lamp "Aladdin." An appropriate name, indeed, for this revolutionary boon to rural America seemed to be nothing short of magical in the intensity of its light.

For those who lit the lamp, trimmed its wick and cleaned its chimney, or just enjoyed its friendly glow, the Aladdin lamp recalls many memories of golden childhood. It made learning possible for many boys and girls; made it possible for them to acquire knowledge that helped them realize their dreams and aspirations.

Later, Aladdin brought this white light to every kind of habitat in every corner of the globe. For many, it has been the only light of their entire life. Even when electricity comes, there are a loyal few who profess to use the electric light only "to find the match" to light their Aladdin.

When I read Professor Courter's book, it not only brought back the nostalgic memories identified with our company's early days and the people who shaped them, but also disclosed much about Aladdin's past that only the inspired resourcefulness and dedication of the author could reconstruct.

I am grateful that he became enamoured with the Aladdin Lamp as a part of Americana. I hope that this book will help you share with him his interest in this part of our prairie past and perhaps you, too, can enjoy not only beginning your Aladdin collection, but adding to its history.

ALADDIN — THE MAGIC NAME IN LAMPS

Aladdin Kerosene Mantle Lamps, Aladdin Electric Lamps, and Alacite by Aladdin

J. W. Courter

INTRODUCTION

There were few country roads in 1909, only well-marked ruts and trails for horses and wagons. Over one-half of the ninety-two million people in the United States lived in small towns or on farms. Most of them had never even seen an automobile. Rural homes did not have conveniences now taken for granted—central heat, rural mail delivery, telephones, running water, indoor bathrooms, or good lighting. Among the many changes that were to come was the bright white light of the Aladdin Mantle Lamp.

The lamp culminated five decades of invention that began when Colonel E. L. Drake drilled the first oil well in Pennsylvania in 1859. Over 1000 gallons of petroleum a day gushed from the well and the price dropped from one dollar per gallon to one dollar per barrel (42 gallons). The resulting plentiful supply of lighting oils, called kerosene, coal oil, and paraffin, stimulated research on lighting devices. During the ensuing years nearly one hundred patents per year were granted for improvements in kerosene-burning lamps.

The popular kerosene lamps in the 1890's used round wicks. They were constructed on the Argand principle of supplying air to the flame through a central draft tube. The round wick provided a larger burning surface and gave more light but it consumed more oil than the common flat wick lamp. Furthermore, the flame was yellow, it flickered, and the lamp emitted smoke and odor in the home. Nevertheless, these lamps were an improvement in kerosene lighting.

Meanwhile in Europe, Baron Carl Freiherr Auer von Welsbach, an Austrian chemist, invented the incandescent mantle. Welsbach received his first mantle patent September 23, 1885. By 1890 he had developed a mantle-impregnating formula which has remained virtually unchanged ever since.

Fig. 1—Aladdin mantle lamp. Model No. 1.

Finally the incandescent mantle was coupled with the "Argand" burner to give the brightest white light ever produced from kerosene. One American lamp—the Aladdin —demonstrated the superiority of this combination more than any other lamp. It was without question the leader in kerosene incandescent home lighting for more than fifty years.

CHAPTER 1

JOHNSON'S VISION

The man who was to make the Aladdin Mantle Lamp a household word throughout America was Victor Samuel Johnson. Born February 6, 1882, in a sod farmhouse five miles south of Minden, Nebraska, he grew up on that farm, studying his school lessons by the weak flame of a common kerosene lamp. He learned his lessons well, and by 1904 was a bookkeeper and salesman for the Iowa Soap Company in Burlington, Iowa.

In 1905 Johnson first saw the superior light produced by a German kerosene mantle burner, the "Practicus." Remembering the flickering light he studied by as a youth, he recognized the potential for sales of mantle lamps in rural areas. At last people without electricity could have good light.

Two years later, Victor Johnson gave up his steady job to form the Western Lighting Company in Kansas City, Missouri. The company imported and sold the Practicus, foreign-made mantles, and other foreign alcohol-burning lamps. Soon after the Practicus was successfully introduced at a hardware dealers' convention in Kansas City, Johnson moved the business to Chicago. In 1908 he changed the name and incorporated the Mantle Lamp Company of America.

Properly adjusted, the Practicus produced white light of about 60 candlepower. The burner was designed to fit common American-made lamp fonts. However, the Practicus frequently smoked and generally proved unreliable. Because of these shortcomings, Johnson searched for an improved mantle lamp.

This improved lamp became a reality when Johnson acquired the patent for a new lamp burner from Charles E. Wirth (assignor to Plume and Atwood Manufacturing Company, Waterbury, Connecticut). Early in 1909, Johnson introduced the Aladdin lamp. He derived the name from the famous story of "Aladdin and His Wonderful Lamp."

The initial sales of the Aladdin were beyond all expectations. It was so much more efficient than other mantle lamps—to say nothing of the conventional flat and round

Fig. 2—Victor Samuel Johnson, 1882-1943.

Fig. 3—Practicus table lamp from original 1907 inventory, Rexroat Bros., Virginia, Illinois.

Fig. 4—Officers of the Mantle Lamp Company. Seated (left to right): Bert S. Presba, Advertising Manager; H. O. Johnson, Sales; Victor Samuel Johnson, President; Charles H. Smith, Vice President; and Theodore French. Standing (left to right): Mr. Weaver, Mr. Kellstedt and Mr. Buettner, regional office managers. Photograph circa 1911. Other officers (not pictured) during the company's early years were Adolph H. Glantz, Treasurer, and W. H. F. Millar, Secretary and Attorney.

Fig. 5—The Chicago home office, June 1909.

wick lamps of the day—that it quickly made all other kerosene lamps obsolete. Soon the Aladdin could be found in nearly all parts of the United States and Canada, and ultimately it made its way around the world.

Remembering the short commercial life of the Practicus, Johnson established a small research department early in the history of the company. His recognition of the need for improving quality through research was ahead of the times. Today, the Research and Development Department is considered vital by virtually all manufacturers.

Undoubtedly the preeminence of the Aladdin through a half-century of competition was due to the continual development of improved models to provide dependable operation, increased illumination, greater safety, and, in general, a "foolproof" lamp. These achievements were largely the results of research accomplishments of Charles H. Smith, Cortland W. Davis, W. B. Engh, and Fred Spangler. The first major breakthrough was Model No. 3, patented in 1911 by Charles H. Smith (assignor to the Mantle Lamp Company of America, Chicago, Illinois). This model featured a new air distributor or gasifier (flame spreader), a combined mantle cap and burner cone (KoneKap Mantle), and improved burner construction for proper mixture of air and kerosene vapor. The KoneKap Mantle was the first mantle to be made by the company itself, Models 1 and 2 having used foreign-made mantles. The

company has continued to make its own mantles throughout the rest of its history. It also furnished mantles for competitive lamps as well as the Aladdin (see pages 135 and 136).

In 1915, Model 6 earned a gold medal and a blue ribbon in competition at the Panama-Pacific International Exposition at San Francisco. The Mantle Lamp Company boldly proclaimed the Aladdin as the best kerosene lamp in the world. An offer of $1000 was made for any oil-burning lamp that could equal the Aladdin in twenty-six important features. This offer was never collected. See page 113 for more information on Aladdin's challenge to the world.

In 1926, the Mantle Lamp Company acquired the Lippincott Glass Company plant on the outskirts of Alexandria, Indiana. A new, large, modern factory was built on the ten-acre site which was later incorporated as a village with the name Aladdin.

The new factory was built at a time when the market for lamps was increasing. As the 1930's approached, an estimated six million farm homes still depended on kerosene or gas for lighting. Acquisition of the Indiana facilities enabled the company to carry out its plans for introducing even better lamps than previous models.

The development of improved Nu-Type side-draft burners in 1932-34 permitted the use of glass for lower cost and also more flexibility for design of fonts. In the ten-year

Fig. 6, 7—The obverse (left) and reverse (right) of the gold medal, 70 mm in diameter, awarded to the Mantle Lamp Company at the Panama-Pacific International Exposition in 1915.

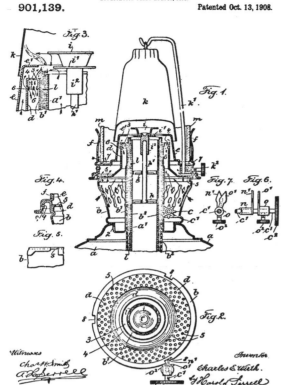

C. H. SMITH.
COMBINED MANTLE CAP AND BURNER CONE FOR INCANDESCENT VAPOR GAS LAMPS.
APPLICATION FILED JULY 8, 1910.

988,902.

Patented Apr. 4, 1911.
2 SHEETS—SHEET 2.

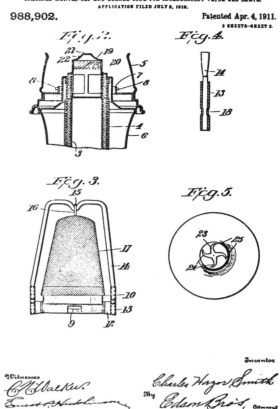

C. H. SMITH.
BURNER FOR INCANDESCENT VAPOR GAS LAMPS.
APPLICATION FILED JULY 8, 1910.

987,022.

Patented Mar. 14, 1911.
2 SHEETS—SHEET 1.

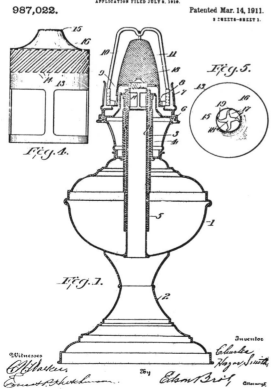

C. H. SMITH.
BURNER FOR INCANDESCENT VAPOR GAS LAMPS.
APPLICATION FILED JULY 8, 1910.

987,022.

Patented Mar. 14, 1911.
2 SHEETS—SHEET 2.

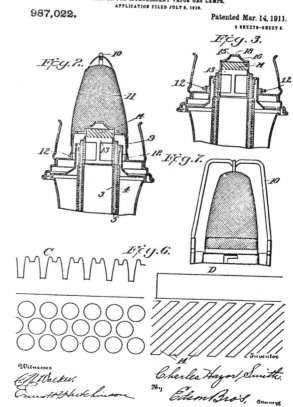

4

period following introduction of Nu-Type burners, Aladdin produced its most beautiful glass kerosene table lamps. (See Chapter 2, "The Colorful Years.")

In 1937, the Ohio River left its banks to flood Louisville, Cincinnati, and other river towns. The emergency call for light was answered by the Mantle Lamp Company. Through the Red Cross, the warehouses were emptied and kerosene mantle lamps were rushed to give life-saving light to thousands stranded without power.

Kerosene lamp-manufacturing operations, by now greatly reduced, were moved from Alexandria to Nashville, Tennessee, in 1952. Domestic manufacture of kerosene fonts came to an end in 1968. However, Aladdin Industries continues to manufacture lamps in England and Brazil to supply worldwide demand. At one time, Aladdins were also made in Argentina and Rumania.

Fig. 8—Model B Aladdin table lamp made in 1939.

Models of Aladdin Kerosene Lamps

Sixteen models of Aladdin lamps were made in the United States from 1909 to 1968. In addition, Models 14 (the Super Aladdin), 21, 21C, and 23 (current) were made in England. Model C lamps, currently manufactured in Brazil, are for sale in domestic and international markets. They utilize a modified Model C burner with both glass and metal fonts.

The brass lamps (font and burner) for Models 1 through 12 and the burners for Nu-Type A, Nu-Type B, and C were made by Plume and Atwood Manufacturing Company, Waterbury, Connecticut. Starting with Model 12, American operations of making mantles, wicks, chimneys, and shades were concentrated at the new plant in Alexandria, Indiana. The fonts for Model C were manufactured by Aladdin Industries in Nashville.

Models 1 through 12 were made of brass finished in bright nickel, satin brass, or dark Old English. Models A and B are made

MODELS OF PRACTICUS & ALADDIN KEROSENE LAMPS SOLD IN THE UNITED STATES FROM 1908 TO PRESENT

MODEL	YEARS SOLD				MONTHS SOLD
Practicus No. 3	May,	1908	— April,	1909	12
1	May,	1909	— August,	1910	16
2	September,	1910	— December,	1910	4
3	January,	1911	— August,	1912	20
4	September,	1912	— August,	1913	12
5	September,	1913	— August,	1914	12
6*	September,	1914	— July,	1917	35
7	August,	1917	— July,	1919	24
8	August,	1919	— August,	1920	13
9	August,	1920	— August,	1922	25
10	May,	1921	— August,	1922	16
11	September,	1922	— May,	1928	68
12**	May,	1928	— April,	1935	84
A	May,	1932	— December,	1932	8
B	February,	1933	— September,	1955	272
C	October,	1955	— April,	1963	91
21C	May,	1963	— December,	1969	79
23	December,	1969	— Present		

*In addition, Model #6 was sold in Canada instead of Models #7 and #8

**A substantial number of Model 12 burners, marked Nashville, Tennessee, were made for the export market from 1949 to 1955.

Be Wise Aladdinize and Save your Eyes

primarily of glass. Model C was made of aluminum with a satin or polished finish. Models 21C and 23 have polished brass or Silcrom (nickel type) finishes.

The first four models are identified primarily by changes in design, although "Model No. 3" is marked on the gallery of that model. Distinguishing construction details of these early models are given on pages 65-77. Starting with Model 5, the model number or letter was placed on the wick-raising button.

The Mantle Lamp Company also sold two side-draft kerosene burners with adapters to fit ordinary lamp fonts. The Sunbeam burner, introduced in 1909, was superseded by the Lumineer, Model A, in 1912. These burners permitted convenient conversion of open flame lamps to mantle lamps by persons who wished to continue to use their old lamp base. See pages 135-136 for more information on the Sunbeam and Lumineer.

Fig. 9 — Models of Aladdin kerosene mantle lamps.

Top Row:

| | Practicus | Model No. 1 | Model No. 2 | Model No. 3 |

Bottom Row:

| | Model No. 4 | Model No. 5 (Transition) | Model No. 5 | Model No. 6 |

Note: There also are Model No. 3 transition lamps.

Fig. 10—Models of Aladdin kerosene mantle lamps.

Top Row:

        Model No. 7   Model No. 8   Model No. 9   Model No. 10

Bottom Row:

        Model No. 11   Model No. 12   Model A   Model B

Note: Model No. 12 burners are often found on Model No. 11 fonts.

Fig. 11—Models of Aladdin kerosene mantle lamps.

Electric   Model C   Model 21C   Model 23
(circa 1950)

Fig. 12—Lamp font made in Brazil of glass and aluminum, discontinued in 1971.

Fig. 13—The Aladdinette Everlasting Candle, circa 1930, served as a night light or as a vaporizer for a child's room.

Fig. 14—The railroad caboose lamp filled a great need for dependable light in railroad cabooses. It was developed by Roy W. Hall and first introduced in 1937.

Fig. 15—The first installation of the Aladdin caboose lamp. Looking on are the conductor and brakeman who pointed out the need for better light and helped in the testing of the prototype models.

Fig. 16, 17—The heart of the Turkey Point Light House in Maryland is its lens illuminated by an Aladdin lamp in 1939. Aladdin lamps were also kept ready in case of power failures in electrically lighted lighthouses.

Fig. 18—Making glass lamp shades at Alexandria, Indiana, circa 1930. (Right to left): two ton day tank, ball gatherer (gathers glass on rod), ball boy (rolls glass into ball), blocker (enlarges ball by gathering more glass), blower (blows glass shade in mold), mold boy (partially hidden), and carry-in boy (checking weight of shade on scale).

11

Lamp Shades

Glass lamp shades were especially designed for Aladdin lamps from 1908 through 1942 (Table page 13). A distinctive new type of shade introduced in 1920 consisted of a white dome and a clear crystal apron which allowed maximum lighting efficiency. Shades of this type were designed for Models 9, 11, 12, and B. Between 1927 and 1929, a relatively few of the domes were hand-decorated.

Shades and tripods sold as extra accessories, thus increasing the cost of an already expensive lamp. Therefore, shades were not purchased with each lamp. Attrition through the years has further increased the rarity of the original glass shades.

Beginning in 1928, parchment shades were made in a myriad of designs and colors. An improved washable parchment, developed to withstand the heat of the Aladdin, was introduced in 1934. It was named Whip-O-Lite after Adolph D. Whipple, the inventor. The patented Whip-O-Lite shades were a significant improvement over all other parchment shades of that era. Made without vegetable or mineral oil, the parchment did not oxidize or turn brown. Nor did it have a greasy feel or appearance. The translucence and diffusion of transmitted light eliminated glare and gave a soft, pleasing light.

More than 230 styles of scenic, floral, and plain parchment and Whip-O-Lite shades, often Parvelour decorated, were made in various shapes, sizes, and color combinations for the metal and glass kerosene lamps.

Today, the ever-popular cabin and duck designs of Whip-O-Lite shades are still available from Aladdin Industries. In addition, a new shade in the style of Aladdin 601 was put into production in 1971 (page 15). It is marked "Aladdin 12." This shade, available in several dome colors, is welcomed by collectors who cannot find the original shades.

ALADDIN PARCHMENT AND WHIP-O-LITE SHADES FOR KEROSENE LAMPS

Size (bottom diameter)	Years Sold	Kind of lamp	Models
15-inch	1928-1931	Table Lamps	12
20-inch	1928-1930	Vase Lamps	12
20½-inch	1928-1931	Floor Lamps	12
17½-inch	1931	Vase Lamps	12
16-inch	1932-1952	Vase and Floor Lamps	A, B
17-inch	1936-1942	Floor Lamps	B
14-inch	1932 to present	Table, Vase, and Hanging Lamps	A, B, C, 21C, 23
12-inch	1937 to present	Caboose Lamp	B, C, 21C, 23

Fig. 19, 20—Model No. 9 (left) and Model No. 11 (right) Aladdin lamps with original shades.

ALADDIN GLASS SHADES FOR KEROSENE LAMPS

Style No.	Size, Bottom Diameter (inches)	Description	Designed for Model	Illus. on Page
201	10	Fancy Opal Shade	Practicus & 1	x, 87, 95
(not listed)	10	Fancy Green Cased Shade for Parlor Lamp	1	87
203	14	Opal Dome for Hanging Lamp	1	95
204	10	Eight-sided Green Cased Shade for Parlor Lamp	3	95
205	8½	White Opal Shade	3	95, 138
206	8½	Art Glass Shade (also used for electric fixtures of the period)	3	95
215	12	White Opal Shade for Hanging Lamp	4, 5, 6	111, 138
301	10	Satin White, Chinese Chippendale	6	98, 110, 138
325	Ball	Satin White Globe with Hand Painted Rose Design for Hanging Lamp	6	110, 138
401	8¾	Artistic Satin White Shade	7, 8	118, 140
416	9¾	Artistic Satin White Shade for Hanging Lamp	7, 8	118, 140
501	10	Satin White Dome with Clear Crystal Prismatic Panels	9	12, 46, 140
501	10	Above design modified for Model 11	11	12
516	11¾	Satin White Design for Hanging Lamp	9, 10	142
550	10	Soft White and Shell Pink Tinted Shade with Medallions Showing Artistic Swiss Mountain Scenes	11	140
601	10	Satin White Dome with Clear Crystal Prismatic Form Apron (1927-1933)	12	15, 122, 124, 142
601 F, S	10	As above with Hand Decorated Dome (1927-1929) (F = Floral and S = Scenic Designs)	12	121, 124, 142
616	14	Satin White Dome with Clear Crystal Prismatic Apron for Hanging Lamps	12	16, 124, 126, 142
616 F, S	14	As above with Hand Decorated Dome (1927-1929) (F = Floral and S = Scenic Designs)	12	16, 125
620	14	Satin White Dome with 1-Inch Rim in Grecian Design for Hanging Lamps	12	142
620 F, S	14	As above with Hand Decorated Dome (1927-1929) (F = Floral and S = Scenic Designs)	12	16, 124
701 (A)	10	Soft Satin White Dome (1932-1942)	A, B	5, 129
701 (B)	10	As above with a Clear Crystal Hobnail Lower Panel. Illustrated in 1935 as new for Model B	B	130
716	14	White Opal Plain Dome for Hanging Lamps (1932-1942)	12	129
N-0392	10	White Swirl (1952-Present)	C	—
N-0393	10	Red Swirl (1952-Present)	C	—
N-0394	10	Green Swirl (1952-Present)	C	—
651, 661 671, 681 series	10	New production of style 601 signed "Aladdin 12" on the edge of the rim. Available in several dome colors and hand painted decoration (1971-Present)	23	15

Fig. 21, 22—Aladdin lamps were made in hanging and bracket (left) and floor styles (right) in addition to table lamps. Circa 1938.

Fig. 23, 24—Parchment 14-inch shades, wild duck scene (left) and log cabin scene (right). 1971.

14

Fig. 25—"Aladdin 12" glass shades are available in several colors. (1971):

N-651 Red   (Opal)
N-652 Green (Opal)
N-653 White (Opal)
N-671 Satin White
N-672 Satin Champagne
N-673 Antique Gold
N-674 Satin Green
N-675 Satin Blue
N-681 Satin White with Hand Painted Dogwood
N-682 Satin White with Hand Painted Violets
N-683 Satin White with Hand Painted Roses

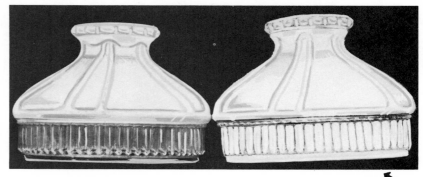

Fig. 26—The new Aladdin 12 Shade (right) is signed on the lower rim edge (arrow). In addition the new shades differ from the original 601 Shade (left) in the design around the upper portion of the shade as well as having a fully colored apron.

15

Fig. 27—Model No. 12 hanging lamp and shades, circa 1928. Top: Shade No. 616s; Bottom: (left) Shade No. 616, (right) Shade No. 620s.

CHAPTER 2

THE COLORFUL YEARS

Some of the most colorful and collectible kerosene lamps ever produced were made by the Mantle Lamp Company beginning in the 1930's. The glass fonts brought the price of lamps down and more people were able to afford them. The company enjoyed some of its best years during this period.

New styles of pattern glass lamps designed for Nu-Type model burners were introduced each year. Fifteen different glass lamps were made as well as two all-metal lamps, two combination glass and metal lamps, and one china lamp (see pages 20-36). They were manufactured at Alexandria, Indiana, except for a china font, which was made by the Metallic Arts Company, Mayfield, Kentucky; and clear crystal lamps made in Fairmount, Indiana (see page 30).

The glass lamps were made of clear and colored crystal, moonstone art glass, and Alacite. The colors of the first glass lamps (Nu-Type Model A) were fired on clear crystal. Subsequently, green and amber were common colors of many different styles, as was clear crystal.

In 1935, Henry T. Hellmers, a specialist in colored glass, was employed as Superintendent of the Glass Department of the Mantle Lamp Company (1935-1942). Hellmers developed several colors of moonstone glass for Aladdin kerosene lamps. White, green, and pink moonstone (a misty translucent glass similar to true moonstone) became popular in several lamp styles. Yellow moonstone, first sold during 1938, apparently was unpopular as the lamps were later offered as a special to reduce unsold stock. Lamps made of moonstone, particularly those with heavy metal bases, as well as lamps made of brilliant ruby and cobalt blue crystal, were higher in original sales price than the clear and more common colored glass lamps. They are shown in sales catalogs and literature, pages 129-134.

Most of the colored glass was melted in day-tanks of two to three ton capacity. The glass prepared in these tanks was made into lamps within a 24- to 48-hour period. In addition, a large forty-ton tank provided clear crystal for lamps, chimneys, and vacuum bottles. In maximum production, 800 to 900 lamps were made from one day-tank or about 2,500 lamps in a 24-hour period.

Unfortunately, nearly all the early factory production records have been lost. However, it is known that well over 2½ million kerosene lamps were sold from 1934 to 1948. The annual totals are given in the following table. In addition to the lamps, approximately 96,000 burners were sold from 1941 to 1948 for Servel and Whirlpool refrigeration units. During 1943 and 1944 the shortage of raw materials restricted production.

The number made in each style can only be left to individual speculation.

The attractive styles, as well as the color variations, set the Aladdin apart from other kerosene lamps. These appealing designs are largely the work of Eugene Schwarz, Chief Designer for the Mantle Lamp Company from 1928 until his death in 1951. He came to the United States from Germany sometime after World War I and worked as an artist in Chicago. Besides having considerable artistic talent, he was knowledgeable in mold making. This combination of abilities helped him to

Fig. 28—Birthplace of the colorful glass lamps, the Aladdin plant in Alexandria, Indiana, circa 1941. Key to buildings: 1—administration, 2—glass plant, 3—assembly, 4—packaging, 5—designing and research, 6—warehouse, 7—shipping, 8—power plant.

create the unique press-blow glass lamps illustrated in this book. Called a genius in his trade, he was the foremost lamp designer in America for two decades. In addition to the kerosene lamps, he designed some of the glass shades, the parchment and Whip-O-Lite shades, and the early glass electric lamps.

Styles of Models A and B Table Lamps

Models A and B table lamps were made in twenty different designs, illustrated in the following color plates. Each design was made in several glass colors or finishes and they were designated by different style numbers. Apparently it was not the general policy of the Mantle Lamp Company to name their designs. And if names were used by Chief Designer Schwarz, they cannot be ascertained. The descriptive names given in quotes are not original with Aladdin but rather are those which have been widely used by collectors.

The years during which the lamps were sold are given after the name. The lighting season, which usually began August 1, extended into the following calendar year. Therefore, a

SALES OF ALADDIN KEROSENE MANTLE LAMPS FROM 1934 THROUGH 1948

Year*	Number Sold
1934	224,152
1935	237,985
1936	272,662
1937	216,940
1938	185,400
1939	156,712
1940	132,186
1941	140,715
1942	176,925
1943	72,100
1944	123,297
1945	192,444
1946	155,283
1947	198,632
1948	182,912

*The company fiscal year (ending April 30) does not necessarily correspond with design or style years.

lamp listed in this book for 1933 was actually sold during the fall of 1933 and the winter of 1934. This lamp would have been described in Aladdin literature as a "new for 1934 style."

The descriptive names of the colored glass, eg. "Green Beta Crystal," were taken directly from advertising literature. The different colors produced for retail lines of glass lamps are shown in the plates.

Collectors observe considerable variation in the shade and intensity of the color of glass lamps, particularly the amber and green crystal and green moonstone. The difference in color of green moonstones was intentional as there were two distinct shades. The darker "bluish-green" moonstone, made in several styles, is referred to as jade green moonstone on the following pages. The black moonstone bases, when held to a strong light, may show cobalt blue, red, amethyst, green, or a dense, near-black opacity. The clear glass lamps range from crystal clear to faint green or grey tints. The differences in color were due to slight variations from one batch of glass to another, in mixing and firing, as well as chemical content.

Replacement bowls and bases were available for those who had broken one part of two-piece glass lamps. Therefore, it is possible to find "hybrid lamps" comprising parts of two different original styles.

Fig. 29—For improved lighting Aladdin oil pots were often installed into lamp bases not made by the Mantle Lamp Company.

18

Fig. 30—Vase lamps of this design were made in two sizes from 1930 through 1934. They accommodate Model No. 12 oil pots. The following colors were made: 1930—Variegated Verde and Duo-Tan, Bengal Red; 1931—Blue and Orange Venetian; 1931 and 1932—Green, Peach, Red, and Ebony Venetian; 1933 and 1934—Green and Amber Marble-like ceramic (shown above).

STYLES OF A AND B TABLE LAMPS

VENETIAN — 1932 and 1933

Model A. Plain design bowl. Two-piece glass with hidden screw metal connector. Height 8½". (Height of lamp base not including the burner.)

Style
100   Satin White Alpha Crystal Art Glass
101   Pastel Green Alpha Crystal Art Glass
102   Pastel Peach Alpha Crystal Art Glass (tan)
103   Pastel Rose (or) Old Rose Alpha Crystal Art Glass

HOBNAIL or "COLONIAL"—1933

Model B. Hobnail bowl with ornate fluted pedestal. Some may be found with Model A burners. Height 9".

Style
104   Clear Beta Crystal
105   Green Beta Crystal
106   Amber Beta Crystal

"CATHEDRAL" — 1934 and 1935

Model B. Convex fluted bowl with fluted and beaded pedestal and hexagon base. Height 9". The style number was preceded by "B" beginning in 1935.

Style
107   Clear Beta Crystal
108   Green Beta Crystal
109   Amber Beta Crystal

1935 only
B-110   Pastel White Moonstone Art Glass
B-111   Pastel Green Moonstone Art Glass (green and jade green)
B-112   Pastel Rose or Flesh Moonstone Art Glass

Fig. 31—Styles of models A and B Aladdin kerosene mantle lamps.

Top Row:	VENETIAN		"COLONIAL"	
	Style 101	Style 103	Style 105	Style 106

Bottom Row:		"CATHEDRAL"		
	Style 108	Style 109	Style B-110	Style B-112

"CORINTHIAN"—1935 and 1936

Model B. Concave fluted bowl. Two-piece glass with brass* or white metal** connector (two styles). Height 9".

Style	1935 only
B-100	Clear Beta Crystal**
B-101	Amber Beta Crystal*, **
B-102	Green Beta Crystal*, **

	1936 only
B-103	Clear Beta Crystal*
B-104	Clear Beta Crystal Bowl with Black Crystal Base*
B-105	Clear Beta Crystal Bowl With Green Crystal Base*
B-106	Clear Beta Crystal Bowl with Amber Crystal Base*
B-114	White Moonstone Art Glass*, **
B-115	Green Moonstone Art Glass (jade green* and green**)
B-116	Rose Moonstone Art Glass*, **
B-124	White Moonstone Art Glass Bowl with Black Moonstone Art Glass Base*
B-125	White Moonstone Art Glass Bowl with Green Moonstone Art Glass Base* (jade green)
B-126	White Moonstone Art Glass Bowl with Rose Moonstone Art Glass Base*

"MAJESTIC" — 1935 and 1936

Model B. Concave fluted bowl and decorated white metal pedestal and hexagon foot. Height 11½".

Style	
B-120	White Moonstone Art Glass Bowl with Rose Gold Plated Base
B-121	Rose Moonstone Art Glass Bowl with Rose Gold Plated Base
B-122	Green Moonstone Art Glass Bowl with Silver Plated Base

"ORIENTALE" — 1935 and 1936

Model B. All metal lamp, brass font, white metal pedestal and hexagon foot. Height 10½".

Style	
B-130	Ivory Lacquer and Rose Gold Trim
B-131	Green Lacquer and Silver Plated Trim
B-134	Oxidized Bronze Plate
	1935 only
B-132	Rose Gold Plate
B-133	Silver Plate

Fig. 32—Styles of model B Aladdin kerosene mantle lamps.

Top Row:		"CORINTHIAN"		
	Style B-102	Style B-106	Style B-115	Style B-126

Bottom Row:		"MAJESTIC"		"ORIENTALE"
	Style B-120	Style B-122	Style B-130	Style B-133

"BEEHIVE" or "WEDDING BAND" — 1937 and 1938

Model B. Horizontal ribbed crystal bowl, round pedestal and base. Height 8½".

Style
B-80   Clear Beta Crystal

1938 only
B-81   Green Beta Crystal
B-82   Amber Beta Crystal
B-83   Ruby Beta Crystal

"DIAMOND QUILT" — 1937

Model B. Quilt pattern bowl with round base. Two-piece glass lamp with brass connector. Height 9½".

Style
B-85   White Moonstone Art Glass
B-86   Green Moonstone Art Glass (jade green)
B-90   White Moonstone Art Glass Bowl with Black Moonstone Art Glass Base
B-91   White Moonstone Art Glass Bowl with Rose Moonstone Art Glass Base

QUEEN — 1937 to 1939

Model B. Vertical ribbed bowl and white base metal pedestal. There are two bowl designs. One is scalloped, the other is plain and is slightly taller. Height 10½".

Style
B-95   White Moonstone Art Glass Bowl with Oxidized Bronze Plated Base
B-96   White Moonstone Art Glass Bowl with Silver Plated Base
B-97   Green Moonstone Art Glass Bowl with Silver Plated Base (jade green)

1937 to 1938 only
B-98   Rose Moonstone Art Glass Bowl with Silver Plated Base

"TREASURE" — 1937 to 1953

Model B. All metal, plain design. In 1937 and 1938 these lamps were the highest priced of the entire kerosene line. Height 8½".

Style
        1937 and 1938
B-136   Chromium Plated

        1937 to 1941 and 1946 to 1953
B-137   Oxidized Bronze Plated
B-138   Nickel Plated

Fig. 33—Styles of model B Aladdin kerosene mantle lamps.

Top Row:	"BEEHIVE"		"DIAMOND QUILT"	
	Style B-82	Style B-83	Style B-86	Style B-90
Bottom Row:	QUEEN		"TREASURE"	
	Style B-95	Style B-98	Style B-136	Style B-137

"VERTIQUE" — 1938

Model B. Vertical ribbed bowl and pedestal. Two-piece glass lamp with brass connector. Height 9½".

Style
B-87   Rose Moonstone Art Glass
B-88   Yellow Moonstone Art Glass
B-92   Green Moonstone Art Glass (jade green)
B-93   White Moonstone Art Glass

"SOLITAIRE" — 1938

Model B. Only 1000 pieces of this design were made. The bowl appears to be the predecessor to the Lincoln Drape. There are different foot designs. Height 9".

Style
B-70   White Moonstone

"WASHINGTON DRAPE" or "REVERSE DRAPE" — 1939

Model B. Scallop design with round base. Height 8½".

Style
B-39   Clear Beta Crystal
B-40   Green Beta Crystal
B-41   Amber Beta Crystal

Fig. 34—Styles of model B Aladdin kerosene mantle lamps.

Top Row: "VERTIQUE"

| | Style B-87 | Style B-88 | Style B-92 | Style B-93 |

Bottom Row: "SOLITAIRE"   "WASHINGTON DRAPE"

| | Style B-70 | Style B-39 | Style B-40 | Style B-41 |

"SHORT LINCOLN DRAPE" — 1939

Model B. Draped bowl with round pedestal and base. Height 8¾".

Style
B-60   Ivory Alacite Art Glass
B-61   Amber Art Glass
B-62   Ruby Crystal Art Glass

"TALL LINCOLN DRAPE" — 1940 to 1949

Model B. Draped bowl, plain pedestal and twelve-sided foot. There are numerous minor designs on the underside of the foot. Some Lincoln Drape lamps have a scalloped rather than plain design on the top of the foot. See below. A few clear glass lamps were made but they were not assigned a style number. The B-75 lamps can be found in near white color. Height 10¼".

Style
B-75   Ivory Alacite Art Glass

       1940 only
B-76   Cobalt Blue Crystal Art Glass

       1941 only
B-77   Ruby Crystal Art Glass

"WASHINGTON DRAPE" or "REVERSE DRAPE" — 1940

Model B. Scallop design with filigree pedestal. B-50 was illustrated as Style No. B-53 in 1947-48. Height 9".

Style
B-50   Clear Beta Crystal
B-51   Green Beta Crystal
B-52   Amber Beta Crystal

"WASHINGTON DRAPE" or "REVERSE DRAPE" — Circa 1940 to 1941

Model B. Scallop design with bell-shaped pedestal. The bell-shaped pedestal was shown in literature as B-53, 54, 55. Height 9".

Style
Not listed   Clear Beta Crystal
Not listed   Green Beta Crystal
Not listed   Amber Beta Crystal

Fig. 35—Styles of model B Aladdin kerosene mantle lamps.

Top Row:	"SHORT LINCOLN DRAPE"			"TALL LINCOLN DRAPE"
	Style B-60	Style B-61	Style B-62	Style B-75

Bottom Row:	"TALL LINCOLN DRAPE"		"WASHINGTON DRAPE"	
	B-76	B-77	B-52	Not listed

"WASHINGTON DRAPE" or "REVERSE DRAPE" — 1941 to 1953
For export from 1950 to 1955

Model B. Scallop design with plain pedestal. There were two designs of the foot in each style, not distinguished by different style numbers. Some of the B-53 lamps, made with the crowfoot base design, do not have an oil fill in the font. Designated as B-53X, it was designed in 1943 apparently to save brass during the war. The mold was reportedly taken to a firm in Fairmount, Indiana, and put into production for a short time in 1946. These lamps apparently were not sold until much later since the burners are addressed "Nashville, Tennessee" rather than "Chicago, Illinois." Height 9″.

Style

B-53 Clear Beta Crystal

1941 and 1942
B-54 Green Beta Crystal
B-55 Amber Beta Crystal

VICTORIA — 1947

Model B. Porcelain china, white glaze, with floral design and gold leaves and stripes. Made by the Metallic Arts Company, Mayfield, Kentucky. Height 11″.

Style
B-25 Decorated China

"SIMPLICITY" — 1948 to 1953

Model B. Tall, smooth design, plain and decorated. The plain ivory Alacite (B-76) carried the same style number as the cobalt blue Lincoln Drape made in 1940. Nashville burners (see above) are found on some of the decorated crystal lamps sold in 1952-53. Height 10″.

Style 1948 only
B-26 Ivory Alacite with Decalcomania
B-27 Ivory Alacite with Gold Lustre
       Decoration
B-76 Plain Ivory Alacite

1949 to 1953
B-28 Rose Decorated Crystal
B-29 Green Decorated Crystal

1949 to 1952
B-30, B-56 White Decorated Crystal

Fig. 36—Styles of model B Aladdin kerosene mantle lamps.

Top Row:	"WASHINGTON DRAPE"		VICTORIA	"SIMPLICITY"
	Style B-54	Style B-55	Style B-25	Style B-26
Bottom Row:		"SIMPLICITY"		
	Style B-27	Style B-76	Style B-28	Style B-29

31

Fig. 37—The Florentine vase lamp, 1935.

Fig. 38—Blown vases of a multi-colored glass, called Velvex, remained in production only a few months. The vases ranged in height from ten to sixteen inches. Circa 1935.

Fig. 39—Alacite glassware. (Left to right): Top—bookend vases, powder dish, candy dish. Bottom—dish, bell, planter, and cigarette container.

Alacite

During its short life, most people did not recognize or appreciate the quality of Aladdin's special glass named Alacite. Developed in 1938, Alacite was used to make not only kerosene and electric lamps, but also dishes and other items. This unique glass was described in advertising literature as "A startlingly beautiful lamp base and pedestal material discovered by Aladdin after many months of research. . . . It resembles many of the semi-precious mineralites in texture and has much of the softness and tone of tusk (genuine ivory)—the only color in which it is available. Alacite has character, class, and plenty of personality."

The name Alacite was a trade name coined by the Sales Department. The "Ala," part of the Aladdin name, was combined with "ite" or "cite," a common suffix in the names of many natural minerals.

Alacite was the creation of H. T. Hellmers. Earlier—between 1930 and 1932—he had developed Crown Tuscan, ruby for blown glassware, heatherbloom, amethyst mulberry, and willow blue, as well as several other colored glasses. At that time he was in charge of glass production and experimentation for the Cambridge Glass Company. He had also developed colored glass for toy marbles, toy dishes, and pressed ware when he was factory superintendent for the Akro Agate Company from 1922 to 1930 and 1932 to 1934.

Alacite has specific composition for ivory color as every colored glass has a special, sometimes secret, formula. It is not a mixture of amber and milk glass. Uranium oxide, a common coloring agent in antique glass, was originally a constituent of Alacite, as well as of yellow moonstone. However, the commercial use of uranium oxide was banned by the government in 1942 because of the development of atomic weapons. Attempts to find a substitute for uranium oxide in the Alacite formulation may explain color variations, particularly in kerosene lamps made between 1940 and 1949.

The color of Alacite varied from a solid light ivory to pinkish-beige. Dark batches of Alacite formulation were discarded. Alacite does not exist in colors other than tones of ivory, although blue, green, and other colors of small glass items may be marked "Alacite by Aladdin." These pieces, usually ashtrays, were experimentally pressed as samples of a new tank of glass. It so happened that the mold plunger with the Alacite mark was used without consideration of the confusion to future collectors.

Fig. 40—Alacite figurine.

Fig. 41—Alacite crucifix figure. This item was not put into production.

Fig. 42—Alacite glassware. (Left to right): Top—pair wall vases and large serving bowl. Bottom—coaster ash tray, small ash tray, large ash tray, wall switch plate and ash tray.

Three distinct designs of kerosene table lamps, fonts for hanging lamps, and numerous electric lamps were made of Alacite. In addition, attractive bowls and other dishware items were made of Alacite to complement lamps in gift shops and in an attempt to keep the glass house working when they were not making lamps. Alacite dishware, made from 1940 to 1943, did not receive sufficient popularity to keep it in production. Because of its cost plus a high loss from breakage (Alacite is brittle), dishware items were only produced in small quantities.

Items made of Alacite included kerosene lamps, electric lamps and parts for electric lamps, finials, planter bowls, berry sets and bowls, nut and candy dishes, wall pockets, electric wall switch plates, bookend vases, candle holders, trays with cigarette box and ashtrays, coaster ashtrays, ashtrays (three styles), divided dishes (two styles), cigarette containers, figurines, egg plates, powder boxes, covers for tissue boxes, and deep fruit bowls. Whimsies made of Alacite by factory glass workers included animals, bells, bottles, canes, coffee cups, cowboy hats, curtain rods, hands, and paperweights. Lamps and ashtrays were made in the greatest quantities. Some of the ashtrays were made with advertising inscriptions for other companies. Alacite dishware items were usually signed "Alacite by Aladdin" in the glass mold or they were marked with a paper label.

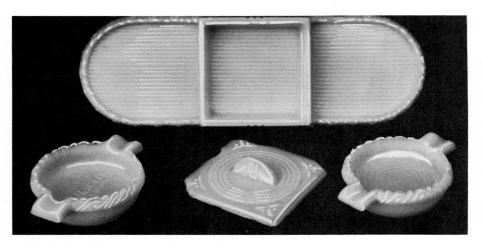

Fig. 43—Alacite cigarette box and tray with two small ash trays.

Fig. 44—Bride and Groom lamp finial.

Fig. 45—Alacite glassware. (Left to right): Top—Nut dish, pair of candle holders. Bottom—egg plate, tissue box cover.

CHAPTER 3

HERE COMES THE HIGH LINE

As the use of electricity for lighting became more and more widespread, Johnson thought it wise to diversify. Beginning in 1915, he made several attempts to establish the Mantle Lamp Company in new markets. The first was the introduction of the Sambo Starter, a mechanical device for starting the Model T Ford. It was similar to the starters now used on outboard motors.

Experience making insulated cooking dishes for the U. S. Armed Services during World War I led to the development of the Aladdin Thermalware Jar, insulated with a material similar to cork. In 1919, the Mantle Lamp Company formed a subsidiary, Aladdin Industries, Inc., to market their new product. Later, Johnson's patents on the common thermos bottle established Aladdin as one of the largest producers of heat and cold-retaining receptacles.

In efforts to diversify during the 1920's, the Mantle Lamp Company founded the Pathfinder Radio Corporation, the Cadillac Phonograph Corporation, the Aladdin Chemical Corporation, and the Aladdin Phonograph Corporation. All of these companies failed. However, Johnson Laboratories, Inc. (radio components), Aladdin Radio Industries (magnetic and radio research), and much later (1957) Aladdin Electronics (electronics engineering) have been very successful.

Aladdin Electric Lamps

As the market for kerosene lamps diminished, the Mantle Lamp Company gradually increased production of electric lamps. Several hundred styles of table and floor lamps have brightened America's homes and at one time the Mantle Lamp Company was one of the largest manufacturers of electric lamps in the United States.

The first electric lamps, the Vogue Vase and Pedestal series, were introduced in 1932. Crystal lamps in many colors and designs, as well as Alacite lamps, soon followed. Decorator lamps displayed statuary, figurines, and later bibelots such as bowling pins. As the 1950's approached, table and floor lamps were made of wood, ceramics, or metal, often in various combinations.

Electric lamps were in peak production by 1940. In that year forty-one table lamps were offered in Alacite, plain and decorated, as well as in decorated crystal. Lighted lamp bases were featured. Thirty new table lamps, mostly Alacite, were offered the following season and more than 273,000 electric lamps were sold. The electric lamps pictured on the following pages plus those in the catalogs reprinted on pages 155-164 show early Alacite and crystal decorated designs. These are only a sampling of the unique lamps created by Eugene Schwarz. The electric lamps featuring figurine and fancy boudoir styles are widely desired by collectors.

Opalique was the name given to crystal lamps, often decorated, made during the 1930's. Opalique was proclaimed as . . . "comparable only to genuine Lalique—a product of a famous French maker of the most expensive and exclusive glassware . . . available in Aladdin table and boudoir lamps in its natural color (clear), etched, or in tantalizing tones of amber and green. Opalique in any color has sparkle, life, and vitality, and molded in Aladdin's original

Fig. 46—Outdoor Exposition in Chicago, 1924.

Fig. 47—Electric Vogue lamps, circa 1932, were made in Green, Blue, Peach, Orange, Red and Ebony.

designs becomes a thing of beauty and a joy forever.''

Virtually hundreds of Whip-O-Lite and fabric shades were designed for Aladdin electric lamps. Many of the attractive scenic designs were carried over from the kerosene shades.

Collectors will find "Aladdin Portable Electric Lamps, Muncie, Indiana." These lamps are not to be confused with the Aladdin electric lamps, described in this book, made by the Mantle Lamp Company. The "Aladdin Portable Electric Lamp" was made by a competitive manufacturer, The Aladdin Lamp Company, who attempted to take advantage of the popular Aladdin radio advertising by

the Mantle Lamp Company. The Aladdin Lamp Company was enjoined by a court decision from using the name Aladdin. They went out of business in the late 1930's.

Several events were to affect the Mantle Lamp Company during the early 1940's. As the nation's war effort intensified, the manufacture of electric lamps was temporarily discontinued in 1943. Glass kerosene lamps continued in production and the Aladdin kerosene burner was used in the famous Servel and Electrolux refrigeration units which preserved serum and plasma on the battlefields. Aladdin was granted permission to use copper by the War Production Board

Fig. 48—The press-blow shop at Alexandria making Alacite lamp bases. (Left to right): carry-in boy, transfer man, presser, punty gatherer, and blow-up boy. The Alacite continuous glass tank (20 tons) is in the background.

during World War II. The usage of Aladdin kerosene lamps saved much precious wiring that would have been required to electrify new homes. The company developed several items essential in the war—a midget foxhole stove and a pressure lantern, both of which burned leaded or white gasoline; a barometric bomb detonation fuse; Permeability Tuning for radios; and precision parts for military radio equipment. Meanwhile, the thermos bottle gained rapidly as one of Aladdin's principal products in the domestic market.

V. S. Johnson died unexpectedly in Washington, D. C., in 1943. His son, V. S. Johnson, Jr., has headed the company since that time, providing leadership for further growth and expansion. He initiated plans to build a new plant in Nashville, Tennessee, to expand the production of Aladdin thermos bottles. The main offices were moved from Chicago to the modern facilities, which opened in 1948.

Aladdin Industries, Inc.

In 1949, the Mantle Lamp Company of America merged with its subsidiary, Aladdin Industries, Inc., taking the latter name as being more representative of its diverse products.

The Alexandria plant was closed in 1952 and all molds for the glass kerosene and electric lamps were destroyed. The production of Aladdin electric lamps ceased entirely in 1956. Aladdin decided it could better use its resources in the production and sale of other products.

Today the principal items manufactured by Aladdin Industries are glass and stainless steel vacuum bottles; children's character school lunch kits; workmen's lunch boxes; Aladdin kerosene lamps and mantles for gas lights; insulated food service trays for hospitals, institutions, and airlines; and electronic components, which were part of man's first steps on the moon.

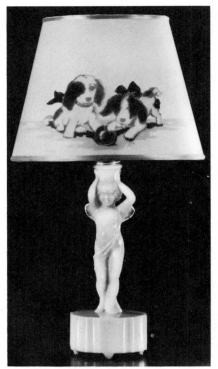

Fig. 50—Alacite cupid lamp (G-24).

Fig. 49—Aladdin electric boudoir lamp, Opalique figure with Alacite base (G-16). This lamp was also made entirely of Alacite.

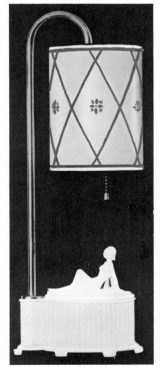

Fig. 51—Powder dish boudoir lamp (G-50).

Fig. 52—Alacite decorative lighted urn (G-375).

40

Fig. 53—Metal figurine lamp (M-123).

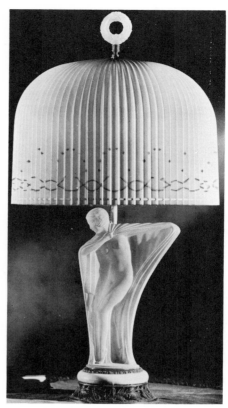

Fig. 54—Opalique figurine lamp (G-130).

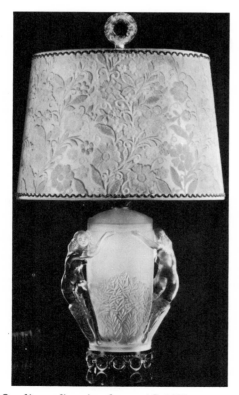

Fig. 55—Opalique figurine lamp (G-163).

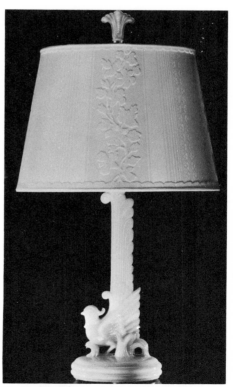

Fig. 56—Aladdin electric table lamp, Alacite Golden Crowned Pheasant (G-234).

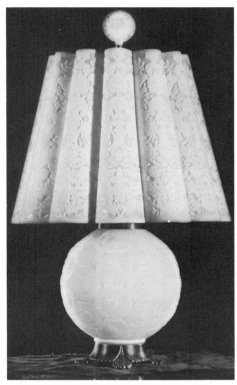

Fig. 57—Opalique table lamp (G-95).

Fig. 58—Alacite lamp with illuminated base (G-195).

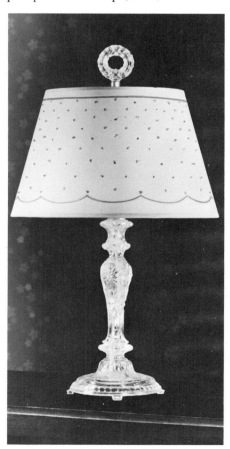

Fig. 59—Opalique table lamp (G-200). This lamp was also made of Alacite.

Fig. 60—Decorated Alacite lamp (G-236).

Fig. 61—Alacite candelabra lamp.

Fig. 62—Electric lamp finials, circa 1940. These designs were made of Alacite as well as several other glass colors.

Fig. 63, 64, 65, 66—Hopalong Cassidy Ranch House Lamps made of Alacite, circa 1950.

Fig. 67, 68—Aladdin Magic Touch lamps, circa 1955, were turned on or off by touching the sensitive lamp bases. On the left is a display control unit and on the right is a complete touch lamp.

Fig. 69—Some of the last designs of Aladdin electric lamps on display in 1955.

CHAPTER 4

MERCHANDISING THE ALADDIN

In the days when automobiles were only for the very rich, Henry Ford built his Model T, "The People's Car." Although there were few roads, Ford's ambition was to build a car that anyone could afford to own. In 1909, when Packards cost $3,500 or more, the Model T was introduced at a price of $850.

In sharp contrast, the new Aladdin Mantle Lamp cost $4.50, more than most kerosene lamps. In 1909, an open-flame kerosene lamp could be purchased for twenty-five cents. To convince prospective buyers that the lamps were worth the extra money, the advantages of the Aladdin had to be demonstrated.

Advertisements in farm publications such as **Successful Farming, Progressive Farmer, Prairie Farmer,** and **National Stockman and Farmer** proclaimed the "new kerosene light" and sought agents. Anyone answering the ads received an Aladdin for free trial with no money down. "We don't ask you to pay a cent until you have used this wonderful modern light in your own home ten days—we even pay transportation charges."

Agents were recruited in each locality. "No money needed, we furnish capital. Agents make big money. Men with rigs make $100 to $300 per month." So it was that each person ordering a lamp might become an Aladdin salesman.

Traveling farmer agents demonstrated the merits of Aladdin lamps, using the "overnight trial and delivery plan." One night's use usually convinced the prospective buyer of Aladdin's superiority. Each agent obtained local merchants to stock supplies—chimneys, wicks, and mantles. The agent was given a free lamp for each Aladdin supply dealership that he established.

The Aladdin was one of the many kerosene, gas, gasoline, and electrical generating systems that competed for sales in rural areas where electricity was not available. Incandescent gas lighting was widespread by 1900. In 1909, nearly 300 towns in the United States used acetylene gas (immersion of calcium carbide in water) and in 1910 nearly 100 Pintsch gas works provided bottled gas for lighting.

Some of the lamps and lighting systems competitive with the Aladdin in the Midwest during the early years of the Mantle Lamp Company follow:

Aida
Akron Lighting System
American Gas Machine Lamps
Angle Lamp
Ann Arbor Lighting System
B & H
Banner

"Aladdinize" Your Own Community Now

Beacon Mantle Lamp
Best Light
Bright As Day
Brite-Lite
Bystrom Gas Lamp
Canchester
Coleman Air-O-Lite
Contraco
Daylight Lamp
Daylite
Felboillin
Foote Kerosene Mantle Lamp
Gasoline Gravity Lamp
Hollow Wire Gasoline Lamp
Ideal Incandescent Lamp
Knight Light
Kronis
Lalley Electro Light
Lumo
Miller
Perfect Lamp
Plumwood
Powerlight Lamp
Practicus
Pyro Alcohol Lamp
Radiant Lamp
Radiosene Wickless Lamp
Rayo Lamp
Rochester
Royal
Saxonia
Success
Sunlight Lamp
Sun Vapor Light
Sunshine Safety Lamp
Vestal
Western Electric Farm Lighting
White Flame Light
Wickless Kerosene Mantle Lamp
Wixon
Wonder Oil Lamp

In advertising literature eighteen reasons were given why Aladdin was superior to its competitors.

(1) Aladdin light is a white light; beautifully brilliant, yet soft and mellow.
(2) Aladdin light is of a quality nearest of all others to sunlight.
(3) Aladdin light is of a strength equal to ten ordinary oil lamps.
(4) Aladdin light is produced from any grade of kerosene (coal-oil).
(5) Aladdin light is a safe light. Women and children can handle it.
(6) Aladdin light is the cheapest white light produced by man.
(7) Aladdin light is smokeless.
(8) Aladdin light is odorless.
(9) Aladdin light is noiseless.
(10) Aladdin light is put in operation and maintained in the simplest manner.
(11) Aladdin light is a quick light—produced and extinguished almost instantly.
(12) Aladdin light is produced without the means of pressure, a pump, preheating with alcohol, or a so-called generator.
(13) Aladdin light is reliable and dependable.
(14) Aladdin light will render a lifetime of service and satisfaction.
(15) Aladdin light is decorative—it will brighten and beautify any home.
(16) Aladdin light may be secured in a variety of styles to fit all needs.
(17) Aladdin light is used and enjoyed by millions of people in all parts of the world.
(18) Aladdin light is the only light of all artificial lights that has all these advantages.

In particular, the safety of the Aladdin lamp was emphasized: " 'Safety First,' both as to lamp and fuel it burns should be the slogan when the purchase of a lighting device is considered. . . . The Aladdin burns from a wick—no needle to clog up, no generating with alcohol, no hissing noise, no pumping up—therefore no pressure or confining of vapors; consequently, the dangers of explosion are eliminated. The fuel used is common kerosene with which every housewife is familiar. When you consider that the Aladdin produces a modern, pure-white light that meets the requirements for the home, introduces no dangerous or new conditions, is there any good reason for considering a lamp which uses an explosive fuel?"

The fact that kerosene does not vaporize readily to form an explosive mixture was an impressive sales point. Dousing a lighted match in an open dish of kerosene was a favorite sales technique. The prospective customer was often immediately convinced.

The quality of light emitted from incandescent kerosene lamps, as well as their efficiency, were favorite research subjects of many universities and private laboratories. The merits of the Aladdin reported by the Lewis Institute (pages 50 and 51) effectively appeared in advertising (page 52).

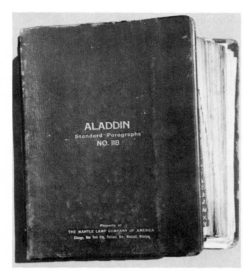

Fig. 70—The Aladdin Standard Paragraph Book.

Another sales technique was the company's detailed correspondence to its customers and agents. The company policy of lengthy explanations (to prevent misunderstanding) soon gained it the nickname — "The House of Long Letters." Sales correspondents used the "Aladdin Standard Paragraph Book" to increase their proficiency in writing letters that would "not conflict in any detail with general policy." This book, weighing more than ten pounds, contained thousands of paragraphs about Aladdin and competitive lamps, dealers, credit, sales and methods, new promotion plans, and complaints. The correspondent selected the paragraphs by number "in proper combination and with good judgment." The secretarial force then quickly speeded the letter on to the addressee.

The following paragraphs, written for persons who had not paid for their trial Aladdin, are examples of the detail in the paragraph book.

(Index Heading) (Subject of Paragraph)
Trial Aladdin — We accept your promise to pay in a few days for trial Aladdin.
Trial Aladdin — Gentle reminder of trial Aladdin unpaid for.
Trial Aladdin — Did not keep his promise to to pay for trial Aladdin.
Trial Aladdin — Additional reminder that trial Aladdin has not been paid for.

V. S. Johnson originated the "multiple card mailing" system of advertising other products to his customers. Furthermore, he developed the machines to gather single copies of assorted advertising cards and stuff them into envelopes for mailing.

"Extra compensation and sales bonus offers" promoted sales of model No. 7 in 1917. The new font design was introduced at a time when the costs for labor and brass were rising. For details on these offers, see the circular reprinted on pages 116-117.

A "new wholesale selling plan" was instituted in 1922 to maintain volume sales at a time when competitive lamps were underselling the Aladdin in price. Letters to sales agents pointed out that the Aladdin was "the most carefully made lamp in the world. All of the burner parts are adjusted to the one-thousandth of an inch; in fact, the lamp is as carefully made as a very fine watch . . . the cost of skilled labor alone on the Aladdin is as much as some lamps sell for at retail, but it is this excellent and careful workmanship that makes the Aladdin so reliable and dependable. . . . There are some people who have the idea and desire to purchase everything at less than the price asked for it. Our New Wholesale Selling Plan is especially devised for these people . . . if our biggest and most successful distributors were able to make $5,000 per year and upwards selling the Aladdin at the regular retail price, it is safe to say that you should be able to do better than that selling the Aladdin at the new wholesale price, without sacrificing any of your profits."

The plan constituted an offer of free lamps which enabled the sales distributor to sell profitably at wholesale price. The number of free lamps varied with the number purchased:

3 lamps free with 6 purchased
8 lamps free with 12 purchased
17 lamps free with 24 purchased
27 lamps free with 36 purchased

As the 1920's boomed, it became increasingly difficult to interest and employ agents. The Mantle Lamp Company turned to franchise dealers, some 15,000 in number by the early 1930's. The company's own sales force coordinated sales programs with the dealers while calling on them and taking orders for lamps and supplies. The dealers sponsored free lamp drawings, lamp trade-in offers, and other promotion contests.

SAFETY FIRST

Gasoline Must Not Be Used In An Aladdin

THE ALADDIN burns any grade of Kerosene (Coal Oil), and will not explode. No pressure, therefore, no noise and no danger. Gasoline is very useful, in its place—in the garage—for running the automobile or an engine—but should never be brought into the house, where there is always the chance of some of the vapor escaping, catching fire and causing a terrible explosion which may endanger the lives of dear ones. On this and the following pages you will find reprints of newspaper articles appearing throughout the country, clipped at random between Feb. 1st and May 31st, 1915, showing the awful losses of property and lives from the use of gasoline in the home.

Several Injured by Gasoline Explosion

(Fargo, N. D., Forum, Feb. 23, 1915)
Devils Lake, N. D., Feb. 23.—In a fire which destroyed their home Sunday evening about 7 o'clock, Mrs. W. F. Wellcome, wife of a well known and pioneer farmer who lives three miles west of Edmore, was seriously injured and her two sons, Guy and Arthur, were badly hurt, while the other members of the family, eight in all, received some injuries.

The fire started with the explosion of a gasoline lamp, which stood near the victim. Her face, arms, hands and back were burned deep. Her two sons who rushed to the rescue and carried her out, were badly burned on their hands and about their faces. Escape through the door was cut off and the family were obliged to get out through the windows. The house was entirely destroyed.

Mrs. Wellcome, nee Miss Stella Sparks, is a sister of Mesdames John Flumerfelt, Wm. Foote and J. C. B. Turner of this city. Guy Wellcome is married and he and his wife were at the parents' home at the time the accident occurred.

Gasoline Starts Fire

(Akron, Ohio, Beacon-Journal, Apr. 26, 1915)
The fire department was called to 894 S. High street Saturday afternoon to put out a blaze caused by the explosion of gasoline which caught fire while being poured into a lamp. The house is owned and occupied by P. J. Romig. The damage was small.

Jewett Stores Burned

Flames Swept West Side of Main Street.
(Houston, Tex., Post, Feb. 9, 1915.)
Houston Post Special.

Jewett, Texas, Feb. 8.—A fire originating from a gasoline lamp in a barber shop swept all the west end of the front street of Jewett about 3 p. m. Buildings burned were a one-story rock building occupied by the Jewett State bank, Coakey Evans drug store, W. T. Evans & Co. drug store, F. P. Harrison furniture, one vacant store, barber shop and four warehouses. Stocks partially lost; buildings total loss. Stocks and buildings were partially covered by insurance. The bank building is still burning and some danger for the balance of the town is felt yet.

Lamp Explosion Burns Man

(Milwaukee Sentinel, Mar. 6, 1915)
Wausau—John A. Socha of Edgar was burned severely when a gasoline lamp he was cleaning exploded. Both his hands and face were burned.

(Davenport, Ia,. Democrat, Feb. 12, 1915)
Albia, Ia., Feb. 12.—June Morrow, son of G. W. Morrow, was severely burned about the face and hands by the explosion of a gasoline lamp with which he was working.

Explosion Occurs at Lodge Meeting

(Nashville, Tenn., Banner, Apr. 17, 1915)
Special to the Banner.

Camden, Tenn., April 17.—A serious and what came near being a fatal accident occurred in the Masonic hall on Thursday night while the Eastern Star members were assembling for the regular meeting. A gasoline lighting system furnishes the light, and just after the tank had been pumped up and the jets were being regulated, one of the lamps exploded, sending parts of it, together with several feet of pipe, flying to all parts of the room. Several persons were struck, but no one was hurt, except Mrs. J. V. Travis, who was struck on the side of the head, just above the edge of the hair, receiving an ugly wound, which was promptly treated by a physician. The wound is very painful, but is not thought to be serious.

Wright Badly Burned

(Oklahoma City Oklahoman, Mar. 24, 1915)
Oilton, Okla., March 23.—(Special.)—Bob Wright of Oilton, brother of Arch Wright of Muskogee, was severely burned here while trying to regulate a gasoline lamp. The bowl was leaking while the lamp was lighted. The gasoline ran down over Wright's face and shoulders. The oil ignited and enveloped him in flames. He placed his hands over his face and in removing them took the skin from his face with them. He had the presence of mind to throw himself flat on the floor and by-standers smothered the flames with rugs. The upper portion of his body and his head are badly burned.

Fire Threatens Village

Gasoline Lamp Explodes, Destroying Hardware Store and Damaging Other Buildings.
(St. Paul Pioneer Press, Feb. 12, 1915)
Special to the Pioneer Press.

Winona, Minn., Feb. 12.—The explosion of a gasoline lamp in the hardware store of E. R. Lydon resulted last night in a fire which for a time threatened the village of Kellogg, near here. The burning fluid was scattered over the storeroom, which burst into flame.

The village bucket brigade enlisted the services of every man and for an hour they fought the fire.

Wabasha was appealed to for assistance when the two adjoining structures caught fire. The brigade finally controlled the flames. The hardware store was destroyed and two other buildings were damaged.

Lamp Explodes; Town Endangered

(Neenah, Wis., News, Feb. 5, 1915)
Athens.—The harness shop of John Cole burned, endangering the entire village. An explosion of a gasoline lamp was the cause. Nearby frame buildings were saved only by volunteers. The loss is $15,000.

$150,000 Fire at Rome, N.Y.

Gasoline Lighting Plant Explodes and Blows Man Out Window.
(Brooklyn Eagle, Feb. 8, 1915)

Rome, N. Y., Feb. 8.—Fire which started in Durfee's candy store, in the Corcoran block, a three-story brick building, shortly before 1 a. m. today, completely destroyed that building badly damaged the three-story Purdy block, on the east, and a one-story frame block on the west.

The loss is estimated at $150,000, with insurance at about 75 per cent. The fire originated from the explosion of a gasoline vapor lighting plant. Mr. Durfee was blown through a rear window and seriously injured.

Lamp Explodes; Small Fire Follows

(Birmingham, Ala., Ledger, Apr. 8, 1915)
The explosion of a gasoline lamp in the Patton-Pope drug store at 300-302 N. Twentieth street started a fire in the building about 7:25 o'clock Wednesday night, which caused a damage of about $15.

All the available apparatus in the down town district was rushed to the scene, and a large crowd gathered. The fire was extinguished with the aid of chemicals.

J. P. Lance, who is said to have been demonstrating the lamp, sustained a slightly burned hand in trying to put out the fire.

Brooklyn Heights Store is Destroyed by Fire

(Ft. Worth, Tex., Record, Feb. 18, 1915)
The two-story brick building of the Mat Atwood drug and grocery store at Brooklyn Heights, a settlement two miles west of Fort Worth, was partially destroyed Wednesday morning about 11:30 by a fire that originated through some unknown cause. The store's stock, which was light, will prove a total loss. The damage is estimated at $3,000.

The fire started in the rear of the building, where a gasoline stove had been left burning. Firemen believe the stove became overheated and ignited some inflammable material. The Fort Worth fire department made a run of about five miles and when they arrived at the scene the blaze had already enveloped the building. Good work on the part of the fire department prevented the flames from spreading.

The greater part of the damage was sustained by the interior of the building. When the blaze was extinguished it was found that the walls were in good condition.

Warsaw Woman Injured in Gas Explosion

(Goshen, Ind., News-Times, Feb. 11, 1915)
Mrs. R. O. Nusbaum of Warsaw is suffering from painful burns received Tuesday evening when a gas stove exploded.

Woman Badly Burned in Gasoline Explosion

Mrs. Peter Luvin Dangerously Seared by Flames from Exploding Cook Stove.

NOT EXPECTED TO SURVIVE.

Husband Burned on Hands and Arms in Attempt to Save Wife, Under Treatment With Her at Virginia Hospital.
(Richmond, Va., Times-Dispatch, Feb. 11, 1915)

Mrs. Peter Luvin, 1716 Venable street, was dangerously if not fatally burned in her home yesterday morning when her clothing caught fire from the explosion of a gasoline stove in the kitchen of her home. Her husband occupies another bed in Virginia Hospital, suffering from severe burns of the hands and arms, received while he endeavored to extinguish the flames which enveloped his wife. Mr. Luvin's condition is not thought to be serious by surgeons at the hospital, but there is little hope of Mrs. Luvin surviving, according to information obtained at the hospital early this morning.

Mrs. Luvin was leaning over the stove, preparing breakfast, when the explosion occurred. Her waist caught fire immediately, and the flames quickly spread over her body. Screaming with pain and fear, the woman rushed to the foot of the stairs leading to her husband's room, and cried for help. Luvin dashed down the steps and his wife ran into the back yard, where he found her, a mass of flame.

Tries to Extinguish Flames With Blanket.

The husband secured a blanket and wrapped it about the body of his wife, beating the flames with the corners as best he could. The blanket quickly ignited, and Luvin's bare hands and arms suffered horribly. Neighbors rushed to his assistance, but they were too late to prove of material assistance.

Ambulance Surgeon Walker had been summoned at 510 N. Eighteenth street and happened to be passing the door soon after the accident occurred. He was notified and, realizing the seriousness of the injuries, abandoned the first call and rushed Mr. and Mrs. Luvin to the Virginia Hospital, where they were turned over to the care of other surgeons while Dr. Walker returned to answer the first call.

Luvin is a tailor in the employ of M. Fisher. He is about 35 years old and his wife is several years younger. They have two small children, who are being cared for by neighbors.

Gasoline Stove Explodes

Mr. Kielmeyer of Nerstrand Is Burned About Face and Hands.
(Faribault, Minn., Journal, Feb. 10, 1915)

J. H. Kielmeyer of Nerstrand was badly burned about the face and hands Sunday evening, caused by a gasoline explosion.

Mr. Kielmeyer was filling the tank of his gasoline stove when in some unaccountable manner a gas was formed and the explosion occurred. His injuries, although painful, are not serious.

LEWIS INSTITUTE

CHICAGO

FRED A. ROGERS, B. S. (E. E.)
DEPARTMENT OF PHYSICS
AND ELECTRICAL ENGINEERING

THE MANTLE LAMP COMPANY OF AMERICA,   September 27, 1915.

Gentlemen:

Complying with your request, I have compared the cost of operating the Aladdin Lamp for a period of five (5) years, with the cost of operating for the same period of time, the open-flame center draught type of lamps. The calculations are based on average values of candle power, or quantity of light, and oil consumption as determined by tests at the Technical Schools and Universities named in the report. (A test made on the Aladdin Lamp at the United States Bureau of Standards at Washington, shows substantially the same values as the average values determined at the Technical Schools and Universities). It is assumed that the lamps are operated three (3) hours each day throughout the year and the cost is determined at oil prices varying from 10 to 40 cents per gallon. The five year period is taken only for the purpose of obtaining a fair comparison--it does not in any way represent the life of the lamps. The accompanying table shows the results of the comparison of the two types of lamps, and also shows the saving of the Aladdin over the open-flame type for the five year period considered.

The first two columns of the table show the expense of operating the open-flame center draught type of lamp and the Aladdin Lamp at different oil prices. The oil bill and the total cost which includes oil and supplies, are given separately.

Column No. 3 shows the saving, lamp for lamp, of the Aladdin Lamp over the center draught open-flame lamp and is obtained by taking the difference between the cost of operation of the two lamps. For example: at the price of 12 cents a gallon for oil, the oil and supplies for the open-flame center draught lamp cost $24.36, while the oil and supplies for the Aladdin Lamp cost only $17.90, giving a saving of $6.46 in favor of the Aladdin. At a higher price for oil, the saving is still greater. It can thus be seen that at a price of 12 cents or more for oil and of $6.00 for the Aladdin Lamp, the lamp will more than pay for itself in five years in the saving of operating expense over the old style lamp, even if the old style lamp is received as a gift. It is not fair, however, to the Aladdin Lamp to make a comparison, lamp for lamp, of the Aladdin with the open-flame center draught lamp, since the Aladdin produces a steady white light equal to 60.3 candles, while the open-flame lamp produces a smoky, yellow light equal to only 24.35 candles. The comparison should be based on equal quantities of light, and such a comparison follows.

Since the cost of operating the open-flame type of lamp for five years, using 12-cent oil, is $24.36 and the candle power is 24.35, it follows that the cost of operating for one candle power for five years is $24.36 (operating expense) divided by 24.35 (candle power), or very nearly $1.00. The Aladdin Lamp produces a volume of light equal to 60.3 candles at the operating cost of $17.90 for five years (Column No. 2). If this volume of light were produced by the open-flame lamps, the cost would be 60.3 (candle power) times $1.00, or $60.30 which is $42.40 more than the same quantity of light would cost if produced by the Aladdin. At a higher price for oil, this saving would be still greater. The saving on 60.3 candle power is shown in Column No. 4. This, however, makes no allowance for the superior quality of the pure white light of the Aladdin over the open-flame lamp.

Column No. 5 shows the amount of money invested at 6% compound interest which will earn as much as one Aladdin Lamp will save in operating expense on the production of 60.3 candle power, over the open-flame type of lamp during a period of five years.

Respectfully submitted,

Fred A. Rogers

Professor of Physics and Electrical Engineering.

Comparison of Operating Expense of Center Draught Open-Flame Oil Lamps and Aladdin Incandescent Oil Lamps

On a 5-year Basis
Lamps burning 3 hours every night at their maximum candle power

Calculations are based on average values of candle power and oil consumed, as shown by reports of tests made at the following Technical Schools and Universities:

Yale University	Leland Stanford University	University of Michigan	Cornell University
University of Arkansas	University of Maine	New Hampshire Agric. College	Pennsylvania State University
University of Idaho	Maryland Agricultural College	Dartmouth College	Carnegie Institute
Lewis Institute	Mississippi Agricultural College	University of Wisconsin	Vanderbilt University
Armour Institute	University of Missouri	University of North Dakota	University of Texas
University of Illinois	Michigan Agricultural College	Syracuse University	Washington State College
Iowa State University	University of Nebraska	Ohio State University	University of Washington
University of Kentucky			

Data on Open-Flame Lamp

Estimated Cost of Supplies

Chimneys $0.90
Wicks ....$.90
$1.80

Candle Power 24.35
1 gallon oil will last ..29.3 hours

Candle Power Hours
per gallon...............718

Data on Aladdin Lamp

Estimated Cost of Supplies

Chimneys $1.00
Mantles 3.25
Wicks 80
$5.05

Candle Power 60.3
1 gallon oil will last ..51.1 hours

Candle Power Hours
per gallon 3080

The Aladdin produces 4.28 times as much light as would be produced by open-flame center draught lamp with the same expenditure for oil.

COLUMN No. 1 — Expense of operating center draught OPEN-FLAME LAMPS

COLUMN No. 2 — Expense of operating ALADDIN INCANDESCENT Mantle Lamp

COLUMN No. 3 — This column shows the saving in cost of operating Aladdin Mantle Lamp over center draught open-flame lamp—lamp for lamp.

This makes no allowance whatever for the great difference in volume of light produced by the Aladdin over the open-flame lamp, nor does it take into consideration the superior quality of the Aladdin light over the flame light.

COLUMN No. 4 — This column shows the saving of Aladdin Mantle lamp over center draught lamp for a 60.3 candle power light.

This allows nothing for the superior quality of the pure, white light of the Aladdin.

COLUMN No. 5 — This column shows the amount of money that would have to be invested at 6% annually to yield interest equal to the saving of the Aladdin over the open-flame center draught lamp for the period shown in this table. In other words, the investment of $6.00 in an Aladdin lamp will save you as much money on 60.3 candle power light as the amount given below will earn for 5 years at 6% compound interest.

	COLUMN No. 1 Oil Bill	COLUMN No. 1 Oil Bill and Supplies Combin'd	COLUMN No. 2 Oil Bill	COLUMN No. 2 Oil Bill and Supplies Combin'd	COLUMN No. 3	COLUMN No. 4	COLUMN No. 5
When the cost of oil is 10c per gal.	$18.80	$20.60	$10.71	$15.76	$ 4.84	$ 35.25	$103.67
" " " 12c "	22.56	24.36	12.85	17.90	6.46	42.40	124.73
" " " 14c "	26.32	28.12	14.99	20.04	8.08	49.58	145.82
" " " 16c "	30.08	31 88	17.13	22.18	9.70	56.75	166.76
" " " 18c "	33.84	35.64	19.27	24.32	11.32	63.92	187.94
" " " 20c "	37.60	39.40	21.42	26.47	12.93	71.08	209.06
" " " 22c "	41.36	43.16	23.55	28.60	14.56	78.26	230.17
" " " 24c "	45.12	46.92	25.69	30.74	16.18	85.43	251.17
" " " 26c "	48.88	50.68	27.83	32.88	17.80	92.61	272.38
" " " 28c "	52.64	54.44	29.97	35.02	19.42	99.77	293.44
" " " 30c "	56.40	58.20	32.13	37.18	21.02	106.92	314.47
" " " 32c "	60.16	61.96	34.26	39.31	22.65	114.10	335.59
" " " 34c "	63.92	65.72	36.41	41.46	24.26	121.26	356.64
" " " 36c "	67.68	69.48	38.55	43.60	25.88	128.43	377.73
" " " 38c "	71.44	73.24	40.70	45.75	27.49	135.59	398.79
" " " 40c "	75.20	77.00	42.84	47.89	29.11	142.76	419.88

Respectfully submitted,

Fred A. Rogers

Professor of Physics and Electrical Engineering.

Lewis Institute, Chicago, Illinois
September 27th, 1915

Form 137

Pouring Oil Down A Rat Hole

would be considered expensive amusement by any sane person. Yet that is virtually what millions of users of the old style open-flame, round wick kerosene (coal oil) lamps are doing every day. You may never have thought of it in just that light, but if you will permit us, we feel sure we can prove to you that you are not getting one-fourth the efficiency you should from the oil you are using. The fault is not in the oil but in the lamp.

Would You Like to Save from $10.00 to $30.00 Per Year on Kerosene Oil?

You can, and we will show you how. According to scientific tests made at the U. S. Government Bureau of Standards and thirty-three different leading Universities throughout the United States and Canada, one Aladdin Kerosene Mantle Lamp gives over twice as much light as round wick, open flame lamps such as the Rayo, Rochester, B. & H., Sears-Roebuck, Success, etc. Each round wick lamp burns over twice as much oil as the Aladdin. So, to get the same amount of light you will be burning over four times as much oil. You may be paying anywhere from 10c to 40c per gallon for kerosene oil (depending on the location.) But let us take 15c per gallon as a fair average. The ALADDIN burns 50 hours on a gallon, which would make its cost for oil three-tenths of a cent or 3 mills, per hour.

The round wick open-flame lamps burn about 24 hours on a gallon that costs 15c or about ⅝ of one cent per lamp per hour. Now suppose we say lamps are burned on an average of three hours per night (in winter it will be more and possibly less in summer.) There are 365 days in a year, which makes 1095 hours that the lamps would be running in a year. At three-tenths cent per hour for operating the ALADDIN, it would cost $3.29 per year for oil at 15c per gallon. To produce about the same amount of light from two round wick, open-flame lamps, would cost 1¼c per hour at 15c per gallon, or $13.68 for the year—a saving of 10.39 in one year on 15c oil.

Burning Candles Would Actually Cost Fifty Times as Much as an Aladdin

A tallow candle that costs one cent will burn only about four hours, or rather one-quarter cent per hour. This would amount to $2.74 per year at three hours per night. It would require 60 candles to equal the volume of light produced by the Aladdin. These would cost about $16.44 per year. As shown above the Aladdin costs $3.29 per year for oil or less than one-fiftieth as much as candle light. And certainly no one would attempt to say that the light of the candle is in a class with the ALADDIN in point of quality.

The More Lamps You are Now Using the Less You Can Afford to be Without the Aladdin

Does it take much figuring to see that if one ALADDIN will save you from $10.00 to $30.00 per year in oil alone, that the more lamps your home requires the better you can afford to set aside all the old lamps and invest in ALADDINS throughout? *They'll help you reduce the high cost of living.* PLACE YOUR ORDER TODAY AND STOP UP THAT "RAT-HOLE."

THE MANTLE LAMP COMPANY OF AMERICA, Inc.

Largest Kerosene (Coal Oil) Mantle Lamp House in the World

Chicago   New York City   Portland, Ore.   Montreal   Winnipeg

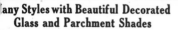

Fig. 71—Dealers offered free lamp drawings to promote Aladdins. The company gave a free lamp ($9.50 value) to dealers with orders totalling $125.00. A National Free Lamp Drawing Day was designated in 1938.

Advertising materials supplied to dealers included counter displays, banners, window posters, and circulars for mailing.

Reminiscent of the "Arabian Nights" story wherein the magician offered "new lamps for old," the company sponsored a national lamp trade-in program from 1938 to 1941. Participation by the dealers was voluntary. One dollar was deducted from the price of a new lamp if an old lamp of any kind was traded in. In areas such as New England, where merchants did not participate in the program, the company honored the trade-in offer by mail.

Every time a dealer made a trade-in sale, he filled out a certificate. A completed book of twelve certificates entitled him to $10.50 worth of free merchandise. The difference between the $10.50 and the $12.00 allowed by the dealers to their customers was used by the company to support a national advertising campaign. The trade-in program was popular with dealers, with many reporting that sales were doubled as a result of the program. The increased sales more than offset their out-of-pocket costs of 12½ cents a lamp.

The success of the trade-in plan was related in a letter from a dealer in Belleville, Illinois:

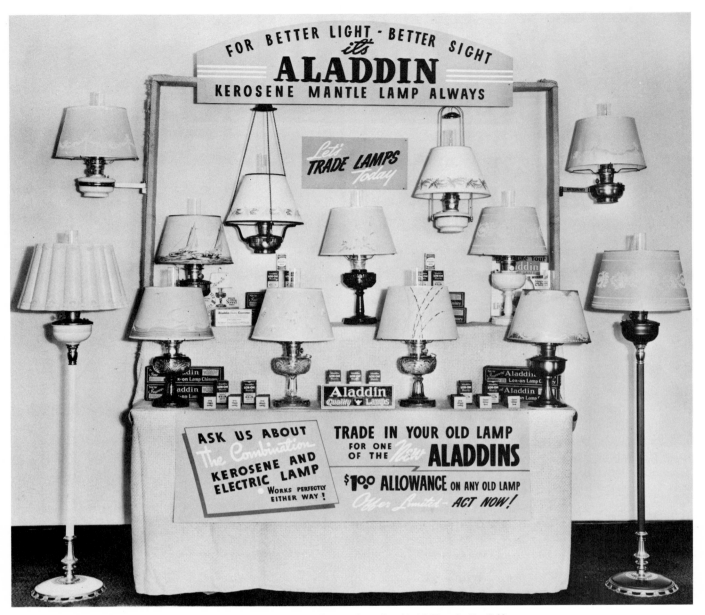

Fig. 72—Display of Aladdin kerosene lamps in 1941 featuring the $1.00 Trade-In Offer.

"The trade-in has helped the sale of Aladdins quite a bit and of course has caused an increase in sale of supplies.

"We traded for forty old lamps—several old=7 brass Aladdins; several Rayo and Rochester lamps; Coleman and Diamond Gasoline Lamps; one old style hanging lamp with glass shade and extension; two large flowered bowl parlor lamps; most of the others were the ordinary glass stand lamps; some with cast iron or marble bases, some with old shapes and designs.

"One small stand lamp with a two-colored glass bowl was considered by antique hunters as a very old lamp.

"We sold quite a few of the old lamps traded in, too. We like this selling plan very much. We found it worked better and created more interest than any other selling plan we ever tried."

The Mantle Lamp Company published the **Aladdin Evening Sun** "in the interests of

Better Light—Better Sight—and Better Lessons.'' The newspaper size tabloid featured articles on home lighting, eye health and care, as well as advertising Aladdin kerosene lamps.

So effective were the company's various merchandising methods that over seven million Aladdin kerosene mantle lamps had been sold by the early 1920's. In total an estimated fifteen million of these lamps have been sold since 1909.

As electricity spread to the rural areas the Mantle Lamp Company promoted their inexpensive Aladdin Convertor. This device, easily inserted into the central air tube, quickly converted the Aladdin to use electricity without sacrificing its capacity to burn kerosene.

The Mantle Lamp Company pioneered in the use of the radio as a new advertising medium. The story of the wonderful Aladdin Lamp was the first paid commercial radio message in the Midwest. In 1927, Bert S. Presba visited the Henry Field Seed Company in Shenandoah, Iowa, and demonstrated the Aladdin to Fred Tunnicliff, Treasurer. He asked if Henry Field would talk about the lamp over the air on his 1000 watt station KFNF.

No, replied the treasurer. That would be worth $500.

Would you do it for $500?

Yes. And, so that evening Henry Field told about the Aladdin Lamp on his "Evening Letterbasket" program. Included was a cash offer of $25 for the best ten-word slogan submitted.

The results of the broadcast were excellent, and the cost per inquiry was less than for publication advertising. About 2200 letters came in and 800 of them did not even submit a slogan. The writers just wanted more information on the Aladdin Lamp.

Many stations in the Midwest started in commercial advertising thanks to the Mantle Lamp Company. So effective were Aladdin radio commericals that other companies emulated these early campaigns.

During the late 1920's most stations did not have established advertising rates and Mr. Edgar Fellers had the job of negotiating with stations around the country. Fellers

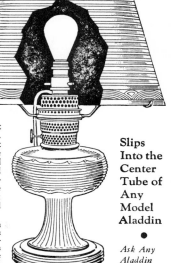
also helped stations with their programming. He often persuaded station managers to hire unknown talent that he had found.

Fellers helped to start the Barn Dance Frolic program, and the Mantle Lamp Company was a sponsor of the live broadcasts from WLS, Chicago, and WHO, Des Moines.

In his search for talent, Fellers heard young Ed McConnell over radio WSB in Atlanta, Georgia. The year was 1926 or 1927. Fellers went to the studio, met young McConnell, and hired him. Shortly thereafter, Smilin' Ed McConnell began his long and productive career advertising Aladdin lamps over WSM, Nashville, Tennessee.

In 1930 Smilin' Ed started making transcription programs in which he sang old favorite songs, told stories, and told about Aladdin lamps. Each program closed with a hymn, Smilin' Ed's desire, reflecting his upbringing as the son of an evangelist.

A series of thirteen radio transcriptions, fifteen minutes long, were offered to any station who could get the local Aladdin franchise dealer to pay the time cost. In 1948, one hundred and forty-five sets were used, primarily by powerful stations dominating large market areas. In addition, five-minute programs were made available to smaller stations.

Look! Who's Here!

Yes! YOU'VE GUESSED IT— IT'S Smilin' Ed McConnell

Star Entertainer and Super-Salesman of the Air. The Friend and Favorite of the Farmer

Smilin' Ed was furnished with scripts which outlined the main commercial points. He ad libbed from these outlines, translating the sales pitch into his own homespun patter and appealing directly to people living in the country beyond the electrical high line.

Smilin' Ed knew his audience. He presented the sales message with an air of joviality. His "soft sell" and his country speech created a rapport which made people trust and believe him. He had the revivalist's ability to project his personality over the air waves directly into the home of the listener. One listener said, "Somehow, just because Smilin' Ed said it was so—then we ought to have some."

Smilin' Ed became "The Aladdin Lamp Man," achieving remarkable success. In the early 1930's, he presented a thirty-minute program of hymns over powerful radio WLW, Cincinnati, Ohio. A disagreement over salary arose. Finally, it was agreed to pay Smilin' Ed twenty-five cents for every inquiry

received about Aladdin lamps. Eight thousand requests poured in after he told his listeners they would do him a great favor by requesting information on this wonderful lamp. The company soon decided to pay him the weekly salary he had been asking.

One Sunday when Smilin' Ed's daughter was very ill, he did the program but only after requesting that he not do any advertising. During the program he told his audience his troubles and asked for their prayers. The next week several thousand cards and notes of sympathy were received. Smilin' Ed McConnell was a very popular man as well as a terrific salesman of Aladdin products.

Aladdin's galaxy of radio stars in the mid-1930's also included Tex Owens, KMBC, Kansas City; Homer Griffith, KFAA, Dallas; Hugh Aspinwall, WCCO, Minneapolis; "Bar Nothin' Ranch Boys," WIRE, Indianapolis; and "The Plainsman," WFAB, Lincoln.

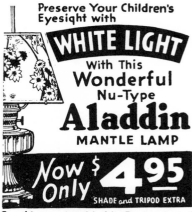

Presentamos LA NUEVA LAMPARA "Aladino" PRODUCE LUZ BLANCA Y ABUNDANTE. USA PETROLEO Q TRACTOLINA. NO NECESITA BOMBEARSE. Sin { OLOR, HUMO, NI RUIDO. ¡CONOZCALA UD.! ¡USELA UD.!

58

Usa petróleo o tractolina. No necesita bombearse.

CHAPTER 5

INSIDE THE ALADDIN

The construction features of the first models of the Aladdin lamp are shown in the accompanying figure (following page). The brass lamps, Models 1 through 12, are center-draft lamps. A central draft tube conducts air up through the lamp directly to the center of the burner. This permits efficient and uniform combustion and helps prevent overheating and smoking.

Before introduction of Model 12, lamps required five to ten minutes to warm up before reaching full capacity light. The Model 12 "Instant Light" was advertised as the "pinnacle of perfection" of central draft burners.

The Mantle

The mantle is the all-important light-emitting part of the Aladdin lamp. It is a very fine filament network of rare earth oxides, 99 percent thoria and 1 percent ceria (by weight), which becomes incandescent when heated. Since these white metals are too hard to be formed or drawn into filaments, the following procedures are followed in manufacturing the delicate mantle.

First, a tubular open-weave knitting is made from a vegetable material such as cotton, linen, ramie fiber, or synthetic material like rayon. The knitting, carefully washed to remove all impurities, is saturated in a solution of thorium and cerium nitrate salts. After drying, the structure is burned to dispose of the supporting vegetable material. The remaining metallic filament structure is then changed from nitrate form to oxide form by intense heat. The final structure is unburnable. It is in the same shape as the original knitting, except that it is considerably smaller because of the burning process. Next, the mantles are dipped in collodion (lacquer) for protection against breakage during handling and shipping. This coating is burned off before the mantle is used on a lamp.

Yarn made of ramie fiber, long considered the best fiber for the original knitting, was used until 1943. Ramie has been cultivated for centuries on swampy land in China and Burma. Until World War II, it was shipped to England, where it was cleaned and spun into yarn. Ramie fiber became difficult to import when the war closed the sea lanes. The company had already investigated substitutes for ramie, and rayon was found to make fine durable mantles. Rayon has since been used to make Aladdin mantles.

The maximum production of mantles reached 8 million per year in the 1930's and during World War II.

Lighting Principle

The Aladdin burner mixes the exact proportion of 94 percent air and 6 percent kerosene vapor for complete combustion. This means maximum heat with no discharge of unburned vapors to deposit soot in the house or on the chimney or mantle. The Aladdin has been described as "almost human" because of its high requirement for oxygen. Many people have related stories about an Aladdin fluttering or going out in church or in rooms where many people were gathered. The problem was quickly remedied, of course, by correcting room ventilation to supply adequate fresh air.

The kerosene is not burned primarily to produce light, but rather to produce heat. The heat of the nonluminous blue flame causes the nonburning mantle to incandesce and emit its characteristic intense pure white light.

The Chimney

The Aladdin chimney, 12½ inches in height, is especially designed for use on Aladdin lamps. It is taller than the usual chimney used on kerosene burners. The extra height draws the proper amount of air for complete combustion of kerosene. In high altitudes it is even necessary to add an extension to the top of the chimney for correct burning.

The first chimneys were ball-style, made of glass with a high lead content. The combination of the ball-style and the improved glass eliminated breakage from overheat-

SECTIONAL VIEW
OF THE
Aladdin Table Lamp
With Model 11 Burner

Refer to this sheet frequently until you thoroughly understand every part of lamp, know what part it takes in the operation and how to remedy anything that gets out of order.

Don't touch the mantle—handle by the wire. Read pages 3 and 4—"How to prevent breaking the mantle."

Only Aladdin size chimneys will work properly; size 12½-inch length with 1⅞ to 2-inch opening at the top. Use only chimneys bearing the above trademark.

Aladdin Hanging Lamps and Bracket Lamps
work the same as the table lamp shown here.

To clean or light the lamp, remove the gallery, mantle and chimney as one piece. See pages 4, 5, 6, 7, 8, 9.

When putting on a new mantle see that it hangs central over the Kone-Kap. If not, bend the wire until it does. Handle by the wire only. Do not touch the mantle.

Chimney should not be removed from gallery except to clean it or adjust a new mantle to the gallery.

Generator must be clean. See generator below.

Wick must be uniform in height, clean and smooth. See wick and cleaner below. Also see pages 11 and 12.

Wick tube flange—scrape it clean before lighting the lamp. See pages 7 and 8.

Kone-Kap must be securely locked under the two catches in gallery.

Chimney must be down on its seat in gallery.

Generator must be down to this stop.

Gallery must be properly locked to burner.

Outside wick tube must be properly locked to burner base.

Button—Model No. of lamp and company address here.

Burner base through which outside air passes to flame.

Tripod (Shade Support) must be fitted to neck of lamp before burner is screwed into bowl, except where burner is used in hanging lamp.

Screw the burner into the bowl; be careful not to cross threads.

Wick Band showing knobs or warts over which the holes in the end of the wick raiser must fit.

Keep the bowl well filled with oil

Wick Raiser and Wick Rack (one piece)

Filler cap.

Sectional View of Aladdin No. 11 Model Wick Cleaner and Shaper
Showing how to use the cleaner to clean wick and wick tube flange

Aladdin Wick Cleaner and Shaper

Wick is turned up until it touches wick cleaner lightly, only enough to clean wick and not roughen it up.

Wick cleaner is pressed down on wick tube flange and turned to the right.

Notice the tapering or slanting edge of wick obtained after using the wick cleaner a few times.

Aladdin No. 11 Model Wick. See page 11.

Sectional View of Aladdin No. 11 Model Generator

Holes through which air passes must be clean and free from dirt (carbon).

The least accumulation of dirt (carbon) on the sides of the generator must be removed. See page 10.

The slightest dent or jam of the perforated part of the generator unfits it for performing its part properly. If dented or jammed use new generator. See page 10.

Perforated part.

Fig. 73—Fitting (modelling) the mantle knitting over a model to give it proper shape.

ing, which had been a problem with earlier foreign-made chimneys. The special glass also enabled the chimneys to withstand the the heat without "blooming" (turning white). Aladdin Lox-On chimneys, introduced in 1928, are still used on current models manufactured in England and Brazil. The Lox-On chimney locks (seats) the chimney in correct position to prevent uneven air supply to the mantle.

Chimneys were made for Aladdin by the Macbeth-Evans Company, Elwood, Indiana, prior to opening the Alexandria plant.
A few Lox-On chimneys of Pyrex glass were made by the Corning Glass Company in Miami, Oklahoma.

Fig. 74—Making Aladdin chimneys at Alexandria. (Left to right): crack-off boy, feeder, and two gatherers.

Fig. 75—Loom weaving Aladdin wicks.

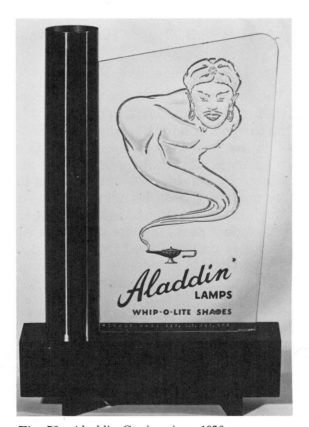

Fig. 76—Aladdin Genie, circa 1950.

REPLACEMENT PARTS FOR ALADDIN LAMPS

Model	Burner	Wick	Mantle	Flame Spreader	Chimney
1	No. 1*	No. 1*	Cap Mantle*	Button No. 1*	Old Style
2	No. 2*	No. 1*	Cap Mantle*	4*	
3	No. 6*	No. 6*	KoneKap	↓	
4					
5				6*	
6	↓	↓		6*	
7	No. 11* or 12*	No. 11		11*	
8					
9					
10					
11	↓	↓	↓	↓	↓
12	No. 12*	No. 12	Lox-on	Nu-Type	Lox-on
A	B*	Nu-Type			
B	B*				
C	C*	↓			
21C	21C*				
23	23	↓	↓	↓	↓

*Obsolete parts no longer available. Other parts listed may be obtained from Aladdin Industries, Inc., Box 7235, Nashville, Tennessee 37210. Additional information may be found in the detailed drawings, pages 65-77.

Note: The Model 23 burner is a direct replacement for Models A, B, C, and 21C. It is available in solid brass or brass with a Silcrom finish.

The Flame Spreader

The small thimble-like part of the burner is called the flame spreader. It insured even air flow to support complete and uniform combustion. The part was originally called the generator but the name incorrectly implied that operation of the lamp required priming or generating. This was not true of Aladdins as it was with some other lamps. The company therefore changed the name from generator to flame spreader in the early 1920's.

The Wick

Aladdin has manufactured its own wicks to insure the finest quality since 1919. Beginning in 1922, Aladdin wicks have had an inner and an outer reinforcement to prevent deformation and insure a symmetrical burning surface. Aladdin wicks will burn reliably for 1000 hours. This fact is extremely important to those who use Aladdin burners in kerosene refrigeration units.

Replacement Parts

The table above lists the replacement parts for those who wish to put their Aladdin lamp in condition for burning kerosene. Even though many of the replacement parts are now obsolete, this table shows which parts are interchangeable. To obtain parts for early models, it may be necessary to search through lamp repair and antique shops. Replacement parts for late models of Aladdin lamps may be purchased from local dealers or from Aladdin Industries, Inc., Lamp Division, Nashville, Tennessee 37210.

Construction Details

The drawings on pages 65-77 show the construction details of burners for Models 1 through B. This information, together with the catalog reprints on pages 85-142, document the improvements made from model to model and will help collectors to properly identify models and burner parts.

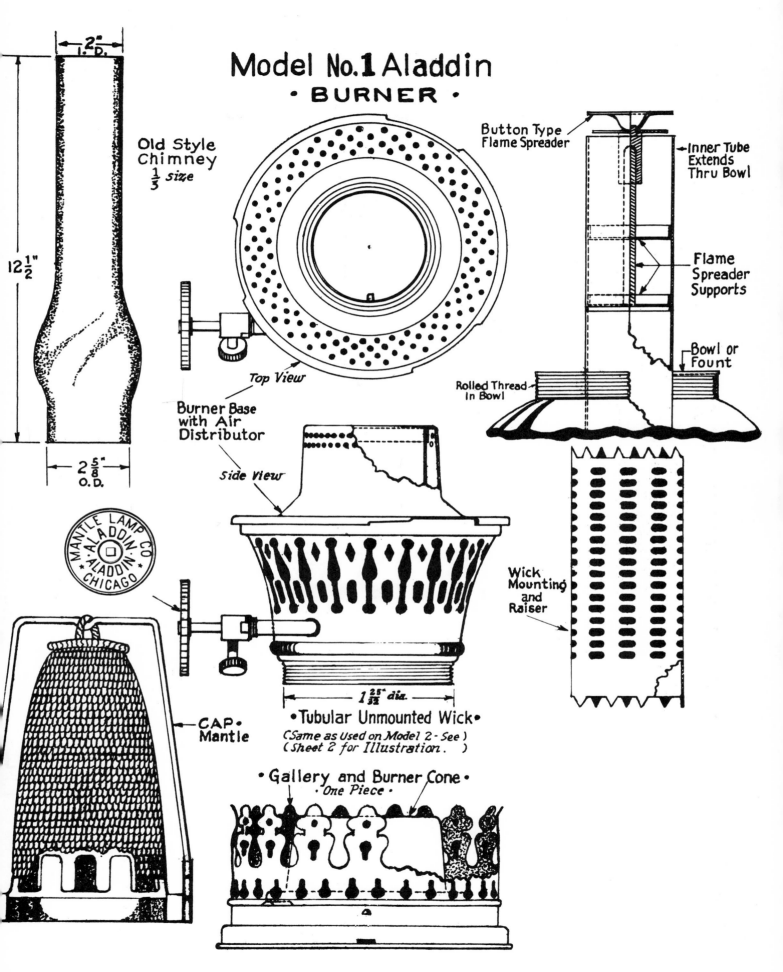

Model No.1 Aladdin
• BURNER •

Old Style
Chimney
⅓ size

2" I.D.

12½"

2⅝" O.D.

Top View

Burner Base
with Air
Distributor

Side View

Button Type
Flame Spreader

Inner Tube
Extends
Thru Bowl

Flame
Spreader
Supports

Bowl or
Fount

Rolled Thread
In Bowl

MANTLE LAMP CO
• ALADDIN •
• ALADDIN •
CHICAGO

CAP.
Mantle

Wick
Mounting
and
Raiser

1 25/32" dia.

• Tubular Unmounted Wick •
(Same as Used on Model 2 - See)
(Sheet 2 for Illustration.)

• Gallery and Burner Cone •
• One Piece •

65

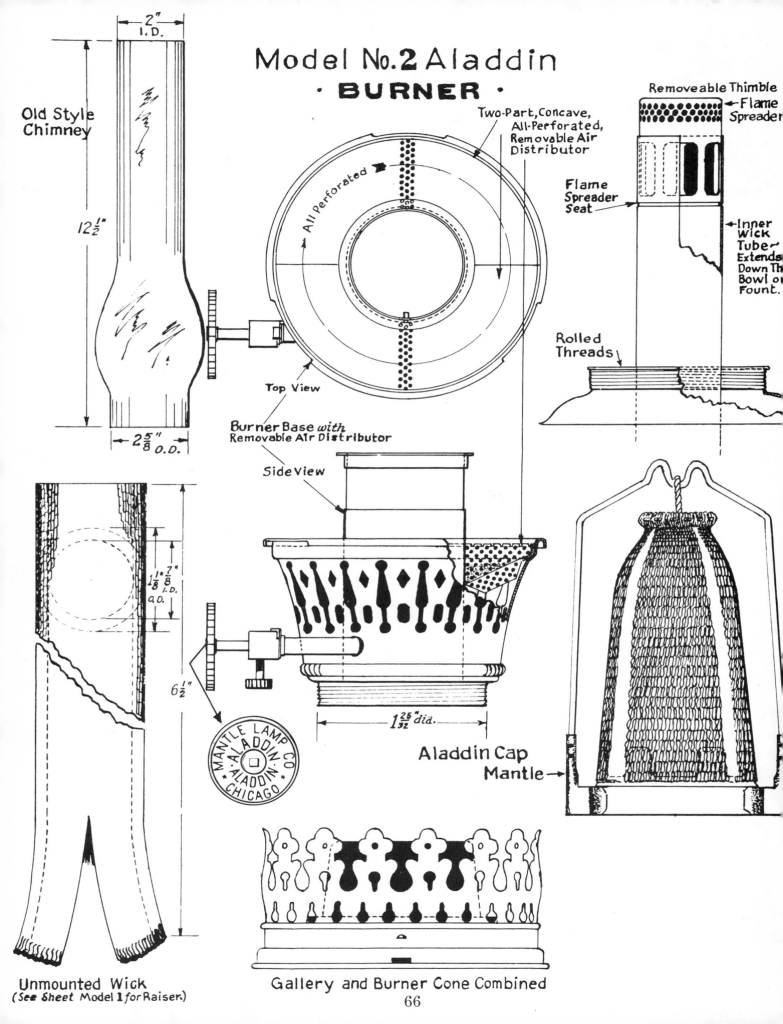

Model No. 2 Aladdin
· BURNER ·

Old Style Chimney

2" I.D.

12½"

2⅝" O.D.

Two-Part, Concave, All-Perforated, Removable Air Distributor

All Perforated

Top View

Burner Base *with* **Removable Air Distributor**

Side View

Removeable Thimble

Flame Spreader

Flame Spreader Seat

Inner Wick Tube Extends Down Th[e] Bowl o[f] Fount.

Rolled Threads

MANTLE LAMP CO · ALADDIN · ALADDIN · CHICAGO

1¼" I.D.
1⅞" O.D.

6½"

1 25/32" dia.

Aladdin Cap

Mantle

Unmounted Wick
(*See Sheet* Model 1 *for Raiser.*)

Gallery and Burner Cone Combined

66

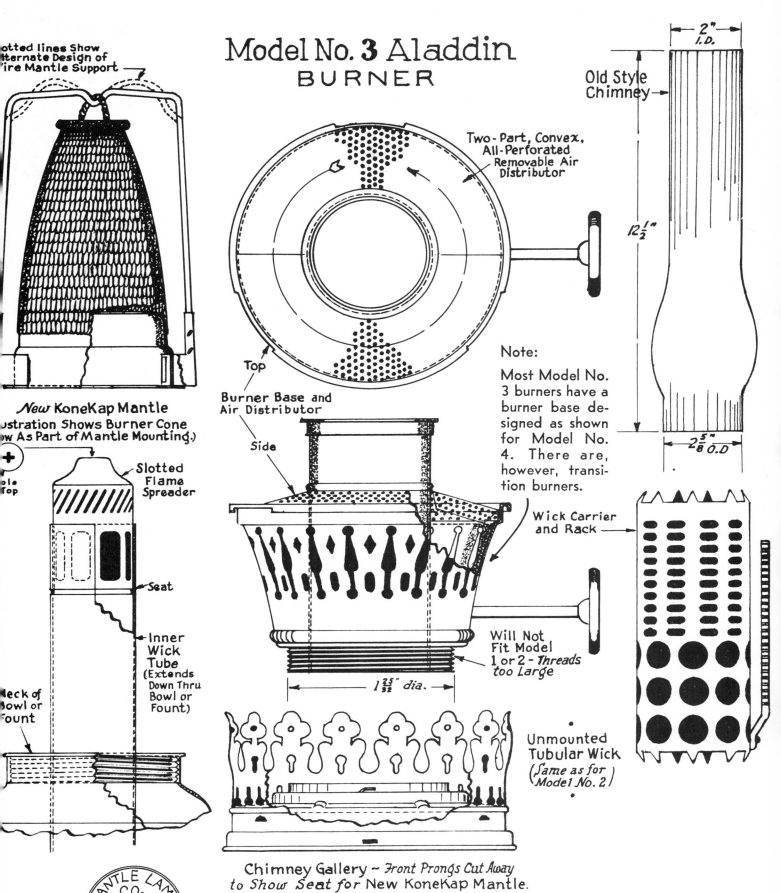

Model No. 3 Aladdin
BURNER

Dotted lines show Alternate Design of Wire Mantle Support

New KoneKap Mantle
(Illustration Shows Burner Cone Now As Part of Mantle Mounting.)

Slotted Flame Spreader

Seat

Inner Wick Tube
(Extends Down Thru Bowl or Fount)

Neck of Bowl or Fount

Hole Top

Top

Burner Base and Air Distributor

Side

Two-Part, Convex, All-Perforated Removable Air Distributor

Note:

Most Model No. 3 burners have a burner base designed as shown for Model No. 4. There are, however, transition burners.

Wick Carrier and Rack

Will Not Fit Model 1 or 2 - *Threads too Large*

$1\frac{25}{32}$" dia.

Old Style Chimney

2" I.D.

$12\frac{1}{2}$"

$2\frac{5}{8}$" O.D.

Unmounted Tubular Wick
(*Same as for Model No. 2*)

Chimney Gallery ~ *Front Prongs Cut Away to Show Seat for* New KoneKap Mantle.

MANTLE LAMP CO. "ALADDIN" ★ CHICAGO

67

Model No.4 Aladdin
· BURNER ·

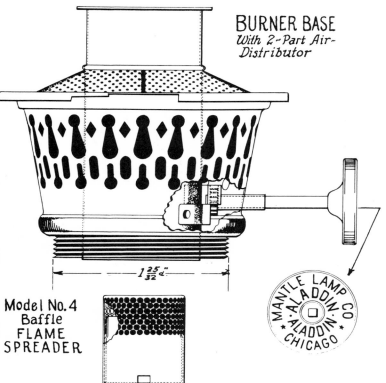

GALLERY ~ For KoneKap Mantle

BURNER BASE
With 2-Part Air-Distributor

USES:
MANTLE ~ Kone Kap
CHIMNEY ~ Old Style
WICK ~ Same as Model No.3 ~
FLAME SPREADER No.4 ~ ~
WICK RAISER ~ Same as Model 3

$1\frac{25}{32}$"

Model No. 4
Baffle
FLAME
SPREADER

MANTLE LAMP CO
· ALADDIN ·
★ ALADDIN ★
CHICAGO

INNER WICK
TUBE
in
Bowl or Fount

Bowl or Fount
Cut Away
to Show Inner
Wick Tube
Extends Down
Into, Thru and
is a Part of
Bowl or Fount

Model No.5 Aladdin
· BURNER ·

GALLERY ~ For KoneKap Mantle

BURNER BASE
with 2-Part Air Distributor

USES:

MANTLE ~ Kone Kap
CHIMNEY ~ Old Style
WICK ~ Same as Model No. 3
WICK RAISER ~ " " "
FLAME SPREADER No. 5

Note: Model No. 5 is also found with the same burner base and gallery as Model No. 6.

THE MANTLE LAMP CO.
OF AMERICA
ALADDIN
MODEL Nº5
CHICAGO, U.S.A.

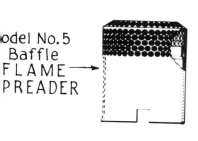

Model No. 5
Baffle
FLAME
SPREADER

INNER WICK
TUBE
in
Bowl or Fount

Seat *for*
Flame
Spreader

Bowl or Fount
Cut Away to
Show Inner Wick
Tube Extends Down
Into, Thru and as
Part of Bowl or
Fount.

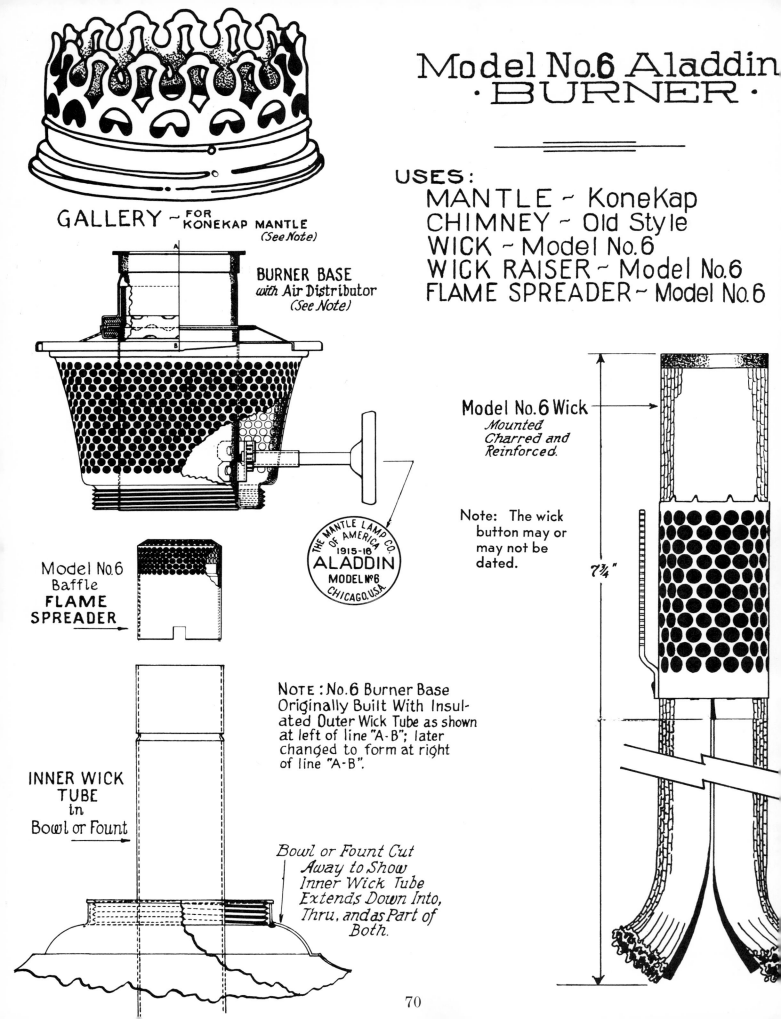

Model No.6 Aladdin ·BURNER·

GALLERY ~ FOR KONEKAP MANTLE
(See Note)

BURNER BASE
with Air Distributor
(See Note)

USES:
MANTLE ~ KoneKap
CHIMNEY ~ Old Style
WICK ~ Model No.6
WICK RAISER ~ Model No.6
FLAME SPREADER ~ Model No.6

THE MANTLE LAMP CO.
OF AMERICA
1915-16
ALADDIN
MODEL №6
CHICAGO, U.S.A.

Model No.6
Baffle
FLAME
SPREADER

Model No.6 Wick
Mounted
Charred and
Reinforced.

Note: The wick
button may or
may not be
dated.

7¾ "

INNER WICK
TUBE
in
Bowl or Fount

NOTE : No.6 Burner Base
Originally Built With Insulated Outer Wick Tube as shown
at left of line "A-B"; later
changed to form at right
of line "A-B".

Bowl or Fount Cut
Away to Show
Inner Wick Tube
Extends Down Into,
Thru, and as Part of
Both.

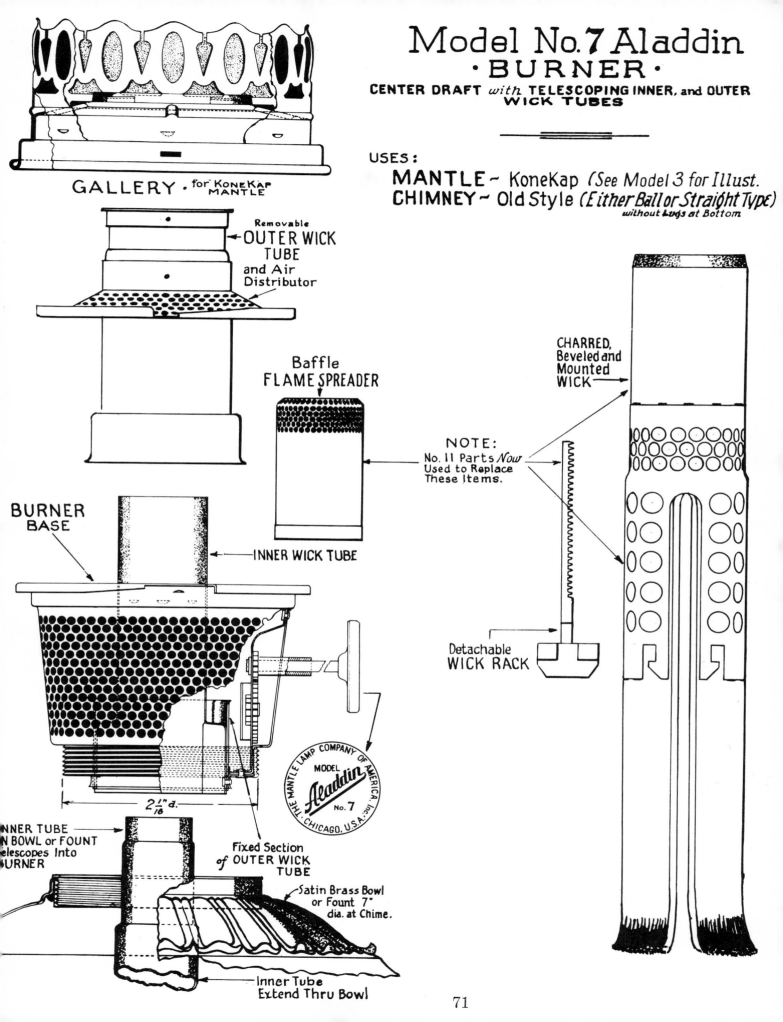

GALLERY · for KoneKap MANTLE

Model No. 7 Aladdin
· BURNER ·
CENTER DRAFT *with* TELESCOPING INNER, and OUTER WICK TUBES

USES:

MANTLE ~ KoneKap *(See Model 3 for Illust.*

CHIMNEY ~ Old Style *(Either Ball or Straight Type)*

without Lugs at Bottom

Removable
→ OUTER WICK TUBE
and Air Distributor

Baffle
FLAME SPREADER

CHARRED, Beveled and Mounted WICK →

NOTE:
No. 11 Parts *Now* Used to Replace These Items.

BURNER BASE

INNER WICK TUBE

Detachable
WICK RACK

2 1/16" d.

THE MANTLE LAMP COMPANY OF AMERICA, Inc.
MODEL
Aladdin
No. 7
CHICAGO, U.S.A.

INNER TUBE N BOWL or FOUNT elescopes Into URNER

Fixed Section of OUTER WICK TUBE

Satin Brass Bowl or Fount 7" dia. at Chime.

Inner Tube Extend Thru Bowl

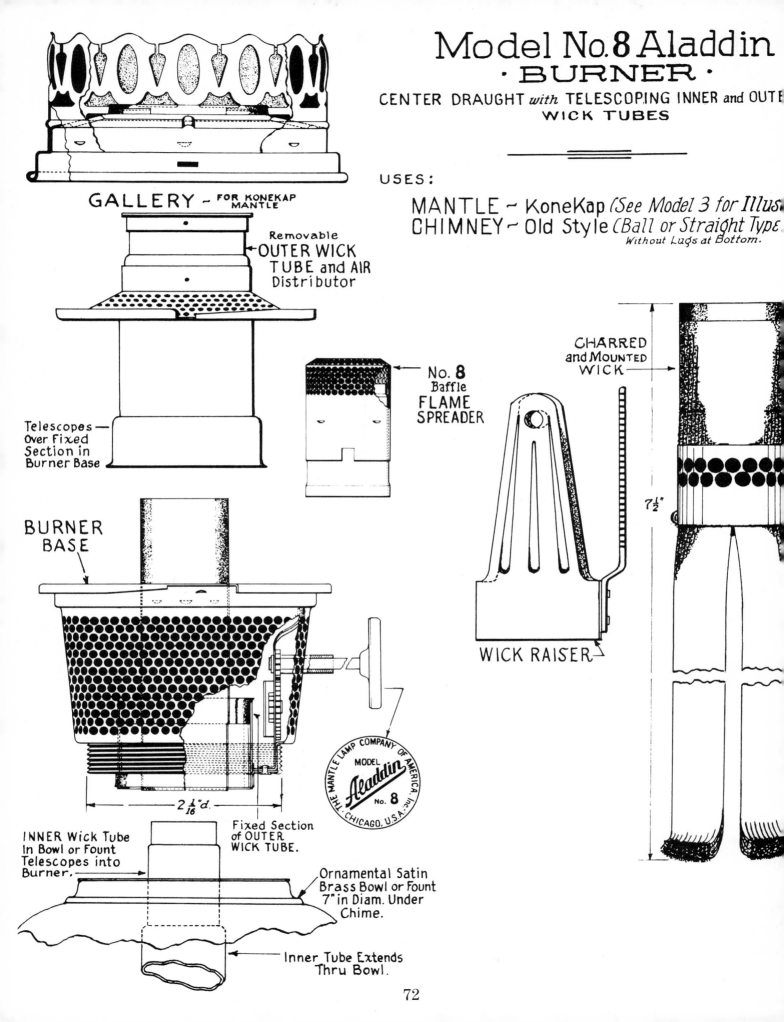

Model No. 8 Aladdin
· BURNER ·
CENTER DRAUGHT *with* TELESCOPING INNER and OUTE[R]
WICK TUBES

USES:

MANTLE ~ KoneKap *(See Model 3 for Illus[.]*
CHIMNEY ~ Old Style *(Ball or Straight Type*
Without Lugs at Bottom.

GALLERY ~ FOR KONEKAP MANTLE

Removable **OUTER WICK TUBE and AIR** Distributor

Telescopes — Over Fixed Section in Burner Base

No. **8** Baffle FLAME SPREADER

CHARRED and Mounted WICK

$7\frac{1}{2}"$

BURNER BASE

WICK RAISER

$2\frac{1}{16}"d.$

MODEL
Aladdin
No. 8
THE MANTLE LAMP COMPANY OF AMERICA, Inc.
CHICAGO, U.S.A.

INNER Wick Tube In Bowl or Fount Telescopes into Burner.

Fixed Section of OUTER WICK TUBE.

Ornamental Satin Brass Bowl or Fount 7" in Diam. Under Chime.

Inner Tube Extends Thru Bowl.

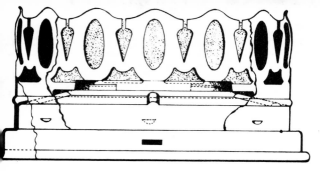

Model No.9 Aladdin
· BURNER ·
CENTER DRAUGHT with TELESCOPING INNER and OUTER WICK TUBES.

GALLERY *for* KoneKap Mantle.

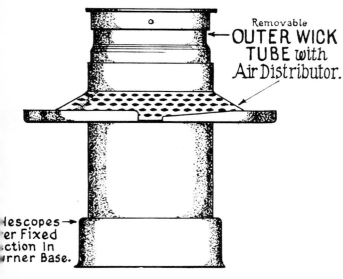

Removable
OUTER WICK TUBE *with* Air Distributor.

Telescopes over Fixed Section In Burner Base.

BURNER BASE

USES:

MANTLE ~ KoneKap
CHIMNEY ~ Old Style

Model No.9 Burner originally fitted with same Wick, Wick Raiser and Flame Spreader as Model No.8. Model No.11 Parts are Replacement Parts for These Items on Model No.9.

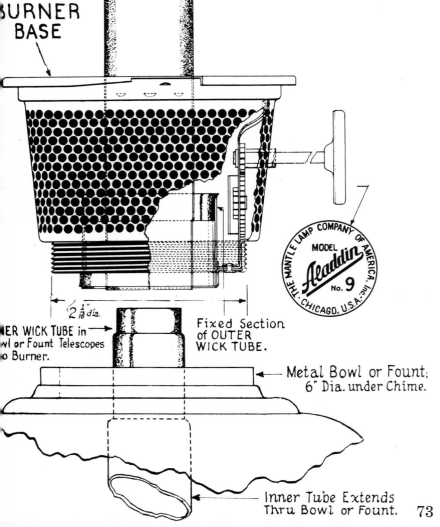

$2\frac{1}{8}"$ dia.

INNER WICK TUBE in Bowl or Fount Telescopes into Burner.

Fixed Section of OUTER WICK TUBE.

Metal Bowl or Fount; 6" Dia. under Chime.

THE MANTLE LAMP COMPANY OF AMERICA, Inc. MODEL *Aladdin* No.9 ·CHICAGO, U.S.A.·

THE MANTLE LAMP COMPANY OF AMERICA, Inc. MODEL *Aladdin* No.10 ·CHICAGO, U.S.A.·

Inner Tube Extends Thru Bowl or Fount.   73

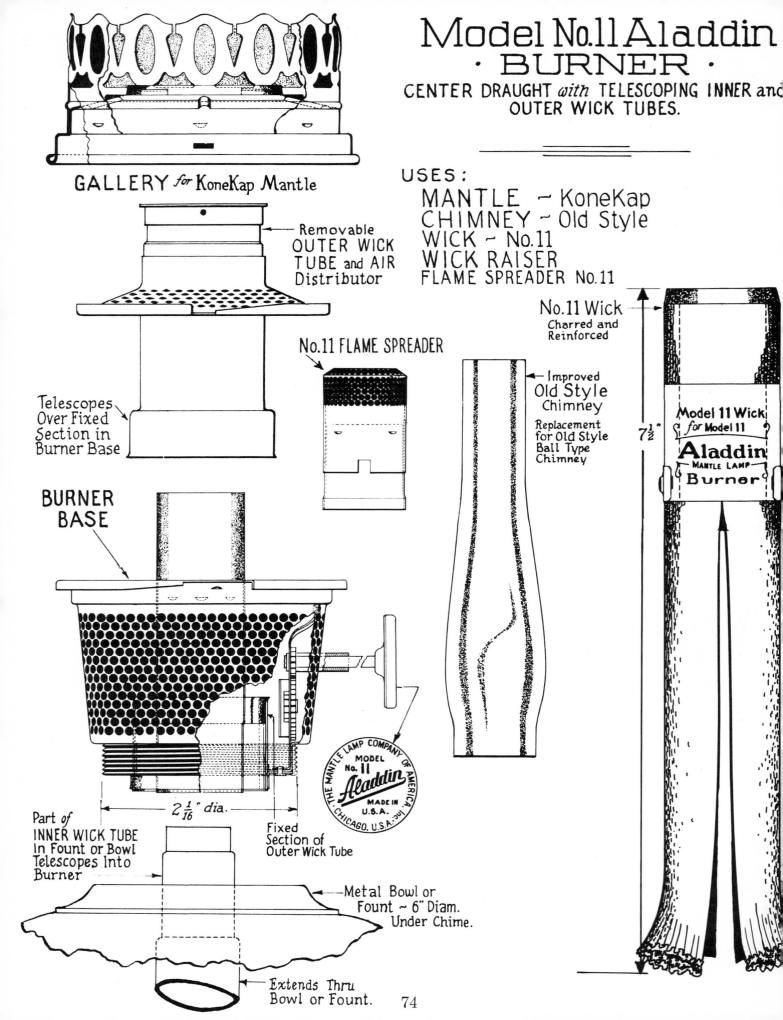

GALLERY *for* KoneKap Mantle

Model No.11 Aladdin
· BURNER ·
CENTER DRAUGHT *with* TELESCOPING INNER and OUTER WICK TUBES.

USES:
MANTLE ~ KoneKap
CHIMNEY ~ Old Style
WICK ~ No.11
WICK RAISER
FLAME SPREADER No.11

Removable OUTER WICK TUBE and AIR Distributor

No.11 FLAME SPREADER

No.11 Wick
Charred and Reinforced

← Improved Old Style Chimney

Replacement for Old Style Ball Type Chimney

Telescopes Over Fixed Section in Burner Base

BURNER BASE

Model 11 Wick *for* Model 11 Aladdin MANTLE LAMP Burner

$7\frac{1}{2}$"

THE MANTLE LAMP COMPANY OF AMERICA, Inc.
MODEL No. 11 Aladdin MADE IN U.S.A. CHICAGO, U.S.A.

$2\frac{1}{16}$" dia.

Part of INNER WICK TUBE In Fount or Bowl Telescopes Into Burner

Fixed Section of Outer Wick Tube

← Metal Bowl or Fount ~ 6" Diam. Under Chime.

← Extends Thru Bowl or Fount.

74

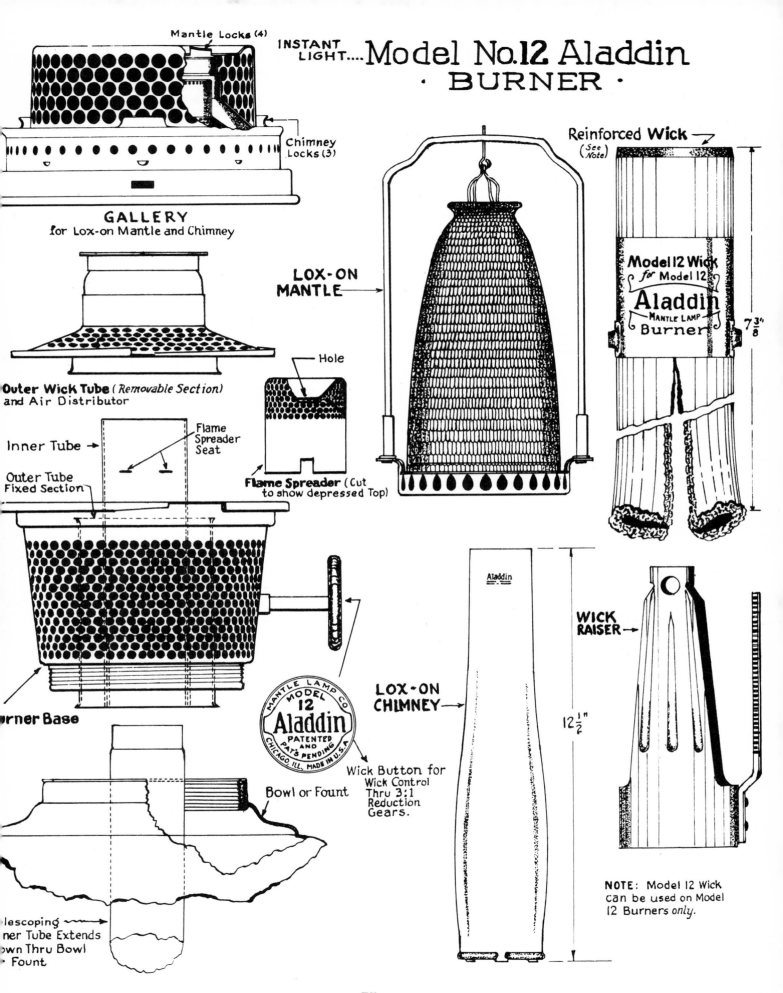

Mantle Locks (4)

Chimney Locks (3)

GALLERY
for Lox-on Mantle and Chimney

Outer Wick Tube (*Removable Section*) **and Air Distributor**

Inner Tube →

Outer Tube Fixed Section

Burner Base

Telescoping Inner Tube Extends Down Thru Bowl or Fount

Flame Spreader Seat

Hole

Flame Spreader (Cut to show depressed Top)

LOX-ON MANTLE

LOX-ON CHIMNEY

MANTLE LAMP CO
MODEL
12
Aladdin
PATENTED
AND
PAT'S PENDING
CHICAGO, ILL., MADE IN U.S.A.

Wick Button for Wick Control Thru 3:1 Reduction Gears.

Bowl or Fount

Aladdin

12 ½"

Reinforced Wick →
(*See Note*)

Model 12 Wick
for Model 12
Aladdin
MANTLE LAMP
Burner

7 ³⁄₈"

WICK RAISER →

NOTE: Model 12 Wick can be used on Model 12 Burners *only*.

75

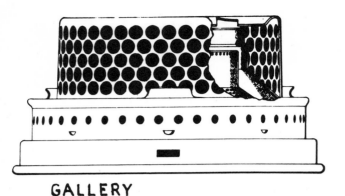

GALLERY

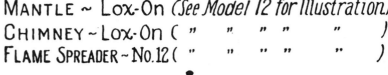

MANTLE ~ Lox-On *(See Model 12 for Illustration)*
CHIMNEY ~ Lox-On (" " " ")
FLAME SPREADER ~ No. 12 (" " " ")

WICK TUBES

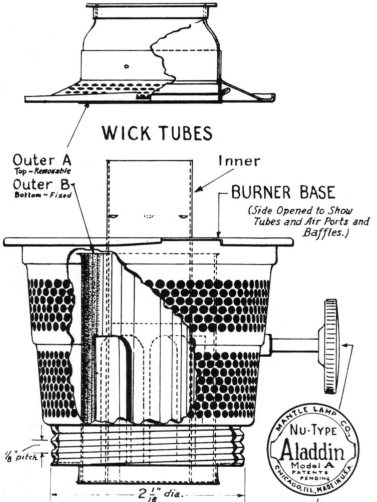

Outer A
Top ~ Removable
Outer B
Bottom ~ Fixed

Inner

BURNER BASE
(Side Opened to Show Tubes and Air Ports and Baffles.)

1/8" pitch

2 1/16" dia.

MANTLE LAMP CO.
Nu-Type
Aladdin
Model A
PATENTS
PENDING
CHICAGO, ILL. MADE IN U.S.A.

WICK BUTTON for Control of Wick Thru 3:1 Reduction Gears and Rack on Raiser

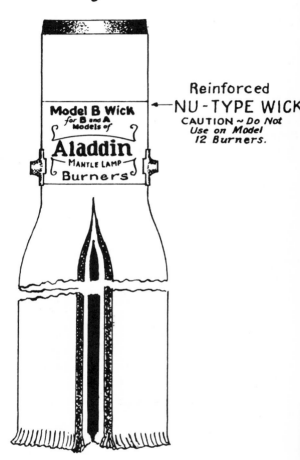

Reinforced
NU-TYPE WICK
CAUTION ~ Do Not Use on Model 12 Burners.

Model B Wick
for B and A
Models of
Aladdin
MANTLE LAMP
Burners

WICK RAISER

76

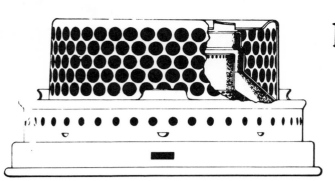

GALLERY

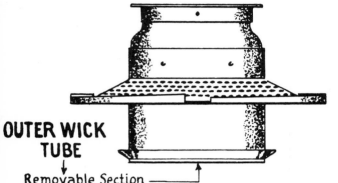

OUTER WICK TUBE

Removable Section
Fixed Section

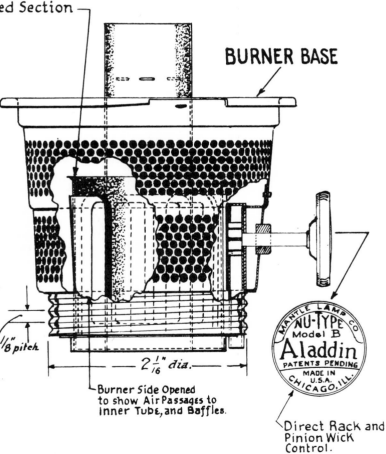

BURNER BASE

$1\frac{1}{8}$" pitch

$2\frac{1}{16}$" dia.

Burner Side Opened
to show Air Passages to
Inner Tube, and Baffles.

MANTLE LAMP CO
NU-TYPE
Model B
Aladdin
PATENTS PENDING
MADE IN
U.S.A.
CHICAGO, ILL.

Direct Rack and
Pinion Wick
Control.

INSTANT LIGHT
Nu-Type Model **B** Aladdin
· BURNER ·
SIDE - DRAUGHT ~ No Central Tube in Bowl or Fount

Complete Burner Consists of Parts Shown On This
Sheet and the Following :
FLAME SPREADER *No. 12* (See Model 12 for Illust.)
WICK ~ Nu-Type B or A (" Model A " " .)

USES :

MANTLE ~ Lox-on (See Model 12 for Illust.)
CHIMNEY ~ Lox-on (" " " " " .)

WICK RAISER

ALADDIN INDUSTRIES INCORPORATED
NU-TYPE
MODEL-B
Aladdin ®
MADE IN
U.S.A.
NASHVILLE. TENN

NOTE : *This Burner Fits All Glass Bowls or Founts,
and All Metal Bowls or Founts Without a
Center Draught Tube.*

CHAPTER 6

LIGHTING THE ALADDIN TODAY

The following directions, reprinted courtesy of Aladdin Industries, Inc., were written for the Model B Aladdin Burner. In general, the same steps are required for successful operation of other models (see page 80 for additional hints to put older model Aladdins in working order).

Assembly (new lamps)

1. Remove all wrappings and cardboard from burner.
2. Screw burner into bowl or font by turning it to the right. When using lamp with shade, attach tripod to gallery as instructed on tripod envelope.
3. Unscrew filler cap and fill bowl or font with good grade kerosene—coal oil. **Never** use gasoline or other dangerous fuels in your Aladdin.
4. Allow new wick to soak in kerosene for at least two hours.

5. Read instructions on Lox-on mantle box, then remove mantle as directed. Place mantle gently on gallery (the upper detachable part of burner which also holds chimney) and lock metal mantle base under all four catches by turning to the right.

6. Place larger end of Lox-on chimney in gallery and lock by turning gently to right just enough so chimney doesn't rattle. If locked too tightly, chimney can't expand evenly when "heated." This produces glass strains which weaken the chimney and may later cause it to break at the bottom.

7. Burn protective coating off by touching flame of match to top of mantle. Don't touch mantle with the matchstick itself as this will damage mantle.

Operation

1. After wick is thoroughly soaked with kerosene, turn gallery to left and lift gallery, mantle, and chimney as a unit.
2. Turn wick up about one-eighth inch above outer wick tube and light. When flame covers entire wick surface, carefully put gallery, mantle, and chimney assembly into place on burner by turning to right. CAUTION! Don't allow gallery to drop into position as this could injure mantle.

3. Turn wick up slowly until part of the mantle glows white and allow it to stand for several minutes to warm up burner. When normal burning warmth is reached, turn lamp up to full light capacity. Never turn lamp up to full capacity immediately after lighting as this will usually cause the lamp to smoke in a short time. A correct lighting condition exists when you have fully lighted mantle without points of flame breaking through the mantle.
4. To put out light, turn lamp down to a low flame and blow across the top of the chimney as with other oil lamps. Don't try to turn it down far enough to go out without blowing as this will not only damage wick-raising mechanism, but also could cause flame to smolder in wick tube. Hanging lamps may be put out by blowing through the burner. When not in use, leave the wick down to prevent oil seeping over the burner parts.
5. Do not clean wick unless it has a formation of carbon crust on it. If it has to be cleaned, remove gallery assembly and turn wick down even with wick tube flange. Then remove flame spreader (thimble-like part) from inner wick tube. Insert

wick cleaner in wick tube, turn wick up until it gently presses against cleaner. Turn cleaner to the right (never back and forth) slowly until wick is smooth. Never permit cleaner to ruffle or gouge wick as this will produce a ragged wick edge and high points of flame when lamp is lighted. If, in cleaning the wick, little threads are accidentally pulled up, carefully remove them with scissors. Otherwise, never trim a wick by cutting with scissors.

6. Sometimes a user will unintentionally allow his lamp to burn dry. This usually burns the wick so badly and unevenly that it is the wisest thing to insert a new wick to insure proper results from your Aladdin. Directions for replacing the wick will be found packed with each new Nu-Type Aladdin Instant Light Wick.

7. If you want a low light, never turn your lamp down so far that the flame becomes yellow. Be sure that there is always a small amount of light in the mantle.

Precautions

1. Never use gasoline or other dangerous fuels in your Aladdin. For best results, use a good grade of fresh, clean kerosene (coal-oil). Be sure that the container in which you keep your kerosene is kept clean at all times. Every time you install a new wick or every six months, empty the bowl of its oil, clean it, and put in fresh, clean kerosene (coal-oil).

AUTHOR'S NOTE: Several brands of scented lamp oils are available through hardware stores, gift shops, antique shops, and other outlets. These lamp oils, in assorted colors, are essentially a high-grade kerosene product. Preferred by most people, they do not emit the objectionable odors of common stove-grade kerosene.

2. Soak new wick at least two hours before using.

3. Handle chimney, mantle, and gallery as a unit. This protects the mantle. Do not remove chimney from gallery except to clean chimney or install new mantle.

4. Allow Aladdin to warm up. When lamp or oil is cold, never turn it up to full light capacity immediately after lighting.

5. Cleaning the wick is very important. Use your wick cleaner carefully. It is designed only to remove carbon and to keep the top of the wick smooth and uniform as on a new wick. If your wick has become too badly charred and too uneven, replace it. Remember an irregular and charred wick produces poor light.

6. Care of flame spreader: This small thimble-like part which rests on the inner wick tube must be kept clean and free from dirt. If it becomes dented, replace it at once.

7. Good air is necessary. Your Aladdin requires good air in order to burn with the blue flame which gives you your good abundant white light. You'll get the best results from your lamp if the room in which it is used is not stuffy.

8. Insure proper performance. Keep Aladdin parts properly assembled! The flame spreader must be seated all the way down—the outer wick tube securely locked in place—the mantle properly and securely locked on the gallery—the chimney properly locked to the gallery, and the gallery properly locked in position on the burner.

9. How to clean sooted mantle: If your mantle should accidentally become blackened from carbon or soot, it may be cleaned by turning the flame low and letting the soot burn off slowly.

10. Satisfaction comes with proper care: Your Aladdin is very reliable and will give perfect results if given the proper care. Given such care, your Aladdin will give you wonderfully white and bright light at extremely low cost. For best results, use only genuine Aladdin parts on your Aladdin lamp. All Aladdin parts have been scientifically designed to give the best lighting results, the most trouble-free service when used together. If you want the best service from each Aladdin part, make sure the others are genuine Aladdin too! Only that way can you be assured of the quality performance built into your lamp.

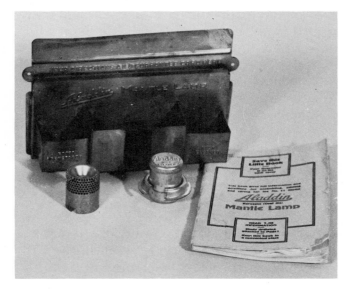

Fig. 77—A combination match box was furnished with early model lamps. The match box, designed to conveniently hang on the wall, contained the wick cleaner, an extra flame spreader, booklet of operating instructions, and the guarantee card.

Fig. 78—New (left) or original (right) burners wired for easy conversion of Model B glass lamps to electricity. The use of the three-way switch and a bulb inside the bowl creates a beautiful night light of the colorful moonstone and crystal lamps.

PUTTING OLD MODELS IN ORDER

If your lamp has not been used for some time, the following procedure will help put your Aladdin in working order.

1. Pour the kerosene out of the lamp. Remove the flame spreader and wick. Thoroughly clean accumulated carbon and dirt from all inner and outer parts of the burner. Clean the inside and outside of the font. The satin brass lamps are lacquered and will retain their finish as long as the lacquer remains intact. Do not use any coarse scouring agent that will scratch the finish. Dull, nickel-plated lamps may be polished in much the same manner as silverware.

2. A new (unused) wick is the quickest and easiest way to remedy problems with old, clogged, and damaged wicks. If a used wick must be reused (models prior to Number 6), it may have to be recharred. To do this, pour the oil out of the lamp. Remove the flame spreader. Lower the wick as far as it will go and scrape any accumulated carbon from inside of outer wick tube and the outside of inner wick tube, so that the wick will move freely. Turn the wick up so that the lowest part of the edge is even with the top of the wick

tubes; light and let it burn dry. Do not blow out, but let it char after the oil is burned out. One burning should char the wick so that it can be wiped smooth and level, but if the wick is in bad shape, it may be necessary to char it more than once. The wick cannot be charred with oil in the lamp bowl.

3. Examine the flame spreader. See that it is free of carbon deposit, that none of the little holes are blocked, and that it is not bent or cracked. Replace with a new flame spreader if the old one is damaged in any way.

4. Replace missing or damaged parts with the proper replacement (see table, page 64).

5. Fill the lamp with clean, fresh oil. Always keep the lamp well-filled with oil.

6. Install a new mantle if the old one is not in perfect condition.

7. Use an Aladdin chimney.

8. Light and enjoy the lamp. Follow the operating instructions given in the manual furnished with the lamp or follow the outline on pages 78 and 79. Models older than No. 12 Instant Light require five minutes burning at low flame to allow the burner to heat up to proper operating temperature.

EPILOGUE

The Aladdin lamp achieved recognition as the pioneer and leader of all kerosene mantle lamps. It remains the ultimate development in incandescent kerosene lighting. Millions of people in rural America depended on the superior quality light of Aladdin lamps for more than half a century.

The Aladdin also furnished a beacon in many remote lighthouses and gave modern white light to forest rangers in isolated watch-towers and cabins. Trainmen on railroads did their clerical work by the much-needed light of the Aladdin caboose lamp. In times of power-crippling hurricanes and floods, the Aladdin brought steady light to hospital operating rooms and flood control centers.

The Rural Electrification Administration (REA), created in 1935 by the Department of Agriculture, brought electric power to rural areas. During the following years, most Aladdin lamps were relegated from an essential source of light to standby service during temporary power interruptions.

Today, in many foreign countries, millions of people still use Aladdin lamps as their source of light. In America, the Aladdin continues to shine in home lighting, although primarily as a decorator lamp. The beautifully designed, brightly colored lamps of the 1930's are in much demand for modern homes. Many purists still use the kerosene Aladdin— only turning on their electric fixtures to light their Aladdin lamp. The truth of an early advertisement lingers on: "There is an Aladdin for every room in your home."

THE PROOF OF THE PUDDING

What Others Say About Their Lamps.

When you recommend your own goods there is an underlying motive! When they are recommended by others with no reason other than the natural outburst of honest enthusiasm, there is a reason why every thinking person should investigate.

Newton, Ill., Jan. 23, 1909.
The Mantle Lamp Company of America, Chicago, Ill.
Dear Sirs:—I have had one of your lamps burning in my store for about two months, and I take pleasure in testifying to its efficiency. It is all the more noticeable from the fact that I am burning twenty incandescent electric lights and the lamp makes them look like tallow candles.
Yours very truly,
C. W. KISER.

De Witt, Ark., Sept. 20, 1909.
The Mantle Lamp Company of America, Chicago, Ill.
Dear Sirs.—I have been using four of your lamps since last December and have only broken two mantles and two chimneys. I discarded electric lights as I find your lights better and cheaper.
Yours truly,
ED. BOWERS.

High River, Alberta, Canada, June 21, 1909.
The Mantle Lamp Co. of America, Winnipeg, Canada.
Gentlemen:—We have disposed of most of the lamps we ordered from you and are getting an immense amount of advertising from them.
The lamp does all that is claimed for it. In fact, one of our customers says that it burns only one-fourth of the oil that an ordinary house lamp uses.
Yours truly,
E. E. THOMPSON & CO.

Unionville, Mo., Oct. 12, 1909.
The Mantle Lamp Company of America, Chicago, Ill.
Gentlemen:—I have been going over some of my territory during the past week to see how those who have been using the "Aladdin" since last fall like them, and I find that they are all perfectly satisfied.
Respectfully,
H. H. TINSLEY.

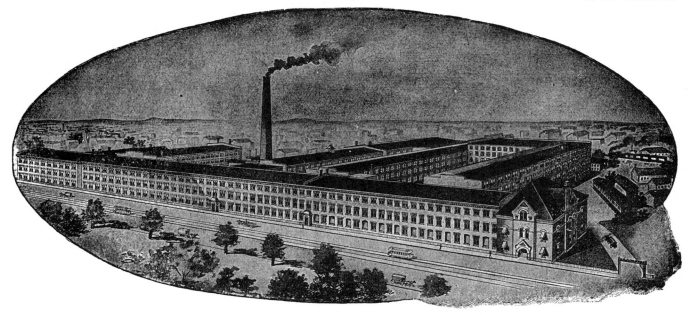

THE HOME OF THE ALADDIN LAMP AND SUNBEAM BURNER.

Buenos Aires, Argentine Republic, Sept. 13, 1909.
The Mantle Lamp Company of America, Chicago, Ill.
Gentlemen:—As we anticipated in our last letter, your "Aladdin" is an excellent affair. We are very willing to undertake the introduction of your lamps which will have a very extensive sale. Gas and electricity are much dearer here than in the States, consequently, the use of lamps is more general and, moreover, your light is **far superior** to gas or electricity.
Yours truly,
MASSALIN & CELASCO.

Carlton, Wash., Sept. 27, 1909.
The Mantle Lamp Company of America, Portland, Ore.
Gentlemen:—Your "ALADDIN" Mantle Lamp is the best in the world. Every family that sees this lamp burn, wants one of them.
Yours truly,
W. H. CARSLEY.

Indian River, Mich., July 28, 1909.
The Mantle Lamp Company of America, Chicago, Ill.
Gentlemen:—I am very much pleased with the "Aladdin" and consider it by all odds the best light that there is; all things considered.
I have given the lamp a thorough trial and I am so well satisfied that I am going to throw over the best acetylene plant that I know of and shall install your lamp.
You may ship me by express or freight three more hanging lamps.
Yours very truly,
C. H. EDWARDS.
Cashier The Indian River Bank.

Cambridge, Wis., Jan. 14, 1909.
The Mantle Lamp Company of America, Chicago, Ill.
Gentlemen:—I received the lamp O. K. It is a most wonderful lamp. I have never seen a lamp give such illumination.
REV. J. BLENKINSOPP.

These are but a mere handful of letters picked from our files. We have thousands of such letters from people everywhere. If the ALADDIN Lamp is proving so satisfactory to others, isn't it reasonable to suppose that it will also please you?

Read the other side and invest and you will find that your investment will pay dividends of several hundred percent.

ALWAYS WRITE OUR NEAREST OFFICE

The Mantle Lamp Company of America

CHICAGO, ILL, 312-320 NORTH MAY ST.   **WATERBURY, CONN., 63 CENTER ST.**
PORTLAND, ORE., 545 FIRST ST.   **WINNIPEG CANADA, 141 BANNATYNE AVE.**
MONTREAL, CANADA, 340 NOTRE DAME STREET WEST.

BIBLIOGRAPHY

Anon. **Aladdin Sales Suggestions for Franchise Dealers and Salespeople.** Publication of the Mantle Lamp Company of America, Chicago, Illinois, circa 1930.

Anon. Growth of an Idea: Mr. Johnson and the Mantle Lamp Company. **A-Ladd-In Service Newsletter.** Employee Publication of Aladdin Industries, Inc., Alexandria, Indiana. September 20, 1943, pp. 3-4.

Anon. His Was a Bright Idea. **Esso Oilways** 8 (12), 1942.

Anon. Lighting. **Encyclopaedia Britannica,** 11th Edition, pp. 651-659.

Freeman, Larry. **New Light on Old Lamps.** Century House, Inc., Watkins Glen, New York, 1968.

Ramsey, A. R. J. The origin and development of the incandescent paraffin lamps. The Newcomen Society for the Study of the History of Engineering and Technology, London, 1968.

Smith, C. H. **How to Sell Lamps.** The Mantle Lamp Company of America, Inc., Chicago, Illinois, 1914.

Thwing, Leroy. **Flickering Flames.** Charles E. Tuttle Co., Rutland, Vermont, 1967.

Weaver, Elbert C. **The Story of Gas.** American Gas Association, Inc., 605 Third Avenue, New York, New York.

CATALOG REPRINTS

Pol. Brass Table Lamp
Complete with Tripod or Globe Ring

Pol. Brass (6 inch) Store or Factory Lamp
Complete as above
Can be screwed on any gas bracket

Pol. Brass, Oil Fount (5 inch)
Fits any Fancy Vase or Hanging Lamp
Complete with Tripod or Globe Ring

Mantles, - - 30c.

Chimneys, - 30c.

18 Inch Heavy Tin Shades
Price 45c. Each

14 Inch Heavy German Opal Dome
Shades. Price $1.00 Each

10 Inch Heavy German Opal Shades
Price 35c. Each

10 Inch Green Dome Shades
Price $1.00 Each

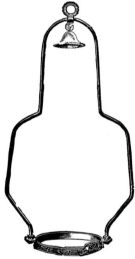

Brass Harp and Bell for Store Lamp
Price 40c.

4 Inch Brass Globe Holder
Price 20c. Each

Brass Tripod for 10 Inch Shades
Price 20c. Each

Brass Harp Crown
for 14 Inch Dome Shade
Price 30c.

Brass Bracket for Store Lam,
Price 40c.

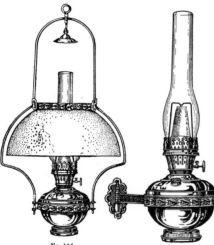

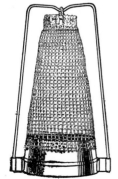

INTRODUCTION

THE MANTLE LAMP COMPANY OF AMERICA

A Corporation

under the laws of the State of Illinois, U. S. A., with principal office in Chicago, and branch offices at Waterbury, Conn.; Montreal, Canada; Portland, Ore., and Winnipeg, Can., with full shipping facilities at each point is the strongest and best equipped institution of its kind in existence.

REFERENCES:

Dun or Bradstreet,
Metropolitan Trust & Savings Bank of Chicago,
First National Bank of Portland, Oregon,
Waterbury Trust Co. of Waterbury, Conn.,
Molson's Bank of Montreal, Canada,
Bank of British North America of Winnipeg, Canada.

The agent of any Express Company doing business at any of our shipping points.

HISTORY

The Mantle Lamp Company of America was well established in the business of importing and distributing foreign incandescent oil and alcohol burners at the time the American Lamp, Aladdin, was brought out.

The Aladdin with its center draught, seamless wick and common shaped chimney gave such great promise of being able to successfully meet the wide range of conditions necessary for a general purpose, rural home lamp, that it was secured by The Mantle Lamp Company and sent out in small lots to its agents in all parts of the country.

The result was far beyond our most sanguine expectations; the demand for the lamp grew by leaps and bounds. Many agents who were induced to take a half-dozen and place them among their friends for trial, sent in their orders for quantities ranging from fifty to one hundred lamps within the first thirty days and the lamp season was nearly over before we could produce lamps fast enough to fill the waiting orders. This was during the spring of 1909.

Now it has found its way into nearly every section of the United States and Canada and several thousand of them are being used in the homes of foreign countries.

The rural-home dweller has passed his judgment on the merits of the Aladdin Lamp and after testing it in every way and comparing it with all other lamps, has pronounced it the "Standard Incandescent Oil Lamp of the World." This verdict assures the Aladdin a place among the necessities of modern life.

CONSTRUCTION

The Aladdin lamp is a mechanical device; as such, it is protected by patents in nearly all of the civilized countries of the world.

Any mechanical device that controls a strong force of nature, such as fire, should be very carefully constructed. Recognizing this fact, we begin at the foundation and every piece of brass that enters into the construction of the Aladdin lamp is made and tempered especially for the requirements of that particular part. The mechanical make-up of the Aladdin is as perfect as money and skill can produce. We are safe in saying that it has no equal.

The Aladdin is constructed on the Argand principle, having a tubular wick and a hollow tube extending from the bottom of the lamp to the top of the burner. This inner tube is a part of the lamp bowl, also a part of the burner. It permits a steady stream of cold air from the bottom of the lamp which meets and checks the heat that is being conducted downward by the metal that comes in contact with the flame at the top of the burner. This cold air equalizes the heat at a point above the danger line and allows the lamp to automatically adjust itself so that just the right amount of heat is maintained to produce the steady flow of vapor required to fill the mantle without overflowing it and causing smoke.

The so-called "lamp" which consists of a burner only and takes its air through the side of the burner, lacks this equalizing power and must be constantly watched to keep it from "crawling up" (over-heating).

The great demand for powerful white lights that are safe and cheap, suitable for churches and other public places, has resulted in the production of specially designed Aladdin lamps that for beauty and reliability have never been equalled.

The new No. 3 Model Aladdin is so constructed that the part most likely to be damaged by the intense heat of the Bunsen flame, is renewed with every new mantle (free of charge).

The "Cone Cap," as its name implies, is a "Mantle Cap," and the actual "Burner Cone," in combination. In all incandescent oil lamps, the cone is the part that comes in contact with the greatest heat, therefore, it is most liable to and often does warp out of shape in such a way that it deflects the flame and destroys the mantle. When this occurs, a renewal of the mantle does not correct the cone which will continue to destroy mantles until the lamp is abandoned in disgust.

The Aladdin is the only lamp that supplies a new cone fresh from the die with each mantle. In all other incandescent oil lamps, the cone is a permanent part of the burner and whenever it becomes damaged by heat or otherwise, the lamp is practically worthless.

This is why other lamps have earned the reputation of being short-lived.

All No. 3 Model Aladdin lamps have the unique and patented feature, the slotted generator. This generator with its oblique slots and ventilated top, creates a perfect mixing of air and vapor in proper proportions; thus, assuring better combustion and less liability of smoking.

PROGRESS

It is conceded by the world at large that this is the most progressive age in man's existence. Every department of science and every field of invention is being pushed by the indefatigable workers of the world; science and mechanics are moving hand in hand for the advancement of civilization.

Crude devices are being replaced by more scientific mechanism with astounding results. Entirely new principles are constantly being discovered and new mechanism is required in order to utilize them.

Electricity furnishes a fair illustration. At one time the Morse instruments gave us the only use of this wonderful power. Today, with entirely different mechanism in each case, we have the telephone, the interurban railways and motive power for all kinds of factory machinery. Other devices give us the spark for gasoline engines, and still another series of mechanism gives us the wireless telegraph and the wireless telephone.

Our own special field "Artificial Lighting" shows most wonderful results from the adaptation of scientific mechanism in connection with kerosene (coal oil) as fuel. The crude lamps of the past with their low grade light and offensive odors are being replaced with mechanism that converts the oil into vapor and automatically produces a gas that burns in a non-luminous flame which heats the modern mantle to a white glow, accomplishing at once the finest high-grade white light from the lowest grade and cheapest fuel.

Mechanical progress is clearly shown by the fact that the old field for labor saving machinery, such as harvesters and sewing machines, is practically full and the inventor must now turn his attention to devices that have to do with the great forces of nature, requiring a thorough knowledge of the laws pertaining to them.

These facts leave scant room for the unscrupulous imitator who knows little or nothing of the scientific principles involved and it is not uncommon to find danger and death lurking in the path of this class of articles which are usually foisted upon an unsuspecting public under the most deceptive and flamboyant advertising.

The Mantle Lamp Company of America has earned the reputation of being the leader in the production of incandescent oil lamps. The Aladdin lamp stands alone; it is the pioneer of its class. It is different from any that preceded it. It has special patented features that cannot be copied. It is the

Patents Applied For.

No. 101

ALADDIN TABLE LAMP
(Center Draught and KoneKap Mantle)

This is an ideal general purpose lamp: is easily carried from room to room; can be temporarily placed in the harp as a hanging lamp for dining room or kitchen. Made entirely of brass, finished in polished Brass or Nickel Plate. The nickel finish is preferable for general use.

Complete as shown with seamless wick, KoneKap mantle, chimney and tripod.

Price $4.50

8

---

homes that are dependent upon kerosene oil for illuminating purposes. Many of these homes enjoy all the modern luxuries, excepting white light. They have telephones, automobiles, R. F. D. service, interurban car lines, music, educated young people and the very acme of social civilization. These people need the Aladdin and we depend upon the agent to show it to them and allow them to test it under their own conditions. The Aladdin agent is a dependable business man and as such is safe to stand between the patron and any possible imposition; he is sole representative of a dignified and prosperous business that is based on the growing demand for a safe, modern light that recommends itself and needs no false representation, and in this connection it is a satisfaction to all concerned to know that The Mantle Lamp Company of America carefully refrains from using any misleading advertising such as is indulged in by venders of spurious or inferior articles.

7

---

highest achievement of science and invention in connection with artificial lighting. It is the most powerful and economical white light ever invented. It is elegantly designed for special purposes and is the only line of incandescent oil lamps that makes a complete lighting system suitable for cottage, palace or public hall.

The Mantle Lamp Company of America is the only lamp house in the world that manufactures its own mantles. These mantles are made and mounted expressly for use on its own lamps. They are produced under the most rigid inspection and are the best and most reliable mantles made.

POLICY

The selling policy of the Mantle Lamp Company of America is so just and equitable between the company and the agent and between the agent and his patron that it has resulted in the strongest organization of its kind.

The Aladdin Lamps are sold only by our agents; they cannot be purchased from wholesalers or mail order houses. Agents are given exclusive selling rights and are restricted to territory allotted to them. The selling price is uniform and the wholesale price is governed entirely by quantity. Terms are absolutely uniform, regardless of financial standing of agents. Agents are backed up by the Company and are authorized to replace any lamp that is found to be mechanically defective. They are also depended upon to canvass their field, install each lamp and show the patron whatever is necessary to insure his success.

The selling possibilities of the Aladdin are unlimited. As an illustration, the average county in the Central States has about 25,000 population. Out of this number some four or five thousand people have access to gas or electricity, leaving a rural population of 20,000 or approximately 4,000

6

90

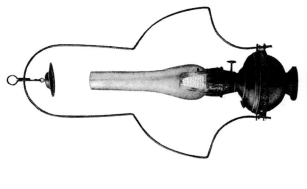

Patents Applied For.

No. 102A

ALADDIN STORE LAMP

(with Harp and Bell)

(Center Draught and KoneKap Mantle)

Made entirely of brass, finished in Polished Brass or Nickel. Same as No. 102 with addition of the Harp and Bell. Complete as shown with seamless wick, KoneKap mantle, chimney and harp and bell.

Price $4.50

11

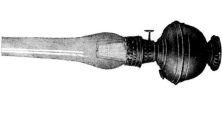

Patents Applied For.

No. 102

ALADDIN STORE LAMP

(Center Draught and KoneKap Mantle)

This lamp is usable in Harp and Bell and Bracket; also in No. 114 Aladdin Bracket and No. 113 Aladdin Hanging Lamp. Made entirely of brass, finished in Polished Brass or Nickel. Complete as shown with seamless wick, KoneKap mantle and chimney.

Price $4.00

10

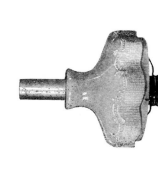

Patents Applied For.

No. 101A

ALADDIN TABLE LAMP

(with Shade)

(Center Draught and KoneKap Mantle)

This lamp is the same as No. 101. It is complete as shown with seamless wick, KoneKap mantle, chimney and shade No. 201, which makes a beautiful lamp for living room or library. The opal shade (our own exclusive pattern) does not darken the upper part of the room but gives a mild, soft light, suitable for aged or weak eyes while the reflected light below the shade is intense and suitable for reading or work that requires a strong light. Polished Brass is preferable for library or drawing room. Made entirely of brass, finished in Polished Brass or Nickel.

Price $5.00

9

91

Patents Applied For.

No. 109

ALADDIN PARLOR LAMP

(Center Draught and KoneKap Mantle)

This lamp is made in Colonial style of heavy brass, finished in Old English (Old Gold color) and Japanese Bronze, (dark oxidization). It is a beautiful lamp in either finish and is fit for the finest living room or parlor. Complete as shown with seamless wick, KoneKap mantle, chimney and 10″ shade ring.

Price $5.50

14

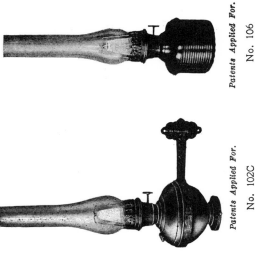

Patents Applied For.

No. 102C

Patents Applied For.

No. 106

No. 102C

ALADDIN STORE LAMP

(Center Draught and KoneKap Mantle)

This lamp is made entirely of brass, finished in Polished Brass or Nickel. Same as No. 102 with addition of bracket. Complete as shown with seamless wick, KoneKap mantle, chimney and bracket.

Price $4.50

No. 106

ALADDIN OIL POT

(Center Draught and KoneKap Mantle)

The universal oil pot is 5″ in diameter and 3¼″ deep (below the rim). It is specially intended for fancy vase stands and will also fit hanging lamp fixtures that are provided with a vase for center draught oil pot of standard size. Made entirely of brass, finished in Polished Brass only. Complete with seamless wick, KoneKap mantle and chimney.

Price $4.00

13

Patents Applied For.

No. 102B

ALADDIN STORE LAMP

(Center Draught and KoneKap Mantle)

Same as No. 102. Made entirely of brass, finished in Polished Brass or Nickel. Complete as shown with seamless wick, KoneKap mantle, chimney, harp and bell, harp crown and 14 inch opal dome shade No. 203.

Price $5.50

12

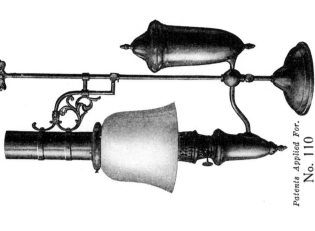

Patents Applied For.

No. 110

ALADDIN STUDENT LAMP

(Center Draught and KoneKap Mantle)

This lamp has many exclusive features found only on Aladdin Lamps: Extension shade holder, adjustable draught and removable oil tank.

The extension shade holder permits the shade to be set at any desired height. It also gives to the lamp a symmetrical and balanced appearance, fully equal to the finest modern gas and electric fixtures.

The adjustable draught makes the lamp suitable for public places where it is required to burn for many hours with little or no attention.

The removable oil tank makes it easy and convenient to refill while the inverted feed keeps the oil at the maximum level around the wick until it is all used up. This keeps the light from sagging and it will burn at its maximum for fifteen hours at a time.

For elegance of design and reliability of action, there is no oil lamp in the world that can compare with this one. It is the ideal lamp for offices, libraries, lodge rooms and pulpits. It is made entirely of brass, finished in Old English (only) and is fit for the finest homes. Complete as shown with seamless wick, KoneKap mantle, chimney and our own special design shade, No. 205. (Is not sold without shade.) Price $15.00

Price, with Art Shade No. 206, $16.50

17

Patents Applied For.

No. 109B

ALADDIN PARLOR LAMP

(Center Draught and KoneKap Mantle)

Made of heavy brass, Colonial Style, Old English or Japanese Bronze finish.

Same as No. 109, excepting that it is furnished with our special Green Cased Shade. This shade darkens the upper part of the room and is especially desirable for use where intense light is required on the table without regard to lighting up the room. It is ideal for reading table in connection with electric or other lighting systems. Complete as shown with seamless wick, KoneKap mantle, chimney, 10-inch shade ring and No. 204 shade. Jap Bronze finish is desirable with green shade.

Price $7.00

16

Patents Applied For.

No. 109A

ALADDIN PARLOR LAMP

(Center Draught and KoneKap Mantle)

This lamp is same as No. 109, made of heavy brass in Colonial Style, finished in Old English or Japanese Bronze. It is furnished with our Special Opal Shade No. 201. This shade in combination with the Old English finish makes a beautiful, medium priced parlor lamp, suitable for any home where the lighting of the upper part of the room is desirable. Complete with seamless wick, KoneKap mantle, chimney, 10-inch shade ring and shade No. 201.

Price $6.00

15

93

Patents Applied For.

No. 111

ALADDIN WALL LAMP
(Center Draught and KoneKap Mantle)

This lamp is made entirely of heavy brass, finished in Old English (only). It has all the features of the Aladdin Student Lamp; extension shade-holder, adjustable draught and removable inverted oil tank and swings on central rod. This is the only wall (or bracket) lamp on the market that uses the inverted oil tank. It is specially designed for side lamp in home, church, office or lodge room and like the No. 110, it has no equal for elegance and reliability. Complete as shown with seamless wick, KoneKap mantle, chimney and No. 205 shade. (Not sold without shade.)

Price $15.00

Price, with Art Shade No. 206, $16.50

18

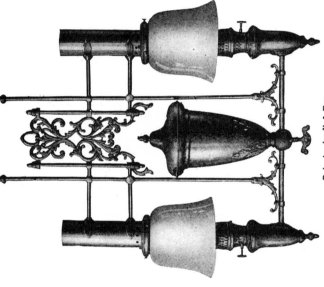

Patents Applied For.

No. 112

ALADDIN CHANDELIER
(Double Lamp)

(Center Draught and KoneKap Mantle)

Made entirely of heavy brass, finished in Old English (only). This lamp has the characteristic features of the Student Lamp, No. 110; extension shade-holder, adjustable draught and removable, inverted oil tank carrying enough oil for both lamps for twenty hours continuous burning.

This lamp is designed especially for large rooms and churches and when used in connection with Wall Lamp, No. 111 and Student (or pulpit) Lamp No. 110, it makes a complete system of inverted tank lamps that has never been equalled for lodge rooms, stores, hotels and churches. Complete as shown with seamless wicks, KoneKap mantles, chimneys and our exclusive shades, No. 205. (Not sold without shades.)

Price $25.00

Price, with Art Shades No. 206, $28.00

19

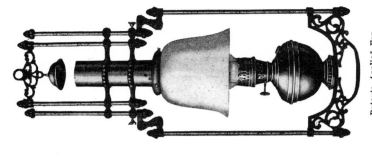

Patents Applied For.

No. 113

ALADDIN HANGING LAMP
(Center Draught and KoneKap Mantle)

This fixture has the special features of extension shade-holder and adjustable draught. It carries our special shade No. 205 or Art Glass Shade No. 206 and Store Fount No. 102. The fixture is made of iron, finished in old gold and ebony color only, and is not sold without shade. Complete as shown with shade No. 205, Store Lamp No. 102 with seamless wick, KoneKap mantle and chimney.

Price $10.50

Price, with Art Shade No. 206, $12.00

20

ALADDIN BRACKET LAMP
(Center Draught and KoneKap Mantle)

Patents Applied For.

No. 114

This fixture has the special features: Extension shade-holder and adjustable draught. It carries our special shades No. 205 and No. 206, and Store Fount No. 102. The fixture is made of iron finished in old gold and ebony color (only) and is not sold without shade. It is our most desirable, medium priced wall fixture for those who desire a fixed light.

Complete as shown with Shade No. 205 and Lamp No. 102 with seamless wick, KoneKap mantle and chimney.

Price $8.50

Price, with Art Shade No. 206, $10.00

21

No. 150
SUNBEAM BURNER
(Side Draught and KoneKap Mantle)

The demand for a cheap burner that is usable on the ordinary lamp is so great that we have provided the SUNBEAM Burner and have given it every advantage possible in a side draught burner. The SUNBEAM is made entirely of brass, uses the same mantle and chimney and burns with all the brilliancy and oil saving of the ALADDIN lamp. It fully meets the requirements for a low-price, incandescent burner, and is emphatically the best side draught burner on the market. It will fit any No. 3 (D) collar, solid bowl, flat wick lamp, and by attaching expander, (not recommended), it may be used on the same style No. 2 (B) collar lamps. The SUNBEAM cannot be used on center draught lamps.

Finished in Polished Brass or Nickel. Complete with flat wick, KoneKap mantle and chimney.

Patents Applied For.

Price $2.75

ALADDIN CAP MANTLE
For use on Model No. 1 and Model No. 2 Aladdin Lamps and Model No. 1 Sunbeam Burners.
Price 25 Cents

ALADDIN KONEKAP MANTLE
For use on Model No. 3 Aladdin Lamps and Model No. 3 Sunbeam Burners.
Price 25 Cents

[NOTE—Where consumers are unable to secure mantles from our agents or dealers, same will be sent direct from any of our offices, prepaid by mail or express at the above price in packages of 4, 6 or 12. Remit by Bank Draft, P. O. or Express Money Order.
We manufacture a complete line of Incandescent Mantles for Kerosene Mantle Lamps.]

ALADDIN CHIMNEY
A 12½-inch high-grade chimney, shaped and proportioned for use on Aladdin Lamps and Sunbeam Burners. **Price 25 Cents**

22

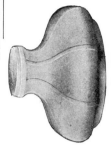

ALADDIN SHADE NO. 201
A pure white 10-inch fancy opal shade. Our exclusive pattern. Diffuses a white light to all parts of the room. Especially adapted to Library Lamp No. 101 and Parlor Lamp No. 109-A, in Dull Gold Finish.

Price 75 cents

SHADE NO. 203
A pure white 14-inch Opal Dome Shade for use on Hanging Lamp No. 102-B.

Price 75 cents

ALADDIN SHADE NO. 204
An eight-sided, green cased, 10-inch shade. Three separate casts are required to make this shade. The inside is opal; the middle, green; and the outside, crystal. It is especially pleasing with Parlor Lamp No. 109-B, Jap Bronze finish.

Price $1.50

ALADDIN SHADE NO. 205
A pure white, special design, opal shade for our new adjustable shade holder lamps (Nos. 110-114 inclusive). A departure in style for oil lamp shades, closely resembling the newest electric shades.

Price 50 cents

ALADDIN ART SHADE NO. 206
Our special design, Art Glass Shade, Brass Mounted. This is one of the most popular styles used with latest electric fixtures. With our lamps having extension holders (Nos. 110-114 inclusive) it makes the most elegant combination ever used in connection with oil lamps.

Price $2.00

AUTOMATIC SPRING EXTENSION
NO. 1
Polished Brass or Nickel. Extends 3 feet, carries 5 to 10 pounds. Its action is smooth and it has an adjustable friction brake. Especially adapted for use with lamps No. 102-A, 102-B and No. 113.

Price $1.75

23

Two views of our offices at Waterbury, Conn.

26

A partial view of our General Office at Chicago.

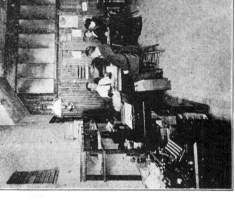

A view of a portion of our office at Portland, Ore.

25

No. 1
BUTTON
GENERATOR
Model No. 1
Price 10 cents

No. 2
THIMBLE
GENERATOR
Model No. 2
Price 10 cents

No. 3
SLOTTED
GENERATOR
Model No. 3
Price 10 cents

These generators are not interchangeable. Must be used with Model designed for them.

No. 2
GALLERY

Model No. 2

For use only on No. 2 Model Lamp and Model No. 1 SUNBEAM Burner in connection with Thimble Generator Model No. 2.

Price 50 cents

No. 3
GALLERY

Model No. 3 (with chimney band cut partly away). Used on No. 3 Model Lamps with KoneKap Mantle. Can be used in combination with Slotted Generator (Model No. 3) and KoneKap Mantle on No. 2 Model ALADDIN Lamps and No. 1 Model SUNBEAM Burners.

Price 40 cents

No. 3
WICK
RAISER
Model No. 3
Not usable in No. 1 or No. 2 Burner Bases
Price 20 cents

No. 1
WICK
RAISER
Model No. 1
For No. 1 or No. 2 Model Burner Bases
Price 20 cents

No. 3
BURNER BASE
Model No. 3

Not usable on No. 1 or No. 2 Model Bowls. (Thread is different on burner bases for No. 1 and No. 2 Model Lamps.)

Price 75 cents

24

TESTIMONIALS

The following letters are from all parts of the world. They are typical and are from people who have used the Aladdin from its earliest introduction. We have thousands of such letters which we esteem highly, because they ring true and voice the real history of the Aladdin.

High Court Vakil, Kaka Tope, Madura, India, July 19, 1910.
The Mantle Lamp Company of America,
Chicago, U. S. A.

Dear Sirs:
In regard to the sample light you have sent me, I may tell you that the ALADDIN Lamp is immensely liked here. It has been burning very well so far, shedding a beautiful, brilliant light and thoroughly answering all the praises you have said about it in your prospectus.
Yours very truly,
S. Harihara Aiyar, B. A. B. L.

San Jose, Calif., October 24, 1910.
The Mantle Lamp Company of America,
Portland, Oregon.

Gentlemen:
I have sold over eight hundred ALADDIN lamps in the past year and a half, requesting every buyer to return the lamp to me at any time they preferred their money back, I have never had a lamp returned that was paid for.
Yours very truly,
T. H. Ball.

Navarre, Kansas, May 19, 1910.
The Mantle Lamp Company of America,
Chicago, Illinois.

Gentlemen:
Yours of 5/17 received to-day. Accept my thanks for your promptness for handling my orders. In regard to the "over-night trial method", I find it is the only practical method, as the lamp sells itself upon its merit and requires no or very little talk. Out of 21 over-night trials and evening demonstrations, I sold 18 lamps. In the very near future, I expect to appoint sub-agents and handle lamps in large quantities.
Yours truly,
J. H. Kauffman.

Van Wert, Ohio, Jan. 3, 1911.
The Mantle Lamp Company of America,
Chicago, Illinois.

Gentlemen:
Please find enclosed Draft of $39.45 for which send me goods as ordered.
I received other order in good condition and was well pleased. Sold all the lamps you sent me, even my sample lamp. Have a borrowed one now. Did not have a chance to leave lamps on trial as you suggested, as each lamp was taken just as soon as demonstrated. 100% of parties called on, bought a lamp. If I had the time, believe could sell hundreds. In six instances I showed your lamp right beside another lamp and effected a sale every time. How is that?
Hoping to receive order soon, I am,
Respectfully,
R. S. Ackom.

Josephine, Pa., Jan. 7, 1910.
The Mantle Lamp Company of America,
Waterbury, Connecticut.

Gentlemen:
Your lamp received and reply will say it is more than we expected.
In order to try it we put 3 ordinary lighted lamps in one parlor, then lit the ALADDIN and extinguished the 3 and you could not tell that they had ever been lit. We think it is simplicity itself.
Now, I am ready to take an agency for Indiana County. Send me a bunch of advertising matter at once.
Yours truly,
A. W. Engle.

29

CANDLE POWER

In advertising artificial lighting devices, the candle power is often grossly over-rated.

Many appliances are advertised as giving 100-200 candle power when by an actual photometric test, they would not rate to exceed 30-35 candle power. This is especially true of advertising pertaining to incandescent oil lamps.

We believe in giving the public the actual facts and are pleased to reproduce below official reports from reliable sources.

LEWIS INSTITUTE
CHICAGO

January 6, 1911.

FRED A. ROGERS, B. S. (E. E.)
DEPARTMENT OF PHYSICS
AND ELECTRICAL ENGINEERING

Mantle Lamp Company,
172 N. Halsted St.,
Chicago, Illinois.

Gentlemen:
This certifies that I have tested in the photometric laboratory of Lewis Institute the Kerosene Mantle Lamps submitted by you for horizontal candle power. The results of the test are given below. The measurements were made by means of a Lummer-Brodhun photometer provided with a 10 c.p. standard pentane lamp.

Data of Tests.

Aladdin Student Lamp .... 76.0 c.p.
Aladdin Table Lamp .... 58.5 c.p.

Respectfully submitted,
Fred A. Rogers.

Ryerson Physical Laboratory
The University of Chicago

Chicago Jan. 11, 1911

The Mantle Lamp Company of America,
Chicago.

Gentlemen:
Your ALADDIN Student Lamp and ALADDIN Table Lamp, have just been given a thorough test. The illuminating power was compared with a Hefner Standard Lamp by means of a Lummer-Brodhun Photometer. The Table Lamp gave a uniform white light of fifty-eight and eight tenths (58.8) candle power and the Student Lamp, seventy-nine and five tenths (79.5) candle power.

Yours very truly,
[signature]
Instructor of Physics,
University of Chicago.

28

A corner of our Winnipeg, Canada, office.

97

A partial view of our office at Montreal, Canada.

27

You Can Make Your Home Bright and Cheerful with
ALADDIN MANTLE LAMPS

YOU want your home to be so cozy and attractive that Happiness and Contentment will be reflected in the face and eyes of every member of the family; so Cheerful that the young folks will not seek their entertainment elsewhere and perhaps fall in with questionable companions, but will take delight in bringing their friends to the house to spend the evening; so Brilliant with white light that all can enjoy comfort in reading, sewing, studying, playing games, etc., in any part of the room and without risk of injury to the eyes; so Tasteful in its equipment and arrangement that the neighbors will point to it with pride as one of the model homes of the community.

Every one of these ideals may be realized, at small expense, with the aid of the wonderful new Kerosene (coal oil) Mantle Lamp—Aladdin.

Solves Your Lighting Problem

Until the invention of the Aladdin, most of the improvements in lighting were for the benefit of City residents.

Very little advancement had been made in town and country lighting facilities. The need for better light was recognized, and people were looking for just such a light as the Aladdin. So, it is only natural that this wonderful new kerosene (coal oil) light should so quickly take the lead.

It is not a "new fangled" experiment, but a practical, modern, scientific method of producing an incandescent light from a common and economical fuel—coal oil. It has been on the market over seven years; has stood the acid test of usage under various conditions; has been examined and endorsed by lighting scientists of numerous Universities; has been awarded the highest prize at the great World's Exposition at San Francisco; has received the unqualified approval of the public; and its beautiful white light is now being enjoyed by several million people throughout the country. The Aladdin is recognized as the highest achievement of science in connection with artificial lighting and is revolutionizing town and country lighting conditions.

Aladdin Stands Guard Between Your Children's Eyes and Spectacles

THE eye is a very sensitive organ. Our eyesight is unquestionably the most important sense we possess. Without good eyesight, we would be pitifully handicapped in any work in which we were engaged. No one can afford to neglect the care of the eye.

In commenting upon a report of the New York State Health Department, an eminent Chicago Physician, Dr. Evans, says: "The figures show defective vision in $5\frac{1}{10}$ per cent of City children against $21\frac{8}{10}$ per cent among country children. *The poor lamps of the country are getting in their work.*"

The report to which Dr. Evans refers covers a very extensive examination of over half a million children, ranging from 6 to 16 years of age, and in various sections of the country. It will be noticed that more than four times as many children from the country were found to have defective vision.

Physicians Say Steady, White, Bright Light Is Best

In this same report, Dr. William T. Powers, A.M., M.D., makes these remarks:

"Of all the physical defects which militate against the comfort, welfare and mental advancement of school chil dren, none is of greater importance than oc ular deficiency.

"The manifestations of eye-strain are numerous. They range from simple Conjunctivitis (inflammation of the mucus membrane which lines the inner surface of the eyelid) to squint, and from headache to severe nervous conditions and mental disturbance. At first, eye-strain may cause simple fatigue after a short time at reading, sewing, writing or other use of the eyes at short range. It may cause drowsiness or simply disinclination for further near work. It may cause a watering of the eyes, redness of eyeball or edges of the eyelids. It may give rise to headache of almost any character. Many cases of vertigo, so-called sick headache or bilious attacks are caused by eye-strain.

"Parents and teachers should see that children in reading, writing or other work, requiring close and accurate vision, assume a proper position, sitting in an erect posture and having the work about fourteen inches from the eyes; *and also that there is sufficient light for the task.*

"Daylight is, of course, the best light. If artificial light must be used, *it should be even, clear, steady, and sufficiently bright.*"

Aladdin Exactly Fits These Requirements

WE could not describe the Aladdin any better than Dr. Powers has:— "Even, clear, steady, bright, nearest to daylight." Just the qualities demanded by Eye specialists.

Foresight May Save Eyesight

Get an Aladdin Now and Preserve the Vision of the Entire Family.

Another Leading Oculist Praises the Aladdin

DR. ELZEAR LA MOTHE, one of the leading oculists of the country and a Professor at Loyola University, Chicago, tested the light of the Aladdin and writes of it as follows:

"Daylight is, of course, the ideal light. Thus it follows that the nearer in color any artificial light is to that of sunlight, the easier it will be on the eye.

"The light of the ordinary open flame kerosene lamps in use in most country homes, is not only very low in intensity but the quality is very poor and injurious to the eye because of its reddish color.

"As an eye specialist, my observation from personal test of the light of the Aladdin (Coal Oil) mantle lamp convinces me that it is almost ideal, as it not only produces the required *amount* of light, but the light is also *more nearly like daylight in color and is soft and steady.*"

Can you afford to continue the risk of injuring your eye-sight and that of the other members of your family by the use of the old style, dingy, flickering, reddish lights when you can have, at small expense, a light that is said by all these great authorities to be the nearest to daylight in quality, and the most ideal artificial light in the world?

Children Run the Aladdin

ANYONE who can handle the old style oil lamp can run the Aladdin. It feeds the fuel through a wick and lights and is put out just like the ordinary oil lamps with which everyone is familiar. It is simple in construction; no complicated parts to get out of order; no pumping up; no pressure—consequently no noise and no danger; no sub-flame; no generating of the burner with alcohol or gasoline; no costly installing necessary; cannot explode and can be carried from one room to another while burning, same as a common lamp. It is no longer necessary to put up with the old style, dingy, dirty, ill-smelling oil lamps, nor throw away money on expensive and dangerous "systems" when you can have the most modern white light, equal to the white light produced by City gas and better than electricity, and yet at less expense than you have had with ordinary oil lamps. The Aladdin makes no noise, throws off no odor, is beautiful in design and finish and an orna ment to any home.

Scientists Have Tested and Approved the Aladdin

More Light on Less Oil

TESTS have been made in the laboratories of 33 of the most important Universities and Agricultural Colleges throughout the country to determine the quantity and quality of the light of the Aladdin as compared with more than a dozen styles of round wick, open-flame lamps.

The average candle power (volume of light) of the Aladdin Table Lamp in all these tests was 60 C.P. while the average candle power of the best round wick, open-flame lamps was only about 25 C.P. In other words, these tests proved that the Aladdin gives more than twice as much light as the best round wick lamps.

At the same time, a record was kept of the oil burned, and the reports showed that the Aladdin averaged 50 hours on a gallon of oil while the round wick lamps averaged only 26 hours on a gallon.

Thus, the Aladdin gives more than double the light on approximately half the oil, making the Aladdin over four times as efficient as any round wick, open-flame lamps such as the Rayo, Rochester, B. & H., Yale, Juno, Champion, Royal, Success, etc.

Aladdin Light Is Pure White

Aside from these remarkable advantages, the *quality* of light is really more important. And that is where the Aladdin so far excels other lights, as shown by the reports of the leading scientists of the country. (Exact copies of any or all of these reports will be supplied on request).

Prof. Fred A. Rogers, the noted Chicago scientist, associated with Lewis Institute, recently made what is known as a Spectrum test of an Aladdin light, a Tungsten electric and one of the best round wick, open flame lamps. This test was for the purpose of determining the quality of the light as compared with sunlight.

His report reads:

"It appears that the light from the Aladdin Lamp approaches nearer to sunlight in quality than that of any of the other lamps tested. The nearer the quality of a light approaches that of sunlight, the greater the sensibility of the eye to that light."

Lighting Engineers at the following Universities also tested the Aladdin and pronounced its light nearest to daylight:

Yale; University of Missouri; Ames Agricultural College; Michigan Agricultural College; Wisconsin University; Cornell University; Illinois University; Leland Stanford University; Maryland Agricultural College; New Hampshire Agricultural College; Dartmouth College; University of Kentucky; University of Michigan; Armour Institute; Mississippi Agricultural and Mechanical College; University of Washington; University of North Dakota; University of Idaho; University of Arkansas; Vanderbilt University; University of Maine; Carnegie Institute; University of Colorado; University of Nebraska.

It is utterly impossible to describe the quality of the light of an Aladdin. It must be seen to be appreciated. However, the statements of these noted scientists that the light of the Aladdin is nearest of any to daylight in quality, cannot be questioned. And you can easily and quickly confirm this with a trial of the Aladdin in your own home.

Expert Lighting Engineers Devoted Years to Perfecting the Aladdin

THE new Aladdin was not simply "discovered" like the mythical fairy lamp from which it derived its name, but has been the outgrowth of seven years of persistent study and toil. The idea of producing vapor from Coal Oil is not a secret but has been known to scientists for years; but to apply it to a low priced lamp, practical and simple to handle, was a big problem that has tested the skill and tried the patience of some of the greatest lighting engineers.

The Mantle Lamp Company of America has spent thousands of dollars in experimental and research work to bring the new Aladdin to its present perfection and place it in a class by itself.

It is made of brass, by the most expert mechanics in the largest and best equipped lamp factory in the world. Some of its parts are made with as much care as a watch. After leaving the hands of the workmen, they are inspected and reinspected several times and if the slightest variation is found, the work must be done over.

All this affords the purchaser assurance that the Aladdin Mantle Lamp is as perfect in construction as money, skill and labor can produce. We can say, without fear of successful contradiction, that the Aladdin has no equal.

Many Inferior Imitations

Don't judge the Aladdin by any experience you may have had with other mantle lamps.

Every success has its imitators. So it is only natural that numerous attempts have been made to mislead the public into buying inferior mantle lamps on the reputation of the Aladdin. Fortunately, however, intelligent people are not so easily "taken in" and consequently these imitators are, one by one, falling by the wayside while the Aladdin goes on more than doubling its sales each season. Of course there have been big improvements in the Aladdin itself, until the Aladdin of today is far superior to the earlier models.

Big Improvement in the Aladdin

One of the biggest improvements on the new Aladdin is the insulated Burner Base, which together with the uniquely constructed Baffle Generator (flame spreader) keeps the lamp cool, and makes it the most reliable mantle lamp ever made. Do not be prejudiced by what you may have seen or heard about cheap, inferior and unreliable mantle lamps but satisfy yourself by trying an Aladdin in your own home.

Lights Entire Room

FATHER can now enjoy his favorite paper; mother can read, mend or sew; sister can play the piano; the children can engage in their games or study—all by the light of the same lamp, if it's an Aladdin. The necessity of huddling around the table or burning several lamps in the same room no longer exists in the Aladdin-lighted home. It lights up every part of the room.

The Aladdin "Shows Off" Everything to Advantage

Every woman takes pride in the furnishings of her home. But no matter how pretty they may be, a poor light will make them look old and dull. The soft white light of an Aladdin brings out the colors of the wall paper, rugs or paintings and makes everything look natural.

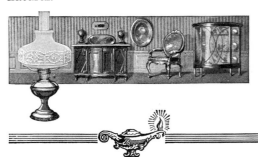

ASIDE from the comfort, convenience, healthful effects and greater efficiency of the workers inside the house during the long Winter evenings, there is a certain sentimental and moral advantage in having a properly lighted home.

Light is one of the essentials of life. Even plants grow toward the sunlight. The attraction of light is a perfectly natural one. Light means cheerfulness. Cheerfulness leads to happiness and good health.

Friends and Neighbors Admire the Aladdin-Lighted Home

Your home can be the center of attraction of your community if well lighted. Passers-by will point it out as the ideal home. Visitors will comment upon it. And after all, there is a great deal of satisfaction in having others think well of what you have.

Half the Oil Goes Over Twice as Far

THE Aladdin costs very little to operate. It burns common Kerosene (coal oil) which is the cheapest, safest and most generally used lighting fuel. Then by mixing 94% air with the 6% of vapor from the oil we get a blue flame which not only heats the mantle to a white glow, but by utilizing all the fuel it is readily seen that much less oil is consumed. In fact numerous tests by many noted scientists at the various great Universities prove that the Aladdin will burn 50 hours on one gallon of oil (70 hours on a Canadian Gallon), while the very best open-flame, round wick lamps burn only about 26 hours on a gallon. In other words, half the oil goes over twice as far in an Aladdin.

Aladdin Saves Money—Ordinary Lamps Burn Money

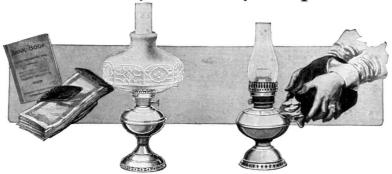

Why Burn Your Money?

THAT is exactly what you are doing when you continue to use open-flame lamps. The Aladdin will pay for itself many times over in oil saved.

For instance, if you are paying 10 cents per gallon for oil the Aladdin will cost you for oil in one year about $2.25; while to get the same amount of light, the round wick, open-flame lamps will cost for oil about $9.00 (based on an average of 3 hours per night). This means a saving in oil of approximately $7.00 per year by using the Aladdin. If you pay 20 cents per gallon for oil the saving will be over $14.00 per year.

The more you pay for oil, of course, the greater will be your saving. The Aladdin is not a luxury but an economic necessity. But aside from the question of economy, one Aladdin is better than 4 round wick open-flame lamps because of the better *quality* of its light— A trial will cost you nothing.

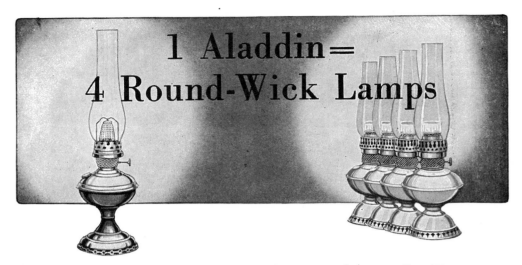

1 Aladdin Equals 4 Round-Wick Lamps

ONE Aladdin Mantle Lamp gives more than twice as much light as one of the best open flame, round wick (center draught lamps).

And each open-flame lamp burns nearly twice as much oil as one Aladdin.

So the open-flame lamps, to produce the same amount of light as the Aladdin, burn 4 times as much oil.

Which makes the Aladdin 4 times as efficient as the best round wick open-flame lamps.

It means more than 4 times as much work for the housewife to keep them clean because they smoke the chimney so badly, while there is no smoke from the Aladdin and so little carbon thrown off that a chimney can be used without cleaning for weeks at a time.

It means many times as many wicks to buy because the open-flame lamp wicks burn out rapidly while so very little of the wick is exposed in the Aladdin that one wick will last from 6 months to a year, with ordinary usage.

It means more than 4 times the chance for breaking chimneys when they have to be cleaned so often.

It means several times as much money tied up in lamps as is necessary, because you are buying weight and not service.

We don't need to tell you which is the most *economical* light.

Every Mail Brings Hundreds of Enthusiastic Endorsements

ALADDIN users soon become Aladdin boosters. Thousands of enthusiastic, complimentary letters pour into our offices each season from satisfied customers. We're proud of these unsolicited endorsements because they tell the story of the superiority of the Aladdin better than anything we could say. The Aladdin is its own best salesman. A trial usually results in a sale because no one would be satisfied to go back to the yellow, flickering light of open-flame lamps after once having the benefit of beautiful white light of the Aladdin.

ABOVE is copy of a Seal of Approval awarded the Aladdin, Feb. 1st, 1915, after a thorough test. It speaks much for the merits of the Aladdin.

You may have heard of the Good Housekeeping Institute, conducted by that great national woman's magazine, Good Housekeeping. It is maintained for the benefit and protection of their subscribers. Without the knowledge of the manufacturers all classes of articles are tested and those that are good enough to pass the exacting requirements are given this Seal of Approval. The subscribers are then told about the article in Good Housekeeping Magazine and in this way they are guided in making purchases.

In describing the results of their test of the Aladdin, they say: "This lamp is well constructed and efficient in operation. It does not require more attention than the ordinary oil lamp. Produces a mild, soft, brilliant white light. Maintenance cost low."

Such remarks, from an outside, uninterested, impartial source, should certainly help you decide to try the wonderful Aladdin and prove these statements to your own satisfaction.

Aladdin Is Perfectly Safe
Will *Not* Explode

THE Aladdin is simple in construction, feeds the oil through a wick, with no pressure, and burns any grade of Kerosene (coal oil.) It is just as safe to handle as the ordinary lamp. Through all the years that Aladdin lamps have been in use there has never been an explosion, but to still further assure the public, we have had some most severe and radical Laboratory tests made—beyond what would ever be called for in everyday use. For instance such as turning a lamp high and allowing it to burn dry; dropping it from a table to the floor while burning; tipping it on its side so the oil could run out and then surrounding the lamp with excelsior which was set on fire and burned, and all through these extreme tests there was not the slightest sign of explosion. A lamp that can endure such treatment can surely be handled with perfect safety by any member of the family.

The Aladdin differs from the old style oil lamps in the method employed to produce a modern white light, but from the same safe fuel—Kerosene (coal oil).

Page Nine

Read What the Bureau of Standards, Department of Commerce, Washington, D. C., Says About the Aladdin

THE United States Government maintains a Bureau of Standards for the purpose of testing any article submitted to them and giving the results to the public. Of course, the equipment used is the best that can be obtained—so perfect, in fact, that practically all of the instruments in the biggest Universities are based on the standards set by the Government's Bureau of Standards. Therefore, the report shown below is unimpeachable. You will note one interesting fact about this report is that it so closely coincides with the average shown by the reports of over 30 Universities referred to in a previous article. We submit, for your careful consideration, an actual reproduction (reduced size) of the letter received from the Director of the Bureau of Standards, Department of Commerce.

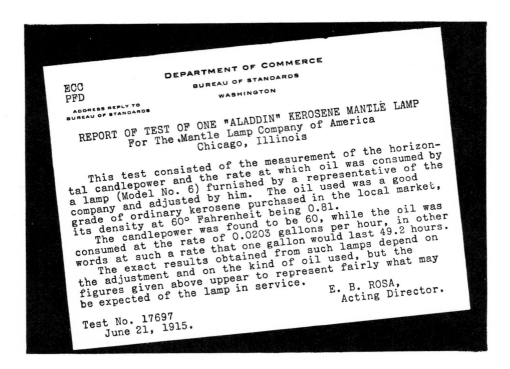

DEPARTMENT OF COMMERCE
BUREAU OF STANDARDS
WASHINGTON

ECC
PFD

ADDRESS REPLY TO
BUREAU OF STANDARDS

REPORT OF TEST OF ONE "ALADDIN" KEROSENE MANTLE LAMP
For The Mantle Lamp Company of America
Chicago, Illinois

This test consisted of the measurement of the horizontal candlepower and the rate at which oil was consumed by a lamp (Model No. 6) furnished by a representative of the company and adjusted by him. The oil used was a good grade of ordinary kerosene purchased in the local market, its density at 60° Fahrenheit being 0.81.
The candlepower was found to be 60, while the oil was consumed at the rate of 0.0203 gallons per hour, in other words at such a rate that one gallon would last 49.2 hours.
The exact results obtained from such lamps depend on the adjustment and on the kind of oil used, but the figures given above appear to represent fairly what may be expected of the lamp in service.

E. B. ROSA,
Acting Director.

Test No. 17697
June 21, 1915.

In another report, which space prevents us from showing here but copies of which will gladly be furnished on request, the Bureau of Standards gives results of tests of three of the best round wick open-flame lamps and adds these remarks in their letter to us—"It will be seen that the Aladdin Mantle Lamp burned about half as much oil as the luminous flame lamps and gave about twice as much light; that is, the use of the mantle practically multiplied by four the amount of light obtained from a gallon of oil."

There is nothing we could add that would be more convincing evidence of the superiority of the Aladdin than these facts from the Government's Bureau of Standards.

You Buy Years of Service, Efficiency, Economy and Satisfaction in an Aladdin

THE first cost of an Aladdin may seem a little greater than the old style ordinary oil lamp, but if you take into consideration the tremendously increased efficiency—how it lights every nook and corner of the room with a soft white light that saves the eye-strain—how it brightens up everything and replaces gloom with cheer and happiness—how it uses about half the oil to produce more than twice the light, and that being made of brass it should last a lifetime, you will then see that the little extra investment in the beginning is real economy, and that the Aladdin therefore, is actually low-priced as compared with the very best open flame lamp that money can buy. And there can be no question about its being far more economical than any "system" —be it acetylene, gasoline or electric.

There's a difference between "cheap" and "economical." Seldom is the so-called "cheap" article real economy in the end. Not always does the original purchase price indicate the real value. The most important considerations are:

—How long will it last and continue to give satisfactory service? How much greater efficiency can I get out of it, and How much will it save me each year as compared with what I have been using?

For instance, a cow costing $50.00 and producing only 100 lbs. of butter per year would certainly not be as good an investment as one costing $100.00 and producing 300 lbs. of butter in a year, and yet the cost of feeding would be the same.

The Aladdin combines highest efficiency with greatest economy, thus meeting the requirements of all classes and filling a long-felt need in country, small town and suburban homes where oil lamps have been in use. Even in the cities many prefer the Aladdin because it produces such a pure white, steady light, about four times as strong as the 16 C. P. electric incandescent, and much more economical. No matter how many lamps you now have you cannot afford to be without the Aladdin.

You Get What You Pay For

IF YOU pay a low price for an article, you buy an article that may be worth the low price you pay, but it will not be worth any more.

When you buy an Aladdin, you receive what every purchaser likes to get—the best possible value for your money.

Just stop and think of some of the lamp troubles you have had—how you have fussed with burners of all kinds, and how you have been annoyed by poor light.

Now, just think what it would be worth to you to have *a flood of daylight* in your house, *every* evening! A few dollars simply cannot measure the value of such an advantage to you and to your family, of the beautiful, white light with which the Aladdin Lamp fills your dwelling. You will say that every dollar you put into Aladdin Lamps is well invested. Such an investment will bring dividends, too, more than a bank's interest on your money, for not only will the Aladdin pay for itself, in oil saved, but

you will say the saving in temper, nerves and time is worth the price of the lamp, for the Aladdin burns steadily and evenly, with the least possible care. Think what could be accomplished in your home, evenings, if your rooms were well lighted.

Aside from all its economic and mechanical advantages, you will remember, the Aladdin is the *only* lamp that has won, from a score of Universities, and from thousands of users, unqualified praise as being the best kerosene (coal oil) lamp on the market, shedding a light that is "next to daylight." Here is a quality not even claimed for electric lighting.

Of course, you do not expect to get all these advantages without paying a little more than you would for the old style ordinary oil lamps. We are willing to aid you, in every way possible, to see that your home is completely lighted with the up-to-date Aladdin Lamps, by giving you a free trial with out paying any money down.

Page Eleven

109

Style No. 101

Aladdin Table or Parlor Lamp

(Illustrated above)

This is an ideal general purpose lamp; is easily carried from room to room, can be temporarily placed in the harp as a hanging lamp or used with our bracket as a wall lamp for dining room or kitchen. Made entirely of brass, finished in satin brass or nickel plate. The nickel finish is preferable for general use.

Complete with seamless wick, KoneKap mantle, baffle generator, wick cleaner, heatproof chimney, a combination match box, an extra KoneKap mantle, an extra baffle generator, and tripod for holding 10-inch shade. Height from table to top of chimney 23½ inches.

Price $6.00

Style No. 101-A

Aladdin Table or Parlor Lamp With Shade

(Illustrated above)

This lamp is the same as No. 101 with the addition of our No. 301 shade, which makes a beautiful lamp for living room or library. The artistic satin white Chinese Chippendale shade (our own exclusive pattern) does not darken the upper part of the room, but gives a mild, soft light, suitable for aged or weak eyes while the reflected light below the shade is intense and suitable for reading or work that requires a strong light. Satin brass is preferable for library or drawing-room. Made entirely of brass, finished in satin brass or highly polished nickel.

Price $7.00

Style No. 125-A

Aladdin Fancy Hanging Lamp

(Illustrated at right)

This is the very latest Aladdin design. Nothing similar has ever been produced in oil lamps. For artistic beauty, elegance and practical efficiency it has no equal. It carries our special design globe No. 325, which is made of pure crystal glass, lined with a very thin inner casing of a high-grade pure white glass that absorbs very little light. The globe is acid etched on the outside, producing an elegant satin white finish and is decorated with a beautiful rose design, hand painted in natural colors.

The No. 325 Aladdin globe compares with the very highest quality of lighting glassware on the market and diffuses the light so as to produce most pleasing results. The globe is so shaped as to produce a semi-

indirect effect, eliminating all glare of the light. Besides giving a beautiful soft white light, this hanging lamp is an elegant decoration in any home and is especially recommended for parlor, dining or living room use. It hangs out of the way of the children.

Complete with seamless wick, baffle generator, wick cleaner, KoneKap mantle, heatproof chimney, No. 325 globe, ceiling hook, fancy harp about 30 inches high with heat bell, Automatic Extension Fixture No. 1, a combination match box and an extra KoneKap mantle and extra baffle generator, finished in satin finish only.

Price $18.00

Style No. 125

Same as No. 125-A in every respect except it is not equipped with Automatic Extension Fixture No. 1.

Price $16.00

Page Twelve

Style No. 116
Aladdin Hanging Lamp
(Illustrated above)

This lamp carries our special 12-inch opal shade No. 215, so designed as to prevent casting a shadow beneath the bowl, and Aladdin Fount No. 102, equipped with seamless wick, baffle generator, wick cleaner, KoneKap mantle, heatproof chimney, harp and bell with shade holder attached, ceiling hook, a combination match box, an extra KoneKap mantle, and an extra baffle generator. The fixture and the lamp is finished in either satin brass or highly polished nickel, and is not sold without shade. It is an elegant and most reliable hanging lamp and is especially recommended for dinning room, over reading table or as a desk light. Height from ceiling hook to bottom of bowl, 32 inches.

Price $7.50

No. 1 Automatic Extension Fixture
(Illustrated above)

This fixture extends 3 feet and is especially designed for Aladdin Hanging Lamps. It has an automatic gravity lock and, like a curtain roller, it will lock at any desired point. It is the only smooth running automatic locking fixture and is designed especially for our No. 116 and No. 125 hanging lamps. It has no friction brake. Finished in satin brass or nickel. When ordering extension fixture state whether for No. 116 or No. 125 lamp.

Price $2.00

Page Thirteen

Style No. 116-A
Aladdin Hanging Lamp
(Illustrated above)

Same as Aladdin Hanging Lamp No. 116 with the addition of Automatic Extension Fixture No. 1, described on left. Height with extension closed 44 inches. Extension 3 feet long.

Price $9.50

Style No. 150
Aladdin Floor Lamp
(Illustrated at left)

This is without doubt the grandest oil lamp ever put on the market. Those who appreciate distinctively elegant parlor furnishings recognize their ideals in this creation. Heavy brass pedestal, with a large base that prevents easy tipping; massive, symmetrical vase for holding oil pot: genuine silk taffeta old rose colored shade, lined with silk and decorated with artistic old rose braid and edged with a heavy 4-inch genuine silk fringe. Size of shade 25 inches in diameter at bottom, 19 inches tall. Shades of this class ordinarily retail for from $30.00 to $35.00. Entire lamp stands 6 feet from top of shade to floor; equipped with removable oil pot, with seamless wick, baffle generator, wick cleaner, KoneKap mantle, a combination match box, heatproof chimney and an extra baffle generator and KoneKap mantle. Finished in beautiful Jap Bronze.

Price $60.00

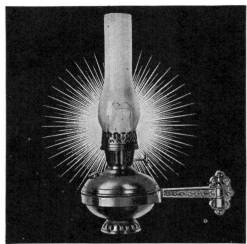

Style No. 102-C   Aladdin Bracket Lamp
(Illustrated above)
Same as No. 102 with addition of bracket and tripod.
This lamp is made entirely of brass, finished in satin
brass or highly polished nickel.   **Price $6.00**

Style No. 102-D
Aladdin Bracket Lamp With Shade
(Illustrated above)
Same as No. 102 with addition of bracket, tripod and
a beautiful Chinese Chippendale design shade No. 301.
This lamp is made entirely of brass, finished in satin
brass or highly polished nickel.
Price $7.00

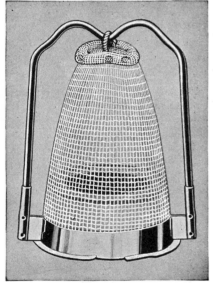

Style No. 102
Aladdin Fount Lamp
(Illustrated at left)

This lamp is usable
in Harp or Bracket,
and is the same lamp
used with the No. 116
Aladdin Hanging Lamp.
Made entirely of brass,
finished in satin brass
or highly polished nick-
el. Complete as shown
with seamless wick,
KoneKap mantle, baffle
generator, wick cleaner,
heatproof chimney, a
combination match box,
an extra KoneKap
mantle, and an extra
baffle generator. Not
suitable for use as a
table lamp. Height
over all 20 inches.
Price $5.50

Style No. 106
Aladdin Oil Pot
(Illustrated at left)

This Universal oil
pot is 5 inches in diam-
eter, 3¼ inches deep
(below the rim). It
is especially intended
for fancy vase stands
with opening in the
bottom and will also
fit hanging lamp fix-
tures that are provided
with a vase for center
draught oil pot of
standard size. Not
suitable for use as a
table lamp. Made
entirely of brass, fin-
ished in satin brass only.
Complete with seam-
less wick, KoneKap
mantle, baffle gener-
ator, wick cleaner, heat-
proof chimney, tripod,
a combination match
box and an extra Kone-
Kap mantle and baffle
generator. **Price $5.50**

Aladdin "KoneKap" Mantle
(Illustrated above)

The brilliancy and candle power of an incandescent oil lamp depends very largely upon the
quality of the mantle. The Mantle Lamp Company of America manufactures its own mantles.
The material used is the best obtainable, the
mantles are produced under the most rigid inspection and are the most reliable made. Each
mantle is mounted on the "KoneKap," so that a
new cone, which is the part most likely to become
damaged by the heat, is supplied with each mantle.
Price 25 cents

Aladdin Chimney

Aladdin chimneys are made of high-grade, heat-
resisting glass. They are scientifically proportioned
to insure best results from Aladdin lamps. 12½
inches tall with 2-inch opening at top.
Price 25 cents

Page Fourteen

Our Standing Reward Offer

To prove that our statements regarding the superiority of the Aladdin Mantle Lamp are not mere idle claims, we have on hand with our bank $1000.00 to be paid to any person who shows us any other oil burning lamp equal to our new model Aladdin in 26 important features, as follows: Quality and Whiteness of light, Strength of light, Steadiness of light, Diffusion of light, Absence of odor, Absence of smoke, Absence of noise, Simplicity of lighting and cleaning, Simplicity of operation, Economy of oil, Cleanliness, Durability, Reliability, Workmanship, Accuracy, Construction, Durability and Perfection of generator, Durability of mantles, Durability and Perfection of chimneys, Simplicity and Economy in renewal of burner cone. Relief of eye-strain, Beauty of design and Elegance of finish.

This challenge has been published broadcast throughout the country for more than two years and to date not one single lamp has been submitted for a test. This would seem like rather significant admittance on the part of other lamp manufacturers that there is no lamp that can compete with the Aladdin.

Our Guarantee Protects You

You take no risk when you buy the Aladdin because every lamp is guaranteed against defect in workmanship or material, and is guaranteed to be mechanically perfect. The Identification Card and Printed Guarantee which accompanies each Aladdin Lamp protects you not merely for 10 days, 30 days, or a year, but for years to come. Then there is our $1000.00 Reward Offer which is positive proof that you are getting the best oil burning lamp in the world when you purchase an Aladdin.

Look Us Up

If there is the slightest doubt in your mind as to our standing in the business world or our reliability, just satisfy yourself by making inquiry of any of the following references:

Duns or Bradstreet's Commercial Agencies.

The Mechanic's and Trader's State Bank, Chicago, Ill.

The Greenwich Bank, New York, N.Y.

The Waterbury Trust Co., Waterbury, Conn.

First National Bank, Portland, Ore.

The Molson's Bank, Montreal, Can.

The Bank of British North America, Winnipeg, Canada.

Or the Agent of any Express Company doing business at any of our shipping points.

Aladdin—the Gold-Medal Lamp

ON the back cover of this book, you will find a reproduction of the First Prize Blue Ribbon awarded to the Aladdin at the great World's Exposition at San Francisco—the highest honor in its class, in competition with various makes of Kerosene (Coal Oil) Lamps. When you stop to think that not only this country but numerous foreign countries as well were represented at this International Exposition, you can appreciate that to be awarded the Gold Medal Prize establishes the Aladdin as the best oil lamp in the world, and puts it in a class by itself.

The Home of the Aladdin

Here is the great big manufacturing plant, splendidly equipped with the most up-to-date labor saving machinery, where the Aladdin is made. You can appreciate that with facilities like this, and with perfectly trained workmen, the highest quality lamps are produced at the lowest possible cost. Then with offices and warerooms in Chicago, New York City, Portland, Ore., Montreal, Can., and Winnipeg, Can., we save excessive shipping costs and can deliver the lamp to any part of the country at a price within the means of everyone and at a price that cannot be duplicated, quality considered.

In this large mill, the brass is specially made up for Aladdin lamps and rolled to perfectly uniform thickness. Every piece is carefully prepared to fit the particular purpose for which it is to be used.

HIGHEST PRIZE

for the

Best Kerosene Lamp
(COAL OIL)

Was Awarded to the

ALADDIN

at the

PANAMA-PACIFIC
INTERNATIONAL
EXPOSITION
SAN FRANCISCO

THE GOLD MEDAL and BLUE RIBBON, representing the very highest honor in the Kerosene (coal oil) lamp class at the World's Exposition, San Francisco, were awarded to the Aladdin.

The International Jury of Awards, composed of great scientists from all nations, selected the Aladdin as the *best* in comparative tests with the numerous other oil lamps from various foreign countries, as well as the United States.

A trial of the Aladdin will convince you that this recognition of merit was well deserved.

115

Sept. 20, 1917

No. 23C

WHOLESALE PRICE LIST OF
Aladdin LAMPS
SUPPLIES AND EXTRA PARTS

TERMS:—Net Cash. Prices Quoted are F. O. B. Chicago. REMITTANCES must be made by P. O. Money Order, Express Money Order or Bank Draft.

This List Supersedes All Issues Previous to this date and is Subject to Change Without Notice

Style	Description	Wholesale Price Each
STYLE No. 701	ALADDIN TABLE OR PARLOR LAMP, complete as illustrated in circular with one Aladdin center draught table lamp bowl No. 701, one Aladdin center draught burner with baffle generator, wick, mechanical wick cleaner, one extra baffle generator, one KoneKap mantle, one Aladdin chimney and one No. 401 Aladdin satin white shade. Finished in beautiful satin brass.	$ 7.50
STYLE No. 705	ALADDIN BRACKET LAMP, complete as illustrated above, consisting of one Aladdin lamp fount No. 716, one Aladdin center draught burner complete with baffle generator, wick, mechanical wick cleaner, one extra baffle generator, one KoneKap mantle, one Aladdin chimney, one Aladdin bracket, tripod and Aladdin satin white shade No. 401. Finished in beautiful satin brass. This lamp is especially suited for use in the kitchen.	7.50
STYLE No. 716	ALADDIN HANGING LAMP (without No. 2 extension fixture.) This lamp is the same as style No. 717 with the exception that it is not equipped with the Aladdin automatic extension fixture No. 2, but is equipped with ceiling hook.	9.50
STYLE No. 717	ALADDIN HANGING LAMP (with No. 2 extension fixture.) Complete as illustrated in circular, with one Aladdin fount No. 716, one Aladdin center draught burner complete with baffle generator, wick, mechanical wick cleaner, one extra baffle generator, one KoneKap mantle, one Aladdin chimney, one Aladdin harp 0716, one heat bell, one Aladdin satin white shade No. 416 and an Aladdin automatic extension fixture No. 2 complete. The fixture and lamp are finished in beautiful satin brass.	11.50

No. 4—Aladdin Carrying Case Size 16 inches long, 12 inches wide and 14½ inches high; made of wood covered with leatherette, equipped with brass finish trimmings. Conveniently partitioned for carrying one Aladdin table lamp complete with the No. 401 shade, chimney, mantle, tripod; an extra chimney, six extra mantles and plenty of room for printed matter. Made to fit a buggy or automobile. Weight empty 6 pounds. Price..................**$2.90**

Suitable Assortments for Beginners

Half Dozen Lot	One Dozen Lot	Two Dozen Lot	Three Dozen Lot
4 No. 701	7 No. 701	14 No. 701	21 No. 701
2 No. 717	5 No. 717	10 No. 717	15 No. 717
1 No. 701 FREE	4 No. 701 FREE	8 No. 701 FREE	12 No. 701 FREE

NOTE—When the Distributor gets into the field he will find many homes where he can place Aladdin Bracket Lamps No. 705. He may also find some homes where the ceiling is too low to require extension fixture No. 2. Therefore he will vary the above assortments by including some No. 705 Aladdins and some No. 716 Aladdins.

The Mantle Lamp Company of America, Inc.
Largest Kerosene (Coal Oil) Mantle Lamp House in the World

Chicago, New York City, Portland, Ore., Winnipeg, Montreal

See Inside for Our Great Free Lamp Offer

Wholesale Price List—Continued

EXTRA PARTS

Description	Wholesale Price	Retail Price
Aladdin Automatic Extension Fixture No. 2 for use with No. 716 Aladdin Hanging Lamp, satin finish....	$2.00	$3.00
Baffle Generator for No. 7 Model Aladdin....	.10	.15
Baffle Generator for Models 5 and 6 Aladdin....	.10	.15
Baffle Generator for Models 3 and 4 Aladdin....	.10	.15
Bracket used with No. 705 Aladdin (can also be used with No. 701) satin finish....	.50	.75
Bug Screen to prevent bugs from getting in chimney and breaking mantles for No. 6 Model Aladdin fount, either satin or nickel finish....	.50	.75
Aladdin Burner Base, satin or nickel finish (state whether for models 2, 3, 4, 5 or 6 and be sure to state finish desired)....	.15	.25
Aladdin Model No. 7 Burner complete with Burner Base, Outer Wick Tube, Gallery, Wick Rack, Mounted Wick, two Generators and one Wick Cleaner, satin finish....	.75	1.25
Ceiling Hook for Aladdin Hanging Lamp No. 716, satin finish....	2.80	3.50
Gallery for Model No. 7 Aladdin, satin finish....	.15	.20
Gallery for No. 2, 3, 4, 5 and 6, satin finish or nickel (state which desired)....	.40	.70
Aladdin Harp No. 0716 (for No. 716 Hanging Lamp) complete with shade holder, lamp supporting band, heat bell and ceiling hook, satin finish....	1.90	2.85
Aladdin Heat Bell for Aladdin Hanging Lamp No. 716 or 717....	.10	.15
Tripod (Model 7) for holding shade No. 401, for use on No. 701 or 705 Aladdin, satin finish....	.10	.20
Tripod (Model 6) for holding shade No. 301, satin or nickel finish....	.10	.20
Wick Cleaners....	.10	.15
Wick Rack....	.05	.10

ALADDIN KONEKAP MANTLES

	PRICE		
	Wholesale		Retail
	By Mail Prepaid	By Express or Freight Not Prepaid	
In lots of 4....	$1.20	$1.50	
In lots of 6....	1.65		
In lots of 12....	2.80	2.65	30c each
In lots of 2 dozen....		2.65 per dozen	
In lots of 3 dozen....		2.60 "	
In lots of 6 dozen....		2.55 "	
In lots of 12 dozen or over....		2.50 "	

If you wish mantles insured when sent by Parcel Post, add 5 cents

ALADDIN CHIMNEYS

Description	Wholesale Price	Retail Price
Aladdin Chimneys are scientifically proportioned for our lamps; therefore to insure best results always use chimneys branded "Aladdin." 12½ inch tall and 2 inch opening at top.		
In lots of less than one dozen....	$ .25 each	30c each
In lots of one dozen or less than one case....	2.40 per doz.	
In six dozen case (original package)....	2.25 "	

ALADDIN SHADES—Our Exclusive Designs

No.	Description	Wholesale Price Each	Retail Price Each
No. 401	Aladdin Satin White Shade for Aladdin Lamps Nos. 701 and 705 (Model 7)....	$ .70	$1.25
No. 416	Aladdin Satin White Shade for Aladdin Hanging Lamp No. 716 (Model No. 7)....	1.60	2.50
No. 301	Aladdin 10 inch Satin White Finish Shade for lamps No. 101, 102C and 106. (Models 1, 2, 3, 4, 5, 6)....	.70	1.25
No. 215	Aladdin Opal Shade for lamps No. 116 and No. 116A, also old style 115 and 115A. (Models 4, 5, 6)....	.95	1.50
No. 325	Aladdin Satin White Finish Globe with hand painted rose design in natural colors; for Lamps No. 125 and No. 125A....	3.75	5.00

Aladdin Wicks (Mounted)

(Be Sure to Specify What Model Wick is Desired)

Description	Wholesale Price		Retail Price
	In lots of 6 and over	In dozen lots	
Aladdin Wicks (Model No. 7) Charred, mounted in Brass Carrier and packed in individual cartons.... (The No. 7 will not fit previous model lamps.)	25c each	$2.40 per doz.	30c each
Aladdin Wicks Models 4, 5 and 6 Charred, mounted in...			

Regular Profits, Extra Compensation and Special Sales Bonus Offers

This information is for Aladdin Distributors and Demonstrators only. It shows the big money that can be made. The exceptionally large profits from free goods—goods that cost you nothing—every cent of the selling price is yours—every dollar stays in your pocket.

The Regular Profits are Liberal. The Extra Compensation Is Attractive, the Special Sales Bonus Is Inviting, But Add the Three Together and the Figures Become Amazing.

The Aladdin, a proven fast seller, should this season surpass all previous records. The public is better educated than ever before to white light. Hence, opportunity now has double the significance and promises of former years. Aim for a big bonus.

EXTRA COMPENSATION

Consists of free No. 701 Aladdins—1 free with every order for 6 and 4 free with every order purchased. In buying 6 lamps, 7 will be sent along with every lamp order purchased. In buying 12 lamps, 16 will be sent.

SPECIAL SALES BONUS

Style No. 701 Aladdins are given free as a reward for effort and ability when sales have reached certain totals. These lamps are sent only when the required number of sales coupons are returned to us as shown in the chart below.

Letters below denote classifications and figures opposite denote the number of sales coupons it is necessary to return to reach classification.		This column shows number of sales bonus lamps given free. Numbers are carried forward so that each classification shows total bonus lamps received on all coupons redeemed from the first 18. No redemption will be allowed until the first 18 coupons are returned, and coupons will be redeemed only in No. 701 Aladdin lamps.	Your profit on total number of bonus lamps received reaching various classifications.	Number of extra compensation lamps given free from the start until reaching various classifications.	Your profit on total number of extra compensation lamps received until reaching various classifications.	Your profit on lamps actually bought and not given free from the start until reaching various classifications.	YOUR TOTAL PROFIT — In this column is shown your total gross profits from the start until reaching various classifications based upon the sale of number of lamps shown opposite various profit figures.
F —	36	Besides the regular sales bonus of 2 complete No. 701 Aladdin table lamps given free with every order for 18 coupons returned, a special class bonus of 1 No. 701 Aladdin will be given when reaching class F. Total sales bonus lamps received will then number 5 giving you a profit of $45.00	$ 45.00	9	$ 81.00	$ 60.50	$ 186.50 for selling 41 Aladdins
E —	90	Besides the regular sales bonus of 2 complete No. 701 Aladdin table lamps given free with every order for 18 coupons returned, a special class bonus of 2 No. 701 Aladdins will be given when reaching class E. Total bonus lamps for this class will number 8. Profit $72.00. Total bonus lamps received 13	$ 117.00	21	$ 189.00	$ 142.50	$ 448.50 " 97 "
D —	180	Besides the regular sales bonus of 2 complete No. 701 Aladdin table lamps given free with every order for 18 coupons returned, intermediate bonuses of 3 No. 701 Aladdins will be given for every 45 coupons returned until reaching class D. Total bonus lamps for this class will number 16. Profit $144.00. Total bonus lamps received 29	$ 261.00	40	$ 360.00	$ 274.00	$ 895.00 " 189 "
C —	315	Besides the regular sales bonus of 2 complete No. 701 Aladdin table lamps given free with every order for 18 coupons returned, intermediate bonuses of 4 No. 701 Aladdins will be given for every 45 coupons returned until reaching class C. Total bonus lamps for this class will number 27. Profit $243.00. Total bonus lamps received 56	$ 504.00	67	$ 603.00	$ 463.50	$ 1570.50 " 324 "
B —	585	Besides the regular sales bonus of 2 complete No. 701 Aladdin table lamps given free with every order for 18 coupons returned, intermediate bonuses of 5 No. 701 Aladdins will be given for every 45 coupons returned until reaching class B. Total bonus lamps for this class will number 60. Profit $540.00 Total bonus lamps received 116	$1044.00	120	$1080.00	$ 838.00	$2962.00 " 596 "
A —	1170	Besides the regular sales bonus of 2 complete No. 701 Aladdin table lamps given with every order for 18 coupons returned, intermediate bonuses of 6 No. 701 Aladdins will be given for every 45 coupons returned until reaching class A. Total bonus lamps for this class will number 143. Profit $1287. Total bonus lamps received 259	$2331.00	230	$2070.00	$1625.00	$6026.00 " 1179 "

NOTE.—Figures showing extra compensation lamps and profits on lamps actually bought, are based on Distributor purchasing dozen orders or more. When nearing a classification, if a dozen is not sufficient to reach it, and a two-dozen order would amount to four or more lamps over, orders for 15 with 6 free, 18 with 6 free, 21 with 7 free, are used. In this way the maximum number of free lamps are obtained and the minimum number of coupons are left over. It is also assumed that all lamps received upon reaching classification are sold and the profits therefrom are given credit to the classification just reached. Coupons will remain after all the lamps are sold and there are carried over into the next classification where they apply toward another bonus. It is further assumed that one-fourth of the lamps sold were style No. 717 and the remainder style No. 701. The total profits shown in the classifications apply only in case of a new distributor continuing to sell from one classification to another until reaching Class A.

Sales Coupons are valuable. On the first redemption their value in Aladdins (retail prices) is equivalent to $1.00 for each. Thereafter they are worth still more because the bonuses gradually increase and coupons on the bonus lamps are used in getting additional bonuses.

Which Bonus are You Going to Strive for? What Amount of Total Profit will You Aim for? Set the Mark High and Strain Every Effort to Reach It. Keep the Goal Clearly Before You—Don't Let It Vanish from Sight—Push Aside Everything that Casts a Shadow Over It. Go Forward Irresistibly. Think of Success—Hope for It—Work for It. Thousands of others have Won—So Can You.

The Mantle Lamp Company of America, Inc.

New York   Montreal   Portland, Ore.

Winnipeg

Chicago

Improvements in the New No. 8 Model Aladdin

The big and far-reaching improvements in the new No. 8 Model Aladdin will please all classes of people.

Not only have all the important and valuable features of all previous Models been retained in the new No. 8, but the mechanical construction has been greatly perfected and the lamp and shade has been so designed as to produce a pleasing and beautifully artistic effect.

One of the splendid mechanical improvements is the new wick raising device which will enable the operator to set the wick with an accuracy and evenness never before attained in any incandescent oil lamp. This is a real advantage and one that will be highly appreciated by all users.

Then the telescopic center tube in the new No. 8 Aladdin makes it possible to retain all the advantages of the center draught and at the same time permits of making the burner complete within itself with its center tube independent of the center tube in the bowl. Hence any ordinary damage to the bowl will not affect the concentric arrangement of the parts in the burner. This also permits the renewal of the burner without regard to the renewal of other parts—a feature that will be recognized as very important to users.

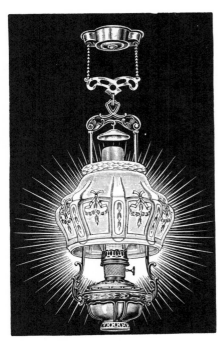

Style No. 817

ALADDIN HANGING LAMP, complete as illustrated above, consisting of one Aladdin fount and Aladdin center draught burner complete with baffle generator, wick, mechanical wick cleaner, one extra baffle generator, one KoneKap mantle, one Aladdin chimney, one Aladdin harp 0816, one heat bell, one Aladdin satin white shade No. 416, an Aladdin automatic extension fixture No. 3 complete, and an extra KoneKap mantle. The fixture and lamp are finished in satin brass and the design of the lamp bowl is made to harmonize with the design of the shade in such a way as to produce the most beautiful effect. This Aladdin is an elegant and most reliable hanging lamp, and is especially recommended for dining room, sitting room or parlor. Height from ceiling to bottom of bowl when extension fixture is not lowered, 32½ inches; with extension lowered 60 inches .... **Price $15.00**

Style No. 805

ALADDIN BRACKET LAMP, complete as illustrated above, consisting of one Aladdin lamp fount, one Aladdin center draught burner complete with baffle generator, wick, mechanical wick cleaner, one KoneKap mantle, one Aladdin chimney, one tripod, one Aladdin satin white shade No. 401, one Aladdin bracket, one extra KoneKap mantle and one extra baffle generator. Made entirely of brass and finished in satin brass. This lamp is especially suited for use in the kitchin .... **Price $9.00**

Style No. 801

ALADDIN TABLE OR PARLOR LAMP, complete as illustrated above. This is an ideal general purpose lamp; it is easily carried from room to room, can be used with our bracket as a wall lamp. Made entirely of brass, finished in satin brass. The design of the lamp bowl and satin white shade are made to harmonize, so that a very artistic effect is produced. Does not darken the upper part of the room, but gives a mild, soft light suitable for aged or weak eyes, while the reflected light below the shade is of the right intensity for reading or work that requires a strong light. Complete with one Aladdin center draught table lamp bowl, one Aladdin center draught burner with baffle generator, wick, mechanical wick cleaner, one KoneKap mantle, one Aladdin chimney, one tripod, one No. 401 Aladdin satin white shade, one extra KoneKap mantle and one extra baffle generator .... **Price $9.00**

Aladdin Lamps

For Every Room in the Modern Home

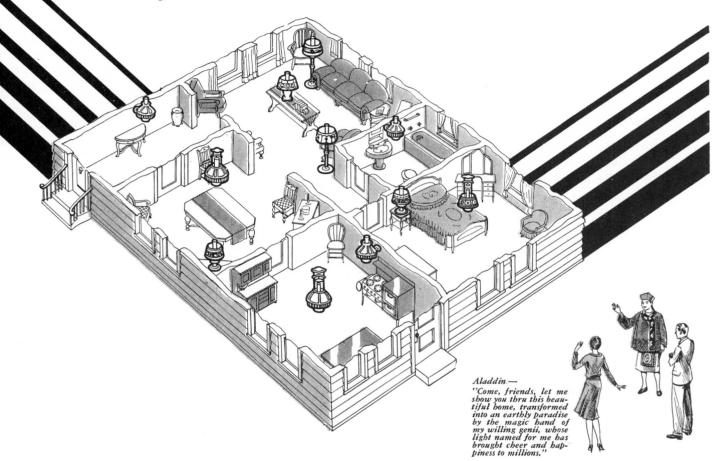

Aladdin.—
"Come, friends, let me show you thru this beautiful home, transformed into an earthly paradise by the magic hand of my willing genii, whose light named for me has brought cheer and happiness to millions."

Instant White Light from KEROSENE

The new instant light Aladdin Mantle Lamp is not a new fangled experiment, but is a time tried and tested device for producing the highest quality of modern white light from kerosene {coal-oil} with the maximum of reliability, safety, convenience and economy. The first Aladdin was invented some twenty years ago, and although a success from the start, has been improved through successive models until today the Model 12 Instant Light Aladdin is regarded as near perfection as seems possible.

The Aladdin is simplicity itself in its operation.

It is lighted and operated much like the old-fashioned wick lamp which makes its care and operation quickly and easily learned even by children. In results, however, the light of the Aladdin is vastly different than the ordinary wick lamp.

The Aladdin is constructed upon highly scientific principles, the fuel being changed into a vapor or gas, and the vapor mixed with air in the proportion of 1 to 16 produces a blue flame {an indication of perfect combustion and extreme economy} and the heat thus secured is transformed into light through the means of an incandescent mantle.

Strength of Aladdin Light

The Aladdin produces a pure white light of full sixty candle power, a light equal to ten ordinary lamps, and will operate for 50 hours on a gallon of fuel. The light is soft and mellow, and of such a character as is best suited for the human eye.

Quality of Aladdin Light

In quality, Aladdin light is the nearest approach to sunlight of all artificial lights. This statement and statements as to strength of light is verified by tests made in the foremost laboratories of the world. It is, therefore, seen that Aladdin light is even more desirable than either electricity or gas.

Economy of Aladdin Light

As the Aladdin produces 60 candle power for 50 hours (68 hours in Canada) on a single gallon of oil, while the best round wick lamp will produce but 25 candle power light for but half the time, it is readily seen that it is over four times as economical. The Aladdin will readily save its cost in a short time in the lesser quantity of fuel consumed, to say nothing of the difference in the quality of its light.

Safety of Aladdin Light

The chief requirement for a home lighting device should be that it be safe both as to the lamp itself and the fuel it uses. The safety of kerosene (coal-oil) as a lighting fuel has long been recognized, and very exhaustive tests of the Aladdin both in laboratories and in millions of homes has proved there is not the slightest danger in its use.

Other Aladdin Features

The new Model 12 Aladdin is the simplest, quickest lighted kerosene mantle lamp ever made. A match and a minute is all that is required to put it in full operation. There is no preliminary heating of a generator, no torch, or no pumping up necessary. The perfect combustion of fuel eliminates

So Simple a Child Can Operate It.

odor and smoke, and as there is no pressure there is no noise. Once properly lighted, the Aladdin will emit a constant, never-varying pure white light hour after hour without any attention. It will be seen at once that the Aladdin combining as it does so many desirable features, is the ideal light for homes without electricity no matter where they may be located. All but a very small percentage of rural homes use oil for lighting, and countless small town and outlying city homes are likewise dependent upon it. The Aladdin is furnished in such a variety of styles that homes may be completely lighted with them, with a style exactly suited to its purpose.

The Aladdin Is Beautiful As Well As Practical

The following pages portray the entire Aladdin line. Aladdins are finished in either highly polished nickel or bronze and may be equipped with plain glass shades in handsome designs or in hand-painted glass or parchment shades as desired. This makes it possible for the user of oil to have his home as artistically and as beautifully lighted as the most modern of city homes. Particular attention is called to the Aladdin Floor Lamp, something never before obtainable in a kerosene lamp.

Aladdin Accessories

It is well known that accessories for Aladdin Lamps, like the lamp itself are manufactured with more care and greater accuracy than any other product of a similar nature. The high standard of efficiency of the lamp itself can only be maintained by always using an equally high standard of accessory. Accessory list is given on page 12 of this booklet.

Its Safety an Outstanding Feature

Aladdin Table Lamps

Aladdin:—
"Here, friends, you see the Aladdin Table lamp in all its glory—its soft, silent, mellow light makes reading and sewing an endless pleasure."

Illustrated above is Aladdin table lamp, No. 1200N {nickel} or No. 1200B {bronze} equipped with Parchment Shade No. 634. {See center spread for shade in full color.}

Above illustration shows Aladdin table lamp No. 1200N {nickel} or No. 1200B {bronze} equipped with Decorated Glass Shade No. 601S. {See center spread for shade in full color.}

Aladdin Table Lamp
Style No. 1200N or No. 1200B

Consists of Aladdin center-draught table lamp bowl, one Aladdin center-draught instant light burner with flame spreader, Lox-on wick and mechanical wick cleaner; one Lox-on mantle, one Aladdin Lox-on chimney, one tripod for holding a 10-in. shade, and one extra Lox-on mantle. This is an ideal general purpose lamp. It is easily carried from room to room, can also be used with our bracket as a wall lamp. Made entirely of brass, finished in highly polished nickel {No. 1200N} or bronze {No. 1200B.} Shade extra if desired.

PAGE THREE

Aladdin *Table Lamps*

Aladdin:—"You see the Aladdin table lamp, again. Here used as a bedroom or night light. In fact it may be used in a great variety of ways, as it is readily portable, therefore the ideal general purpose lamp."

Illustrated above is Aladdin Table lamp, No. 1200N {nickel} or No. 1200B {bronze} equipped with Plain Glass Shade No. 601.

Aladdin Table Lamp
Style No. 1200N or No. 1200B

As illustrated in center above, consists of the various parts as listed on page three. It is the base lamp for all Aladdins of this style, and is finished in highly polished nickel {No. 1200N} or bronze {No. 1200B}. It may be equipped with plain glass shade No. 601, or decorated glass shade No. 601S, or with any 15-inch parchment shade of No. 630, 631, 632, 633, 634, or 635. Prices quoted on this style do not include shade or 15-inch tripod.

Aladdin Oil Pot
Style No. 1220S or No. 1220B

Illustrated above consists of all essential parts, ready for operation with one extra Lox-on Mantle. The No. 1220 Aladdin Oil Pot is the lighting unit for all Floor and Vase lamps. Finished in Satin Brass or Bronze to harmonize with finish of fixture with which used.

Aladdin *Vase Lamps*

Illustration above shows Aladdin Vase Lamp, No. 1240, equipped with Parchment Shade No. 640. Vase finished in Variegated Verde. Lighting Unit is Aladdin, No. 1220S in Satin Brass finish.

Shown above is the Aladdin Vase Lamp, No. 1242, equipped with Parchment Shade No. 642. Vase finished in Bengal Red. Lighting Unit is Aladdin No. 1220S in Satin Brass finish.

Aladdin Vase Lamp, No. 1241, above is shown equipped with Parchment Shade No. 641. Vase is finished in Variegated Two-tone Tan. Lighting Unit is Aladdin, No. 1220S in Satin Brass finish.

THESE new Aladdin Vase Lamps are unquestionably the most decorative kerosene lamps ever made. Not only do they provide an abundance of modern white light, but with the splendid assortment of both vases and shades from which to choose a charming combination may be found which will harmonize with any color scheme of home decoration. These Venetian Vases are artistically hand decorated and fired, therefore the finish is as permanent as that of a china dish, and may be washed as easily. All vase lamps are supplied with an Aladdin collapsible tripod by which any shade of Design No. 640, 641, 642, 643, 644 or 645 (See page 6) may be fitted. Prices on Vase Lamps No. 1240, 1241 and 1242 include Aladdin Oil Pot, No. 1220S, Venetian Vase and Collapsible Tripod. Shade extra, if desired.

Hand Decorated Parchment Shades to Beautify Your Home

For Vase Lamps and Floor Lamps

For Table Lamps and Hanging Lamps

In the decoration of a home there is nothing that plays so important a part as artistic artificial lighting. While the Aladdin lamp itself has always provided the proper quality and quantity of light, the recent demand for color in the home has prompted us to now supply a full line of beautifully hand decorated shades in both glass or parchment with which Aladdins may be equipped. All Aladdin shades are hand-decorated in our exclusive designs created by expert shade designers, are in the most popular motifs, and are pleasingly proportioned for each style of Aladdin for which they are recommended.

Aladdin parchment of which all our Parchment Shades are made is an exclusive Aladdin product. It has a high degree of transparency—does not warp or buckle or turn yellow and is moisture proof. Permanent transparent oil paints are used exclusively and preserve the brilliance and beauty of the shades indefinitely. Aladdin Parchment may be readily cleaned with a damp cloth in case it becomes necessary. A heavy gold braid at both top and bottom is applied as the final touch to these masterpieces of the shade makers art.

Aladdin:—
"Can you imagine a more beautiful and striking array of shades than these? Certainly here one may find a shade to suit every type, every whim, in any American home. All the art and witchery of the Arabian Nights of old could scarcely make them more alluring."

No. 631

No. 634

No. 630

No. 632

No. 633

No. 635

Aladdin Parchment Shades, Nos. 630, 631, 632, 633, 634 and 635, shown above are 15" diam. at bottom, 9" diam. at top and 8¾" high. These shades are all interchangeable on Table Lamps, Nos. 1200N or 1200B and on Hanging Lamps, Nos. 1214N or 1214B.

PAGE SEVEN

Hand Decorated-GLASS SHADES—Plain Glass

To those who prefer shades of the more conventional type, these new plain and hand-decorated Aladdin glass shades will have an instant appeal. The table and bracket lamp shade, No. 601 and the hanging lamp shade, No. 616, shown below at right, are finished with a satin white dome with a clear crystal glass panel below. This combination produces a very striking shade. The surface of the crystal panel represents crystal drops, and while permitting the passage

and the No. 620S is 14" in diameter, while the table and bracket lamp shades, Nos. 601 and 6015 fit a 10" diam. tripod. No matter which style or type of shade you may select for your Aladdin you may be assured that it will prove an exceptionally practical and decorative addition to your home.

No. 616

No. 620 S.

No. 601 S.

No. 642

No. 643

No. 645

No. 641

No. 640

No. 644

Aladdin Parchment Shades, Nos. 640, 641, 642, 643, 644 and 645, shown above, are 20½" diam. at bottom, 11" diam. at top and 10½" high. These shades are all interchangeable on all Vase Lamps, Nos. 1240, 1241 and No. 1242 and on Floor Lamps Nos. 1252 and 1253.

PAGE SIX

Aladdin *Hanging Lamps*

Aladdin:—
"Compare this beautifully lighted room with any other you ever have seen lighted with an ordinary oil lamp. Note the atmosphere of joy and happiness and of brightness and cheer the Aladdin creates."

Shown above is a reproduction of Aladdin Hanging Lamp, No. 1214N {nickel} or No. 1214B {bronze} as it would look equipped with Aladdin Parchment Shade, No. 632. {Shade is illustrated in full color on page 7.}

Above is an illustration of Aladdin Hanging Lamp, No. 1214N {nickel} or No. 1214B {bronze} shown equipped with a decorated glass shade No. 616S. {See center spread for shade in full color.}

Aladdin Hanging Lamp
Style No. 1214N or No. 1214B

Consists of one Aladdin Fount equipped with one Aladdin Instant Light Burner complete with flame spreader and Lox-on wick and mechanical wick cleaner; one Aladdin Lox-on Mantle; one Aladdin Lox-on Chimney; one Aladdin Lamp Hanger, No. 01214; one ceiling hook; and one extra Aladdin Lox-on Mantle. Finished in highly polished nickel or bronze. This Aladdin without shade or extension fixture {see page 10 for illustration} is the base lamp for all Hanging Lamps. Shade or Extension Fixture or both, extra if desired.

PAGE NINE

125

Aladdin *Hanging Lamps*

Aladdin:—

"Where will you find a better lighted kitchen. Is it not fitting that the place where a housewife spends so much time should be correctly lighted. The Aladdin here surely adds much to her comfort and makes her tasks lighter."

The lamp shown above is the Aladdin Hanging Lamp of style No. 1214N (nickel) or No. 1214B (bronze), which has been equipped with Plain Glass Shade, No. 616.

Aladdin Hanging Lamp
Style No. 1214N or No. 1214B

This style of the Aladdin is an ideal parlor, dining or living room lamp. It can be hung from a hook in the ceiling, or used in connection with the Aladdin Extension Fixture, No. 3 illustrated above, (see description below.) It may be equipped as an extra with plain glass shade No. 616 or with hand-decorated glass shades, Nos. 616S or 620S, or with any of the hand-decorated Aladdin Parchment shades, Nos. 630, 631, 632, 633, 634 or 635. Choice of highly polished nickel or bronze finish.

Aladdin Extension Fixture No. 3

The Aladdin Extension Fixture illustrated in center above, is recommended for use in connection with all Aladdin Hanging Lamps. It provides a neat and convenient way to adjust the height of the lamp above a dining or reading table. Many people equip their Aladdin Hanging Lamps with extension fixtures no matter where used as it enables them to elevate the lamp up out of the way and out of the reach of children when not in use. For full details of the construction and operation of this fixture see page 12 of this booklet.

The No. 1214N (nickel) or No. 1214B (bronze) Aladdin, pictured above is the base lamp for all Hanging Lamps. Shade Ring (not shown in illustration) necessary for attaching glass or parchment shades is regularly furnished with this lamp. Shade or Extension Fixture or both, extra if desired.

PAGE TEN

Aladdin *Fount and Bracket Lamps*

Aladdin—
"You see here another example of how completely a home may be Aladdin lighted. There's an Aladdin for every purpose, and now that you have seen them in actual service you will no doubt agree that no home by whatever means lighted could be brighter cheerier or more artistically decorative."

Illustration above shows Aladdin Bracket Lamp, Style No. 1204N (Nickel) or No. 1204B (Bronze), which has been equipped with Plain Glass Shade No. 601. Decorated Glass Shade No. 601S may be used if desired.

Aladdin Fount Lamp
Style No. 1203N or No. 1203B

As illustrated above, consists of one Aladdin Fount, one Aladdin Instant-light burner complete with Flame Spreader, Lox-on Mantle, Lox-on Wick, Lox-on Chimney, Mechanical Wick Cleaner and one Extra Aladdin Lox-on Mantle. Finished in highly polished nickel or bronze. This fount is the Lighting Unit on all Aladdin Hanging and Bracket Lamps.

Aladdin Bracket Lamp
Style No. 1204N or No. 1204B

As illustrated above, consist of one Aladdin Fount Lamp No. 1203N (Nickel) or No. 1203B (Bronze) complete as described at left, but in addition is supplied with an Aladdin Lox-on Lamp Bracket consisting of wall arm and lock ring for 10" diameter shade, combined, four removable shade arms, and one slotted basket. Bracket and parts, finished in either nickel or bronze to match finish of Lamp selected. This Aladdin makes an ideal wall lamp for the bedroom, hall or kitchen. May be equipped with plain glass shade No. 601 or hand decorated glass shade No. 601S. Not arranged for Parchment shade.

PAGE ELEVEN

Beautify Your Home With these

STRIKING
hand decorated
ALADDIN
SHADES

ALADDIN FLOOR LAMP NO. 1250 SHADE NO. 680

ALADDIN FLOOR LAMP NO. 1251 SHADE NO. 681

Aladdin Floor Lamps

These beautiful and artistic creations are designed to meet for the first time the ever increasing demand among kerosene users for a modern floor lamp. They are made entirely of wrought iron and steel, are handsomely finished in lacquer in two harmonizing combinations—blue and gold—and black and gold. The three shades, in parchment, are hand-decorated in 5 colors and crystal beads and may be used on either pedestal as desired. No home is quite complete without one or more of these striking creations.

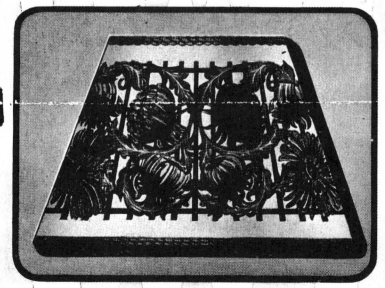

ALADDIN FLOOR LAMP SHADE NO. 682

There is an Aladdin for Every Room in Your Home

Nu-Type Aladdin Table Lamps

In Beta Crystal Clear and Colored

This new 1934 line of Nu-Type Aladdin Table Lamps in Beta Crystal is undoubtedly the most beautiful and practical ever presented. The lighting unit on these lamps is the famous Nu-Type Aladdin Burner, complete with Lox-on Mantle and Chimney. The Bowl is of handsome hobnail design with an ornate fluted pedestal and is available in sparkling crystal (No. 104) or in Green (No. 105) or Amber (No. 106). Any one of these Aladdins will add charm and beauty to your home.

Illustration at right shows Nu-Type Aladdin No. 104, 105 or 106, complete as priced below.

Illustration at left shows No. 104, 105 or 106, fitted with Satin white glass shade No. 701 and 10" Tripod.

Illustration at right shows No. 104, 105 or 106, fitted with Whip-o-lite Shade, No. 156 and 14" Tripod.

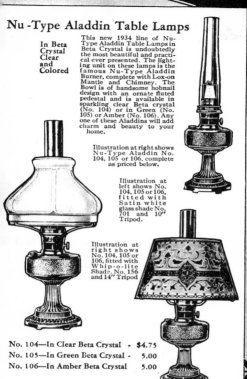

No. 104—In Clear Beta Crystal - $4.75
No. 105—In Green Beta Crystal - 5.00
No. 106—In Amber Beta Crystal 5.00

{ Add $1.00 for Satin White Glass Shade No. 701, and 20c for 10" Tripod
Add $1.95 for any design 14" Whip-o-lite Shade, and 25c for 14" Tripod }

Model 12—Aladdin Vase Lamps

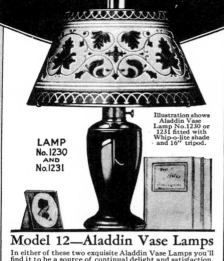

LAMP No. 1230 AND No. 1231

Illustration shows Aladdin Vase Lamp No.1230 or 1231 fitted with Whip-o-lite shade and 16" tripod.

In either of these two exquisite Aladdin Vase Lamps you'll find it to be a source of continual delight and satisfaction. They are ultra modern in design and colorings and will add just the proper note to any room to make it a brighter, happier, more cheerful place in which to live.

The lighting unit in these lamps is No.1220S Satin Finish Oil Pot with Model 12 Satin Brass Burner complete with Lox-on Mantle and Chimney. The Vases are 10¾" high x 5¾" diam. Available in choice of two colors — Green or Amber.

Add $2.25 to above prices for 16" Whip-o-lite Shade of any design or color as illustrated on reverse side of this folder and 25c for tripod.

No. 1230, In Green, $8.00
No. 1231, in Amber, $8.00

Nu-Type Aladdin Table Lamps

For those who prefer an Aladdin in simpler, plainer design, this Alpha Crystal line will have an irresistible appeal. The lighting unit on these lamps is the famous Nu-Type Aladdin Burner complete with Lox-on Mantle and Chimney. The Bowl is of Alpha Art-crystal, the design of which will harmonize with practically all surroundings. Available in Satin White (No. 100) and in beautiful pastel tones of Green (No. 101), Peach (No. 102) and Rose (No. 103).

In Alpha Art Crystal, White and Pastel Green, Peach and Rose

Illustration at left shows Nu-Type Aladdin No. 100, 101, 102 or 103 complete as priced below.

Illustration at right shows No. 100, 101, 102 or 103, fitted with Satin White Glass Shade and 10" Tripod.

Illustration at left shows No. 100, 101, 102 or No. 103, fitted with Whip-o-lite Shade No. 160 and 14" Tripod.

No. 100, In Satin White Alpha Crystal, $5.00
No. 101, In Pastel Green   "   "   5.00
No. 102, In Pastel Peach   "   "   5.00
No. 103, In Pastel Rose   "   "   5.00

{ Add $1.00 for Satin White Glass Shade No. 701, and 20c for 10" Tripod
Add $1.95 for any design 14" Whip-o-lite Shade, and 5c for 14" Tripod }

Model 12—Aladdin Table Lamps

In All-Metal, Highly Polished Nickel Finish

Many people prefer Aladdins of the all-metal type, and to those we offer Aladdin No. 1200N. This style of Aladdin is fitted with Model 12 Burner complete with Lox-on Mantle and Chimney. The Bowl is of high-quality brass, of semi-ornate design, and is heavily coated in highly polished nickel with burner to match. For a practical all-purpose lamp it can scarcely be improved upon, and will render a life-time of service and satisfaction.

Illustration at right shows Model 12 Aladdin No. 1200N, complete as priced below.

Illustration at left shows No. 1200N, fitted with Satin White Glass Shade, No. 701 and 10" Tripod

Illustration at right shows No. 1200N fitted with Whip-o-lite Shade No. 141 and 14" Tripod

No. 1200N—In Highly Polished Nickel—All Metal - $6.30

Add $1.00 for Satin White Glass Shade No. 701, and 20c for 10" Tripod, Add $1.95 for any design 14" Whip-o-lite Shade, and 25c for Tripod.

Aladdin Floor Lamps

No matter which of these handsomely designed and finished Aladdin Floor Lamps you may select you may be sure it will add a touch of modernism never before thought possible in a kerosene lamp. With the addition of one or more of these exquisite floor lamps in your home you have the assurance that no home, city or country will be more artistically and beautifully lighted.

Illustration shows Aladdin Floor Lamp No. 1254 or 1255 fitted with No. 470 Whip-o-lite Shade and 18" Tripod.

No. 1254 and No. 1255

These two new Aladdin Floor Lamps consists of a beautiful open-work fluted base, and a heavy fluted riser, with solid intermediate breaks, surmounted with handsome design receptacle for No. 1221S or No. 1221B Oil Pot supplied complete as lighting unit. Choice of two combination lacquer finishes; No. 1254 in Bronze and Gold; No. 1255 in Green and Gold. Either Finish Each, $10.50

Illustration shows Aladdin Floor Lamp No. 1256 or 1257 fitted with No. 468 Whip-o-lite Shade and 18" Tripod.

No. 1256 and No. 1257

In order that a wider choice of design and finishes may be afforded in Aladdin Floor Lamps, these two new numbers were also added to the line. The base of these lamps are solid in reed and ribbon design, with the fluted riser in complete harmony with it. Oil Pot No. 1221S or 1221B complete supplied as lighting unit. Choice of two combination lacquer finishes; No. 1256 in Bronze and Gold; No. 1257 in Ivory and Gold. Either Finish Each, $10.50

Add $2.75 to prices quoted for Floor Lamps for Any Design or Color. 18" Whip-o-lite Shade, and 25c for 18" Tripod.

See Reverse Side for Aladdin Bracket Lamps, Fount Lamps and Oil Pots, and illustrations of complete line of Aladdin Whip-o-lite Shades for all Aladdin Lamps.

Model 12 Aladdin Hanging Lamps

This remarkable Aladdin Hanging Lamp will have a strong appeal to those who wish a premier lighting device that may be located above a dining or reading table and is up out of the reach of children. The No. 1214N Aladdin Hanging consists of Aladdin Fount Lamp No. 1203N fitted with Model 12 Burner complete with Lox-on Mantle and Chimney, and a Nu-Type Hanger of the most improved type with ceiling hook. Tilting ring in hanger permits lamp to be quickly removed and inserted for filling and cleaning. Illustrated at left.

In All-Metal Highly Polished Nickel Finish

No. 1214N Aladdin, in All-Metal, highly polished Nickel. $7.50

Add $1.95 for Satin White Glass Shade No. 716 (as illustrated) or for 14" Whip-o-lite Shade. Any design or color.

Illustration at right shows No. 1214N Aladdin fitted with 14" Whip-o-lite Shade No. 150.

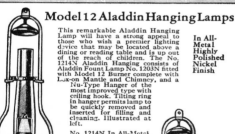

Illustration above shows No. 1214N Aladdin fitted with Satin White Shade No. 716.

Extension Fixture

For conveniently raising or lowering Aladdin Hanging Lamp. (Polished Nickel) $2.75 Extra

The Mantle Lamp Company of America, Inc.

Largest Kerosene (Coal Oil) Mantle Lamp House in the World -- 609 W. Lake Street, Chicago -- Portland, Ore., Toronto, London, Paris, Sydney, Wellington, Buenos Aires

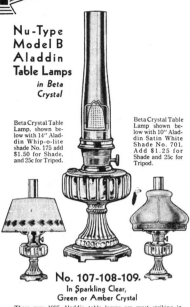

Brighten the Home

With These Wonderful

Aladdin

KEROSENE (COAL OIL)

Mantle Lamps

Aladdin TABLE LAMPS

Illustration at left, above, B-103 Aladdin equipped with 14-in. Whip-o-lite shade No. 203, and 14-in. nickel tripod.

Illustration at right shows B-104 Aladdin equipped with 14-in. Whip-o-lite shade No. 198 and 14-inch nickel tripod.

ALADDIN TABLE LAMP
B-103

…strated *in inset* at left above, consisting of all clear crystal …No. 0103; Model B Nu-Type burner, nickel finish; one … mantle and chimney, with directions and ready to operate.

PRICE . . . $4.95
Shade and Tripod Extra

…described Aladdin when equipped with any design 14-inch …-lite shade and tripod, as illustrated above—

PRICE . . . $6.70

ALADDIN TABLE LAMPS — B-104, B-105 or B-106

As B-104 illustrated *in inset* at right above, consisting of a combination clear crystal and black bowl No. 0104; Model B Nu-Type burner, nickel finish; one Lox-on mantle and chimney, with directions and ready to operate. Or as B-105 with combination clear crystal and green bowl, No. 0105, or as B-106 with combination clear crystal and amber bowl, No. 0106.

PRICE $4.95 *(Shade and Tripod Extra)*

Any above described Aladdin when equipped with any design 14-inch Whip-o-lite shade and tripod, as illustrated above—

PRICE . . . $6.70

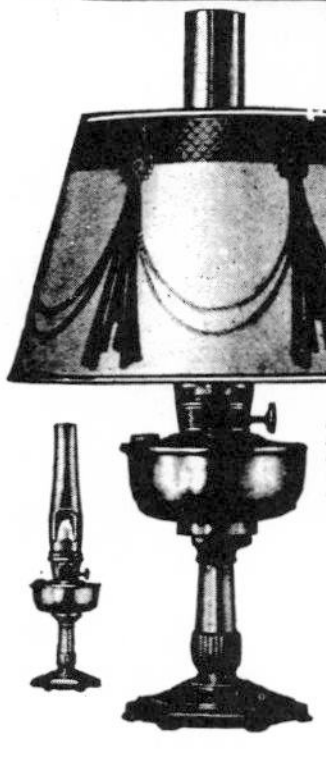

Illustration at left shows B-130 Aladdin equipped with 14-in. Whip-o-lite shade No. 213 and 14-in. rose-gold tripod.

Illustration at right shows B-120 Aladdin equipped with 16-in. fluted Whip-o-lite shade No. 294, and 14-in. Tripod.

ALADDIN TABLE LAMPS
B-130, B-131, B-132, B-133 or B-134

As B-130 illustrated *in inset* at left above, consisting of all-metal ivory and rose-gold bowl No. 0130; Model B Nu-Type burner, rose-gold finish; one Lox-on mantle and chimney, with directions and ready to operate. Or as B-131 with green and silver bowl No. 0131 and nickel burner; as B-132 with all rose-gold bowl No. 0132 and rose-gold burner; as No. B-133 with all silver bowl No. 0133 and nickel burner; or as B-134 with all oxidized bronze bowl No. 0134 and oxidized burner.

PRICE $6.25 *(Shade and Tripod Extra)*

Any above described Aladdin when equipped with any design 14-inch Whip-o-lite shade and tripod, as illustrated above—

PRICE . . . $8.00

ALADDIN TABLE LAMPS
B-120, B-121 or B-122

As B-120 illustrated *in inset* at right above, consisting of a combination white moonstone and rose-gold metal bowl No. 0120; Model B Nu-Type burner, rose-gold finish; one Lox-on mantle and chimney, with directions, ready to operate. Or as B-121 with combination rose moonstone and rose-gold metal bowl No. 0121 with rose-gold burner; as B-122 with combination green moonstone and silver finish bowl No. 0122 and nickel burner.

PRICE $6.50 *(Shade and Tripod Extra)*

Any above described Aladdin when equipped with any 16-inch fluted Whip-o-lite shade and 14-inch tripod as illustrated above—

PRICE . . . $9.50

Aladdin TABLE LAMPS

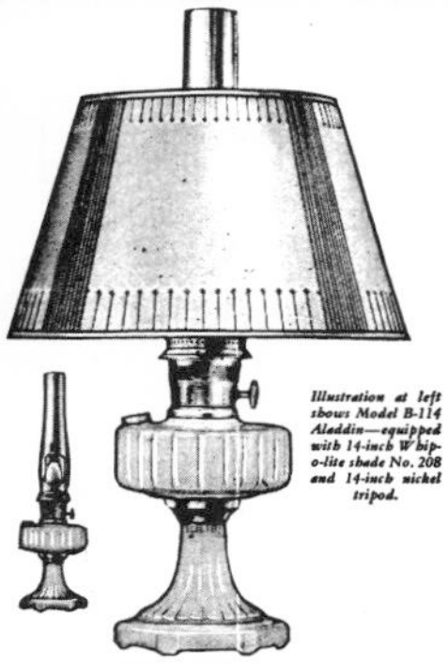

Illustration at left shows Model B-114 Aladdin—equipped with 14-inch Whip-o-lite shade No. 208 and 14-inch nickel tripod.

Illustration at right shows Model B-124 Aladdin—equipped with 14-inch Whip-o-lite shade No. 144 and 14-inch nickel tripod.

ALADDIN TABLE LAMPS — B-114, B-115 or B-116

As B-114 illustrated *in inset* at left above, consisting of all white moonstone bowl No. 0114; Model B Nu-Type, nickel finish burner; one Lox-on mantle and chimney, with directions, ready to operate. Or as B-115 with all green moonstone bowl No. 0115 with nickel burner; or as B-116 with all rose moonstone bowl No. 0116 with nickel burner.

PRICE $5.45 *(Shade and Tripod Extra)*

Any above described Aladdin when equipped with any design 14" Whip-o-lite shade and 14" tripod, as illustrated above—

PRICE . . . $7.20

ALADDIN TABLE LAMPS — B-124, B-125 or B-126

As B-124 illustrated *in inset* at right above, consisting of combination white moonstone and black bowl No. 0124; Model B, Nu-Type burner, nickel finish; one Lox-on mantle and chimney, with directions and ready to operate. As B-125 with combination white and green moonstone bowl No. 0125 with nickel finish burner, or as B-126 with combination white and rose moonstone bowl No. 0126 with nickel burner.

PRICE $5.45 *(Shade and Tripod Extra)*

Any above described Aladdin when equipped with any design 14" Whip-o-lite shade and 14" nickel tripod, as illustrated above—

PRICE . . . $7.20

Aladdin HANGING LAMPS

Illustration at left shows B-200 fitted with 14-inch satin white glass shade No. 216.

ALADDIN EXTENSION FIXTURE No. 03N

For use in raising and lowering Aladdin Hanging Lamps. Simple and easy to operate. All metal-finished in oxidized nickel. Add extra to any hanging lamp price, if desired.

PRICE $2.75

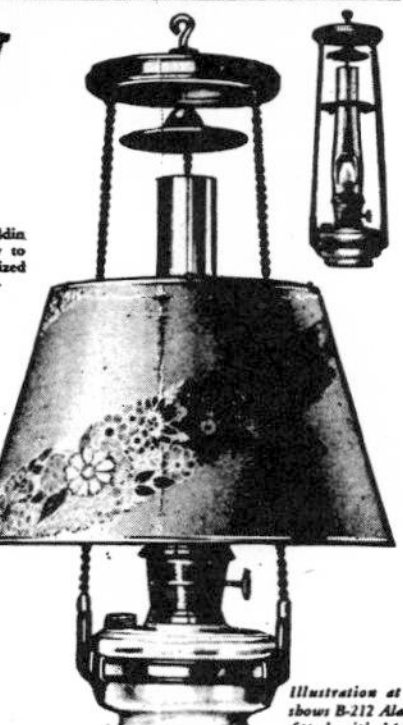

Illustration at left shows B-212 Aladdin fitted with 14-inch Whip-o-lite shade No. 197.

…DIN HANGING LAMPS — B-200 and B-201

…00 illustrated *in inset* upper left, consisting of white …one fount No. 0152, silver trimmed; Model B Nu-Type … nickel finish; Nu-Type hanger No. 0210, nickel finish; …x-on mantle and chimney, with directions and ready to … Or as B-201 with green moonstone fount No. 0151, silver …d, with burner, Lox-on mantle and chimney, etc., as above.

PRICE $6.25 *(Shade and Extension Extra)*

…of above described Aladdin, when equipped with 14-inch …hite glass shade No. 716 as illustrated above—

PRICE $8.20 *(Extension Extra)*

…er of above described Aladdins when equipped with any …14-inch Whip-o-lite shade (not illustrated)—

PRICE . . . $7.75

ALADDIN HANGING LAMPS — B-212 and B-213

As B-212 illustrated *in inset* upper right, consisting of white moonstone fount No. 0152, silver trimmed; Model B Nu-Type burner, nickel finish; chain type hanger No. 0212 in oxidized nickel; one Lox-on mantle and chimney, with directions, ready to operate. Or as B-213 with green moonstone fount No. 0151, silver trimmed, with burner, mantle and chimney, etc., as above.

PRICE $7.25 *(Shade and Extension Extra)*

Either of above described Aladdins when equipped with any design 14-inch Whip-o-lite shade, as illustrated above—

PRICE $8.75 *(Extension Extra)*

Aladdin satin white shade No. 716 cannot be used on above styles.

Aladdin HANGING LAMPS

Illustration below at left shows B-210 Aladdin fitted with 14-inch Whip-o-lite shade No. 169.

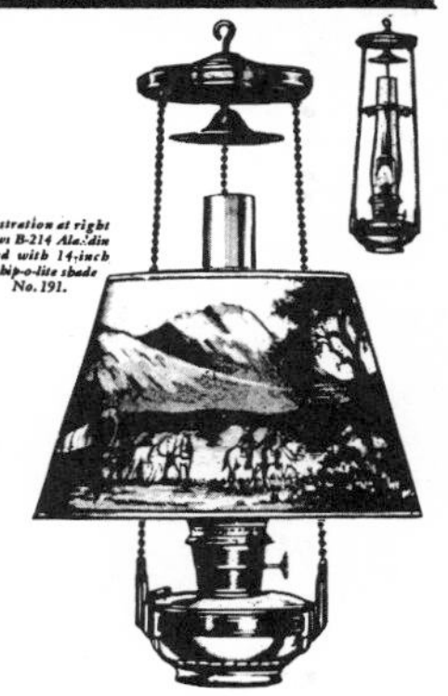

Illustration at right shows B-214 Aladdin fitted with 14-inch Whip-o-lite shade No. 191.

ALADDIN HANGING LAMP — B-210

As B-210 illustrated *in inset* upper left, consisting of all-metal nickel plated fount No. 0160; Model B Nu-Type burner, nickel finish; Nu-Type hanger, nickel finish, No. 0210; one Lox-on mantle and chimney, with directions, ready to operate.

PRICE $7.00 *(Shade and Extension Extra)*

Or B-210, above described, when equipped with any design 14-in. Whip-o-lite shade, as illustrated above—

PRICE $8.50 *(Extension Extra)*

Or B-210, above described, when equipped with 14-inch satin white glass shade No. 716 (not illustrated)—

PRICE $8.95 *(Extension Extra)*

ALADDIN HANGING LAMPS — B-214 and B-215

As B-214 illustrated *in inset* upper right, consisting of all-metal, nickel plated fount No. 0160, Model B Nu-Type burner, nickel finish; chain type hanger No. 0212, oxidized nickel; one Lox-on mantle and chimney, with directions, ready to operate. Or as B-215 with all-metal, oxidized bronze fount No. 0162, with oxidized burner, and mantle and chimney as above.

PRICE $8.00 *(Shade and Extension Extra)*

Either of above described Aladdins, when equipped with any design 14-inch Whip-o-lite shade, as illustrated above—

PRICE . . . $9.50

(Aladdin satin white glass shade No. 716 not adaptable to above styles.)

Aladdin FOUNT LAMPS

STYLES B-151 and B-152

Aladdin Fount Lamp B-151, illustrated at left, consists of an Aladdin oil fount No. 0151 in green moonstone art glass with silver plated metal trim; a Model B Nu-Type burner in nickel finish; and one Lox-on mantle and chimney, with directions, ready for operation. (This complete Aladdin Fount Lamp is the lighting unit on hanging lamps of Styles B-201 and B-213, and on bracket lamp Style B-178.

Aladdin Fount Lamp B-152 consists of an Aladdin oil fount No. 0152 in white moonstone art glass with silver plated metal trim; and burner, mantle and chimney as above. (This complete Aladdin Fount Lamp is the lighting unit on hanging lamps of Styles B-200 and B-212 and bracket lamp Style B-177.)

PRICE $4.75
Shade and Tripod Extra

Illustration at left shows the Aladdin Fount Lamp B-151 or B-152.

STYLES B-160, B-161, B-162

Aladdin Fount Lamp B-160 illustrated at right consists of all-metal Aladdin oil fount No. 0160 in nickel plated finish; Model B Nu-Type burner, nickel finish; one Lox-on mantle and chimney, with directions, ready to operate. (This complete Aladdin Fount Lamp is lighting unit on hanging lamps B-210 and B-214, bracket lamp B-187 and on floor lamps B-270 and B-273.)

Aladdin Fount Lamp B-161 consists of all-mteal Aladdin oil fount in rose-gold finish No. 0161; Model B Nu-Type burner, rose-gold finish; one Lox-on mantle and chimney, with directions, ready to operate. (This complete Aladdin Fount Lamp is lighting unit on floor lamps B-269, B-272, B-275.)

Aladdin Fount Lamp B-162 consists of all-metal Aladdin oil fount in oxidized bronze finish No. 0162; Model B Nu-Type oxidized finish burner; one Lox-on mantle and chimney, with directions and ready to operate. (This Aladdin Fount Lamp is lighting unit on hanging lamp B-215, bracket lamp B-188, and floor lamps B-268, B-271, B-274 and B-276.)

PRICE $5.50
Shade and Tripod Extra

Illustration at left shows Aladdin Fount Lamps — B-160, B161, and B-162.

Aladdin BRACKET LAMPS

Illustration at left shows B-177 fitted with 14-inch Whip-o-lite shade No. 210.

ALADDIN BRACKET LAMPS — B-177, B-178

As B-177 illustrated at lower right, consisting of white moonstone fount No. 0152, silver trimmed; Model B Nu-Type nickel finish burner; bracket No. 0177, in ivory and nickel finish; one Lox-on mantle and chimney, with directions, ready to operate. Or as B-178 with green moonstone fount No. 0151, silver trimmed, with burner, bracket, mantle and chimney, as above.

PRICE $5.35 *(Shade and Tripod Extra)*

Either of above described Aladdins, when equipped with any design 14-inch Whip-o-lite shade, as illustrated at left—

PRICE . . . $7.10

Either of above described Aladdins, when equipped with satin white shade No. 701 (not illustrated)—

PRICE . . . $6.80

Illustration at left shows Aladdin B-177 or B-178

THE Aladdin Mantle Lamp is one of the greatest and most practical inventions of the century. It is an outstanding achievement of science in connection with artificial lighting. It has gone a long, long way toward solving the lighting problem for rural homes, with its abundance of soft, mellow, modern, white light. Aladdin light makes evening reading, writing or sewing a pleasure. It costs very little to operate. It burns commen kerosene (coal-oil) which is generally regarded as the cheapest, safest and most readily procurable of fuels. The average consumption is a single gallon to 50 hours of service, with an average candle power of 60—a striking example of its remarkable efficiency.

It is simple—anyone can operate it. It lights and is put out just like the ordinary kerosene wick lamp. It lights instantly and burns without noise, odor, smoke or trouble. It is safe—cannot explode. The importance of a good light in the home cannot be overemphasized. Poor light is depressive, dismal, gloomy, while the white light of the Aladdin is full of cheer and generates joy and happiness. Good light of the correct quality is also a preventive and protection against injury and strain upon the eyes. No user of the old-style open flame lamp can, in view of the many advantages of having a well-lighted home, afford to let another evening pass without one or more of these efficient, beautiful, modern Aladdins in their home.

(Aladdin Floor Lamps, Glass and Whip-o-lite Shades are illustrated and described on reverse side of this folder.)

Aladdin BRACKET LAMPS

ALADDIN BRACKET LAMPS — B-187 and B-188

As B-187 illustrated at lower left consisting of all-metal fount No. 0160 nickel plated finish; Model B Nu-Type burner nickel finish; bracket No. 0177, ivory and nickel finish; one Lox-on mantle and chimney, with directions, ready to operate. Or as B-188 with all-metal fount No. 0162, Model B Nu-Type burner, oxidized finish; bracket No. 0188, oxidized bronze plated and bronze lacquer finish, with mantle and chimney, etc., as above.

PRICE $6.10 *(Shade and Tripod Extra)*

Either of above described Aladdins, when equipped with 10-inch satin white shade No. 701 and 10-in. tripod, as illustrated at right

PRICE . . . $7.55

Either of above described Aladdins, when equipped with any design 14-in. Whip-o-lite shade and 14-in. tripod (not illustrated)—

PRICE . . . $7.85

Illustration at right shows B-187 or B-188.

Illustration at right shows B-187 Aladdin fitted with 10-inch satin white shade No. 701.

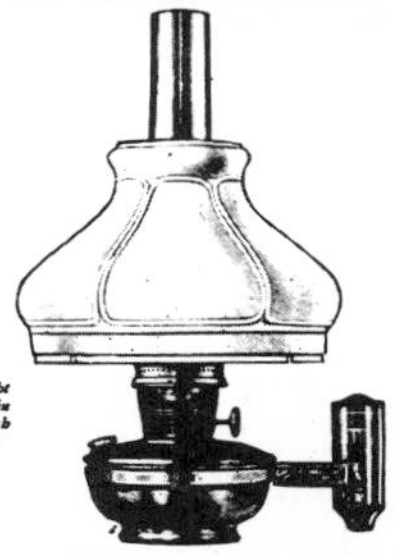

THE MANTLE LAMP COMPANY OF AMERICA, INC.
609 WEST LAKE STREET, CHICAGO, ILL.

…RGEST KEROSENE (COAL OIL) MANTLE LAMP HOUSE IN THE WORLD

Chicago, Portland, Ore., Toronto, London, Paris, Sydney, Wellington, Buenos Aires

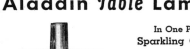

Aladdin *Table* LAMPS

GOOD Light is as important as good air or good food. In fact there is nothing that adds more to the healthfulness, happiness, comfort and convenience of a home than good light. Eyesight is a priceless possession and every possible safeguard should be used to preserve and protect it. For many years the old-style yellow-flame oil light has been the only light available for homes without electricity, and the damage it has done to the eyes of millions cannot be figured even in billions. It's small wonder that the Aladdin Mantle Lamp with its abundance of modern white light, its amazing economy, its safety and simplicity has won its way into the hearts and homes of over 7,000,000 of users throughout the world.

Aladdin Table Lamps

B-87—*Rose*
B-88—*Yellow*
B-92—*Green*
B-93—*White*

In Moonstone Art Glass

In Moonstone Art Glass and Cast Metal Base

Shown with 14" Whip-o-lite Shade No. 241 and 14" Tripod

Shown with 16" Fluted Whip-o-lite Shade No. 265 and 14" Tripod

B-95—*White, Moonstone, Bronze*
B-96—*White, Moonstone, Silver*

B-97—*Green, Moonstone, Silver*
B-98—*Rose, Moonstone, Silver*

In Moonstone Art Glass in choice of B-87, B-88, B-92 or B-93 with any design of 14" Whip-o-lite Shade shown in this circular, including 14" Tripod.

Price, *Each*, $7.50

With 10" No. 701 Satin Glass Shade...**$7.20**
Without Any Shade or Tripod........**$5.75**

In combination Moonstone Art Glass (bowl) and Metal (base) of B-95, B-96, B-97 or B-98, with any design of 16" Fluted Whip-o-lite Shade shown in this circular, including 14" Tripod.

Price, *Each*, $9.50

(*Neither* 14" *Whip-o-lite or* 10" *Glass Shades Adaptable*)
Without any Shade or Tripod, Each...**$6.50**

Table Lamp B-80

IN THIS new one-piece, all crystal glass Aladdin the artist and the artisan have produced a table lamp of unusual beauty. Neutral in color and simple in design it harmonizes perfectly in practically any setting.

In Clear, Sparkling Beta Crystal *only*

As shown complete with any design Standard 14" Whip-o-lite Shade and Tripod. Each..... **$6.70**

Complete with 10" Glass Shade No. 701, instead of Whip-o-lite (*Not shown*). Each...... **$6.40**

Complete, but without either Shade or Tripod. Each............. **$4.95**

B-138 Nickel
B-137 Bronze
B-136 Chromium

THOSE who prefer an all metal table lamp, will find this new Aladdin very sturdy, and chock full of arresting eye appeal. Very beautifully plated in all of its several finishes. You'll make no mistake in choosing an Aladdin of this style.

In All-Metal—In Plated Finishes

B-137 or B-138 as shown, Complete with Any Standard 14" Whip-o-lite Shade. Each............... **$8.70**

As above, with 10" Glass Shade No. 701 instead of Whip-o-lite. Each.... **$8.40**

As above, without any Shade or Tripod. Each **$6.95**

For B-136 in Chromium, Add 75c to Price Quoted Above

HERE in this new and handsomely designed Moonstone Glass table lamp, you'll find a lighting device, as beautiful as it is practical. Among the many colors in soft pastel tones, you're sure to find one exactly suited to your needs and taste.

In Beautiful Moonstone Art Glass.

As shown, complete with choice of any Standard 14" Whip-o-lite Shade. Each............. **$7.50**

With 10" Glass Shade No. 701, instead of Whip-o-lite. Each.. **$7.20**

Without Shade or Tripod. Each...... **$5.75**

Choice of Any Style Listed at Right

B-85 All-White
B-86 All Green

B-90 White Bowl Black Base
B-91 White Bowl Rose Base

THIS Aladdin has been acclaimed, and rightfully so, as the Queen of all Aladdins. Beautiful design, metal base handsomely finished, and bowls of delicate pastel Moonstone glass, form a lamp of an irresistible appeal even to the most discriminating.

In Combined Metal and Moonstone

As shown, complete with any 16" Fluted Whip-o-lite Shade and 14" Tripod. Each..... **$9.50**

With special 14" Whip-o-lite Shade, instead of Fluted. Each...... **$8.50**

Without any Shade or Tripod. Each.... **$6.50**

Choice of Any Style Listed at Right

NOTE—Glass Shade No. 701 not suitable to these styles.

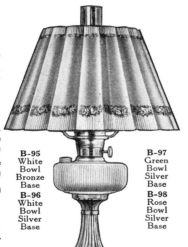

B-95 White Bowl Bronze Base
B-96 White Bowl Silver Base

B-97 Green Bowl Silver Base
B-98 Rose Bowl Silver Base

The Mantle Lamp Company of America, Inc., 223 W. Jackson Boulevard, Chicago, Illinois

SUPPLIES FOR OTHER KEROSENE LAMPS

The Mantle Lamp Company supplied parts for competitive mantle lamps as well as the Aladdin. The following list was taken directly from the Aladdin Paragraph Book, dated August 2, 1920.

The Chicago, New York and Portland offices are prepared to supply loop mantles for the following different makes of kerosene mantle lamps and burners.

AIDA—German manufature—uses No. 3 Practicus mantle.

BEACON BURNERS AND LAMPS—Sold by the Home Supply Company of Kansas City, Missouri, have been on the market for several years. The early Beacon burners use the Aladdin cap mantle and the later burners use the Aladdin Konekap mantle. The Konekap mantle will fit all Beacon burners sold beginning with the season 1913-14.

Aladdin Standard Chimneys will fit all Beacon burners. We can supply wicks used by Beacon burners. They are known as Tubular Wicks for Beacon burners.

BRIGHT-AS-DAY lamp—Sold about 1912-1914 by Sears, Roebuck & Company. Advise Customers we are not in position to furnish supplies.

CANCHESTER Lamps and Burners—Manufactured by the Canchester Lamp Company of Chicago. This company went into bankruptcy in 1912. It is impossible to get supplies for the Canchester.

CONTRACO—Sold by Connecticut Trading Co., of Clinton, Connecticut. This concern sold a number of German burners and lamps under the name of Contraco during the season of 1908-1909, and this early Contraco lamp used both the No. 2 and No. 3 burners, therefore, they will take the No. 2 or No. 3 Practicus mantle.

DAYLITE Lamps—Manufactured by Edward Miller & Co. for the Daylite Company, Chicago. Aladdin cap mantle, Aladdin Chimney, and Aladdin model 6 mounted wick can be used.

FELBOILLIN—German manufacture, uses No. 3 Practicus Mantle.

KRONIS—German manufacture, uses No. 3 Practicus Mantle. It was sold by W. R. Noe of New York City.

LUMINEERS—The Lumineer is a burner put out by the Mantle Lamp Company of Chicago during 1912-13. It was sold mostly to merchants. Only a few thousand of these burners were marketed and their manufacture was discontinued. They were not very satisfactory as they proved to be very susceptible to slight changes in temperature. Lumineers all use the Konekap mantles and standard Aladdin chimneys and tubular burner wicks. Whenever a Sales Correspondent has orders or correspondence pertaining to supplies for this burner, he should call the matter to the attention of the Sales Manager.

LUMO—This lamp was sold by John S. Noel Company, Grand Rapids, Michigan. The early lamps put out by this company consisted of a variety of German burners which required different sizes of mantles and it is almost impossible to determine from a description what particular style of mantle or chimney would be required. The later lamps put out by this company and also called Lumo were of American make, using the Aladdin tubular unmounted wick, and the Aladdin cap mantle same as used on the early models of No. 1 and No. 2 Aladdin.

PRACTICUS LAMP BURNERS—The No. 2 Practicus takes the No. 2 Practicus mantle. The No. 3 Practicus takes the No. 3 Practicus mantle.

The No. 3 Practicus burner which The Mantle Lamp Company sold was also sold by the Connecticut Trading Company as their No. 1 burner. The No. 2 burner sold by the Mantle Lamp Company, was also sold by the Connecticut Trading Company as their No. 2 burner. For several years, the lamps put out by the Connecticut Trading Company were of American make and the Aladdin cap mantle will fit them. These American made lamps also bear the name Contraco.

RADIANT LAMPS AND BURNERS—Sold by Montgomery, Ward & Company about 1913-1916. Uses a standard 12½" Aladdin chimney, the Aladdin Konekap mantle and the same tubular wick as the Beacon burner. Side draft burner same as we sold to Home Supply Company.

SAXONIA—German manufacture. Neither mantles nor chimneys can be supplied for this burner.

SOLAR—Sold by Solar Mantle Lamp Company (formerly Home Supply Co.) Kansas City, Missouri. Same as Model 6 Aladdin. Aladdin Konekap mantle, Aladdin 12½" chimney, Aladdin model 6 wick can be used.

SUNBEAM BURNERS—Manufactured and sold by The Mantle Lamp Company of America. The early models use the Aladdin cap mantle and the later models of 1911-1912 use the Konekap mantle. All Sunbeam burners use the Aladdin standard chimney.

SUNLIGHT—Sold by Montgomery, Ward & Co.,—same as Daylite lamp. Aladdin cap mantle, Aladdin chimney, Aladdin model 6 mounted wick can be used.

WIXON—German manufacture, uses No. 3 Practicus mantle.

WONDER LAMP—German manufacture, uses No. 3 Practicus mantle, and was sold by the United Factories Company, Kansas City, Missouri, but they are now out of business, or at least not operating under this name.

136

Aladdin Supplies and Extra Parts

The Aladdin Lamp has been improved from time to time, and to make it convenient for our customers to order supplies and extra parts, we have carefully described each part of the different models.

Mantles

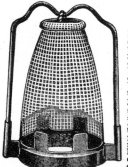

NOTE—Where consumers are unable to secure mantles from our distributors or dealers, same will be sent direct from our offices, prepaid by mail or express at the below price in packages of 4, 6 or 12. Remit by Bank Draft, P. O. or Express Money Order. Owing to cost of handling, packing, etc., we cannot accept orders for less than $1.00 worth of supplies. Mantles do not spoil with age.

Mantle cut away to show Mounting
Aladdin Cap Mantle—For use on Models No. 1 and No. 2 Aladdin Lamps.
Price 30c

Mantle cut away to show Mounting
Aladdin KoneKap Mantle—For use on Models No. 3, No. 4, No. 5 and No. 6 Aladdin Lamps.
Price 30c

Important: *When ordering Mantles, be sure and state whether you want Cap or KoneKap Mantles. It will be easy for you to determine what kind of Mantles you require if you will refer to the illustration above. If you are then in doubt, note generator used in your lamp—under illustration of same shown on the right you will find the style of mantle you should order.*

Galleries

Gallery for Cap Mantle—For use only on No. 2 Model Aladdin in connection with Thimble Generator Model No. 2 and Cap Mantle. Be sure to state finish desired.
Price 50c

Gallery for KoneKap Mantle—(chimney band cut partly away.) Used on No. 3, No. 4, No. 5 and No. 6 Model Lamp with KoneKap Mantle only. Be sure to state finish desired.
Price 50c

Special Notice: We aim to establish headquarters for Aladdin Supplies with a reliable merchant at every point where Aladdin Lamps are used. It sometimes happens, however, that a patron is unable to secure Mantles, Chimneys, Wicks or other parts, and in such instances we shall be pleased to fill orders direct from here at prices quoted in this circular. On account of the expense involved in packing and handling small orders for supplies we have found it necessary to ask that orders be sent to us for no smaller amounts than $1.00. Remittances to be made in advance by P. O. or Express Money Order or Bank Draft. On supply orders for $1.00 or over we will pay parcel postage — but if you wish shipment insured, send 3c additional.

Generators

These Generators are not interchangeable but must be used on the Model Aladdin for which they were designed, except No. 4 Baffle Generator, which we recommend for use on Model No. 3 Aladdin. Be sure to note the difference in number of rows of holes in Generators.

No. 1
Button Generator
For Model No. 1 Aladdin. Used in connection with the Cap Mantle.
Price 10c

No. 2
Thimble Generator
For Model No. 2 Aladdin. Used in connection with the Cap Mantle.
Price 10c

No. 3
Slotted Generator
For Model No. 3 Aladdin. Used in connection with the KoneKap Mantle.
Price 10c

No. 4
Baffle Generator
For Model No. 4 Aladdin. Can be used on Model No. 3 Aladdin. Used in connection with the KoneKap Mantle.
Price 15c

(No. 6—Same as No, 5)
Baffle Generator
For Models No. 5 and 6 Aladdin. Used in connection with the KoneKap Mantle.
Price 15c

Wick Cleaner

Wick Cleaner
For cleaning wick and wick tube flange—see directions. Can be used on all Aladdin Lamps except Model No. 1.
Price 15c

The Mantle Lamp Company of America, Inc.

168-172 N. Halsted St. *Largest Kerosene (Coal Oil) Mantle Lamp House in the World* **Chicago, Ill.**

— — — — — — T E A R   H E R E — — — — — — —

If there is no Supply Dealer in your vicinity, you may use this blank and mail your order to us, with remittance to cover.

Mantle Lamp Company,

_____
P. O. _____ State or Prov. _____ Date _____

Enclosed find _____ *in payment for supplies listed below.* **Ship by** _____
Amount

_____ *to* _____
Parcel Post or Express   *Name of Station*

Number	Article	Amount	Number	Article	Amount
	Aladdin KoneKap Mantles				
	Aladdin Chimneys				
	Aladdin Mounted Wicks				
	Total			Total	

Add 3c to your remittance if you wish to insure parcel post shipment against loss or breakage. All mail shipments sent at owner's risk unless insured.
No. 7—8-2-17

Sign Your Name Here

Aladdin Supplies and Extra Parts (continued)

Chimneys

The Standard Aladdin Chimney is 12½ inches long with 2-inch opening at the top, inside measurement. It is a high-grade chimney, scientifically shaped and proportioned especially for use on Aladdin Lamps. To insure best results, use only chimneys branded "Aladdin."

Price 30 Cents Each

Bug Screens

Made to fit snugly over top of chimney. Will prevent bugs or large flies from falling into chimney and breaking mantle.

Price 25 Cents Each

ALADDIN Mounted Wicks

(Illustrated at Left)

With the Wick charred and inserted in Wick Raiser, ready for use on Models 3, 4, 5 and 6. Packed in individual carton.

Price 30 Cents Each

No. 1 Wick Raisers

(Illustrated at Right)

For No. 1 or No. 2 Model Aladdin Lamps.

Price 15 Cents Each

Unmounted Aladdin Wicks

(Not Charred)

All Aladdin Lamps use the same size and style tubular wick, specially woven. Models Nos. 3, 4, 5 and 6 take the mounted wick illustrated above. Models 1 and 2 cannot use the mounted wick, but an Aladdin tubular wick can be set in Wick Raiser No. 1, illustrated above, for use on these models.

Price 20 Cents Each

Shades

Aladdin Shade No. 301

A pure white 10 - inch fancy shade. Our exclusive Chinese Chippendale design, white satin finish. Diffuses a white light to all parts of the room. Especially adapted to Table or Library Lamp No. 101.

Price $1.25

Aladdin Shade No. 215

Our own exclusive design. Made especially and only for old style Aladdin Hanging Lamp No. 115 or new style No. 116. White fancy opal, 12 inch diameter at bottom.

Price $1.25

Aladdin Shade No. 325

Beautiful hand painted rose design, in natural colors. Satin white finish. Made from pure crystal glass with a very thin casing of pure white glass which absorbs small amount of light. Nothing better made at any price. 12¾ in. diameter, 11¾ in. high. Exclusively for No. 125 and 125-A Fancy Hanging Lamps.

Price $5.00

Aladdin Shade No. 205

A pure white, special design, opal shade for our old style lamps No. 110, 111, 112, 113 and 114.

Price 75c

Aladdin Brackets

Used in connection with Aladdin Fount No. 102 as a wall lamp. Can also be used with Aladdin Table Lamp No. 101. Made in either Satin or Nickel. State which finish is desired. **Price 75 Cents.**

No. 6 Burner Base

(Illustrated at Right)

For Models No. 3, No. 4, No. 5 and No. 6 Aladdin. Not usable on Models No. 1 or No. 2 Aladdin. (Thread is different on burner bases for No. 1 and No. 2 Model Lamps.) Be sure to state whether Satin Brass or Nickel finish is desired.

Price $1.25

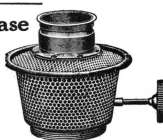

Tripod

For holding 10-in. shade. State finish desired.

Price 20c Each

Add 3c to your remittance if you wish to insure parcel post shipment against loss or breakage. Mail shipments sent at owners' risk unless insured.

Aladdin Extension Fixture No. 2

(Illustrated at Left)

This fixture, unlike any other on the market, is designed to fit snugly against the ceiling, giving it a very neat and firm appearance. It can be extended 3 feet 6 inches and will carry from 8 to 11 lbs. Has an automatic lock and like a curtain roller, will lock at any desired point. Has no friction brake. It is the only smooth running automatic locking fixture, and is designed especially for Aladdin hanging lamps. Be sure to state whether Satin Brass or Nickel finish is desired. **Price $3.00**

Mantle Lamp Company of America, Inc.

Largest Kerosene (Coal Oil) Mantle Lamp House in the World

168-172 North Halsted Street   **Chicago, Illinois, U. S. A.**

Aladdin Supplies and Extra Parts

The many improvements made in the Aladdin from time to time, have necessitated new designs of certain parts that could not always be made interchangeable in all the different models. Therefore, to make it convenient for our customers to order supplies and extra parts, we show herein the parts that fit the different models of the Aladdin. In ordering, it is well to always specify the model of your Aladdin, as well as the finish. The model number appears on the button of wick ratchet of No. 5, No. 6, No. 7, No. 8 and No. 9. Previous models can be determined by comparing the illustrations shown in this circular with the parts on your Aladdin.

Mantles

(Mantle cut away to show Mounting)
Aladdin Cap Mantle—For use on models No. 1 and No. 2 Aladdin.

Price 35c

NOTE—Where customers are unable to procure mantles of our distributors or dealers, they will be supplied direct from our office, prepaid by mail or express at price quoted if quantity ordered is not less than 4. Remit by Bank Draft, P. O. or Express Money Order.

Owing to cost of handling, packing, etc., we cannot accept orders for less than $1.40, the amount necessary to cover an order for 4 mantles. Mantles do not spoil with age.

Aladdin KoneKap Mantle—For use on Models No. 3, No. 4, No. 5, No. 6 No. 7, No. 8 and No. 9.

Price 35c

IMPORTANT: *When ordering Mantles, be sure and state whether you want Cap or KoneKap Mantles. It will be easy for you to determine what kind of Mantles you require if you will refer to the illustration above. If you are then in doubt, note gallery used in your Aladdin—under illustration of same shown below you will find the style of mantles you should order.*

GALLERIES

Gallery for Cap Mantle — For use only on No. 2 Model Aladdin in connection with Cap Mantle. Satin and Nickel finish.

Gallery for KoneKap Mantle—Used on No. 3, No. 4, No. 5 and No. 6 Model Aladdin with KoneKap Mantle only. Satin and nickel finish.

No. 9 Gallery — Used on No. 9, No. 8 or No. 7 Model Aladdin with KoneKap Mantle. Satin and nickel finish.

In ordering specify Model Number and finish desired

Price each, any style, 70c

TRIPOD Tripod for holding 10" shade (No. 501 or old No. 301) for use on Model No. 9 Aladdins. Satin or Nickel finish.

Tripod for holding 10" shade (No. 501 or old No. 301) for use on Model 6 or earlier model Aladdins. Satin or nickel finish.

Tripod for holding 9" shade (No. 401) for use on Model 7 or 8. Satin finish.

Be sure and state Model No. of lamp and finish desired.

Price 20c

GENERATORS

These Generators are not interchangeable but must be used on the Model Aladdin for which they were designed, except No. 4 Generator, which we recommend for use on Model 3 Aladdin, and No. 6 Generator which can be used on both Model 5 and 6. Be sure to note the difference in number of rows of holes in Generators.

No. 4 Generator
For Model No. 4 Aladdin. Can be used on Model No. 3 Aladdin. Used in connection with the KoneKap Mantle.

No. 6 Generator
(Same as No. 5)
For Models No. 5 and 6 Aladdin. Used in connection with the KoneKap Mantle.

No. 9 Generator
(Same as No. 7 and 8)
For Model No. 9 Aladdin. Also used on No. 7 and No. 8. Used in connection with KoneKap Mantle.

Price each, any model, 15c

Aladdin Bracket

Bracket 6" diameter opening used with No. 904, No. 905, No. 900 and 901. Can be used also for all No. 6 or earlier Models. Satin or nickel finish. Bracket 7 in. diameter opening for Models 7 or 8 in bracket or table lamps: satin finish only. (Give Model No. of your lamp and finish desired.)

PRICE 90c

Wick Cleaner

For cleaning wick and wick tube flange—see directions. Can be used on all Aladdin Lamps.

Price 15c

CHIMNEYS

The Standard Aladdin Chimney is 12½ inches long with 2-inch opening at the top, inside measurement. It is a high-grade chimney, scientifically shaped and proportioned especially for use on Aladdin lamps. To insure best results, use only chimneys branded "Aladdin."

Price each 35c

SPECIAL NOTICE We aim to establish headquarters for Aladdin Supplies with a reliable merchant at every point where Aladdin Lamps are used. It sometimes happens, however that a patron is unable to secure Mantles, Chimneys, Wicks or other parts, and in such instances we shall be pleased to fill orders direct from here at prices quoted in this circular. On account of the expense involved in packing, handling, etc., on small orders for supplies we have found it necessary to ask that orders be placed so that the total amount of the order will not be less than $1.40. Order may consist of all mantles, all chimneys, all wicks, or a combination of any of these in such proportion as may be desired. Remittances to be made in advance by P. O. or Express Money Order or Bank Draft. If more convenient to send personal check, add 5c for exchange. On supply orders for $1.40 or over, at prices shown in this circular, we will pay parcel postage — but if you wish shipment insured, send three cents additional. Parcel post shipments are sent at owner's risk unless insured. **See suggested assortments on other side.**

The Mantle Lamp Company of America, Inc.

609-613 W. Lake Street   *Largest Kerosene (Coal Oil) Mantle Lamp House in the World*   **Chicago, Ill.**

- - - - - - - - - - - - - - - - - - TEAR HERE - - - - - - - - - - - - - - - - -

August 1, 1921   *If there is no Supply Dealer in your vicinity, you may use this blank, and mail your order to us, with remittance to cover.*

The Mantle Lamp Company of America: _____ P. O. _____ State _____ Date _____

Enclosed find _____ *in payment for supplies listed below.* Ship by _____ to _____
Amount   Parcel Post or Express   Name of Station

How Many	Article	Amount	How Many	Article	Amount
	Aladdin KoneKap Mantles				
	Aladdin Chimneys				
	Aladdin Mounted Wicks (Be sure to give Model No.......)				
	Supply Assortment No....(Be sure to give Model No......)				
	Total				Total

Add 3c to your remittance if you wish to insure parcel post shipment against loss or breakage. All mail shipments sent at owner's risk unless insured.   Sign Your Name Here

You cannot expect perfect results without a perfect generator. It is always well to have a new one constantly on hand.

SHADES

Table Lamp Shade No. 501

A beautiful shade with satin white finish dome and crystal prismatic panels. Most artistically designed and scientifically constructed. Our own exclusive pattern, made especially for Model 9 Aladdin in styles 900, 901, 903, 904 and 905. Can also be used on Model 6 Aladdin in table and bracket lamp styles. Can also be used on Models 7 and 8 if you purchase a new tripod 10" in diameter. (See tripods.) 10 inches in diameter at bottom.
Price $2.50

Swiss Scenic Table Lamp Shade No. 550

A beautifully soft white and shell-pink tinted shade with four medallions showing an artistic Swiss mountain scene, hand painted. Our own exclusive design. Will appeal to those who desire something unusually attractive. Can be used on all model Aladdin table lamps, except No. 7 and 8; and on these also if new 10 in. tripod is ordered with shade.
Price $6.00

Hanging Lamp Shade No. 215

Our own exclusive design. Made especially for and to use only on Model 5 and 6 Aladdin Hanging lamps, styles No. 115 and 116. White opal glass, 12 inches in diameter at bottom.
Price $3.00

Table Lamp Shade No. 401

A beautiful satin white shade, artistically designed to conform with the lines of the bowl. Our own exclusive design, made especially for model 8 Aladdin, styles Nos. 800, 801, 804 and 805. Used also on Model 7, No. 701 and 705. Nine inches in diameter at bottom.
Price $2.50

Hanging Lamp Shade No. 416

A beautiful, artistic satin white shade, designed especially for Aladdin Hanging Lamp, styles No. 816 and No. 817, and for use on No. 716 and No. 717 Hanging Lamp.
Price $3.75

Aladdin Extension Fixture No. 3

This new patented fixture, unlike any other on the market, is made entirely of pressed steel, therefore virtually indestructible. It is designed to fit snugly against the ceiling like a canopy, which gives it a neat and trim appearance. It can be extended approximately 3 feet and 6 inches. Its locking device is very unique, permitting the fixture to carry any load that can be safely put upon the chains and at the same time will lock at any desired point. It is positive in action and has no friction brake. Very smooth and quiet in operation. While designed especially for Aladdin Hanging Lamp can be used on any style hanging lamp. Satin or nickel finish. State finish desired.
Price $3.00

Ceiling Hook

For Aladdin Hanging lamps No. 914 and 916. Can be used on any Aladdin Hanging lamp which requires a ceiling hook.
Price 20c

Aladdin Mounted Wicks
(Be sure and state model desired)

Aladdin Mounted Wicks are charred and inserted in wick raiser ready for use in model for which they are intended.

No. 6 — No. 6 mounted wick can be used also on Models 3, 4, and 5. **Price 35c each**

No. 7 — For Model No. 7 only. **Price 40c each**

No. 9 — For Model 9. Can also be used on Model 8. **Price 35c each**

Wick Raiser
For Model Nos. 8 or 9 Aladdins. Also for Model 7 Aladdin, which have Model 8 or 9 wicks installed.
Price 25c each

Aladdin Burner Base No. 6

(Illustrated at left.) For Models No. 3, No. 4, No. 5 and No. 6 Aladdin. Not usable on Models No. 1, No. 2 or No. 9 Aladdin. Thread is different on burner bases for No. 1 and No. 2 Model Lamps. Be sure to state whether Satin Brass or Nickel finish is desired.
Price $1.50

Bug Screens

Made to fit snugly over top of chimney. Will prevent bugs or large flies from falling into chimney and breaking mantle.
Price 40c

Heat Bell

Made especially for Aladdin Hanging Lamps. Can be used on any Aladdin in Hanging lamp style.
Price 15c

Aladdin Unmounted Wicks

Models No. 1 and 2 Aladdins cannot use mounted wicks; but an Aladdin tubular wick can be set in Wick Raiser.
Price 30c

Aladdin Burner
No. 9

Complete as illustrated above, with Burner Base, Outer Wick Tube, Gallery, Double Swivel Wick Raiser, Mounted Wick, two generators, and one Wick Cleaner. Nickel finish only. Designed especially for Model No. 9 Aladdin. Cannot be used on Model 6 or earlier models.
Price $3.50

QUICK SERVICE ASSORTMENTS OF SUPPLIES

In order to give Aladdin lamp users the quickest possible service on their supply orders we have made up ready for immediate shipment, several assortments of supplies. It can be readily seen that by having these standard size packages prepared for immediate shipment, goods can move forward more promptly than otherwise. You can therefore secure quicker delivery by ordering in the assortments shown below. Small items such as generators or wick cleaners may be added to any assortment, simply add them on the order blank and include additional remittance to cover. Order the assortment wanted by its number in space provided on order blank on opposite side; for instance for 4 KoneKap mantles, you would specify Assortment No. 1, etc. Prices include postage. You are in no way obligated to order in assortments shown—you may make up your order as best suits your requirements, so long as it amounts to not less than $1.60. We can, however, assure you quicker service where supplies are ordered in the assortments shown.

Order Assortments by Number below	Assortment	Price	Order Assortments by Number below	Assortment	Price
No. 1	4 KoneKap Mantles	$1.40	No. 5 (Give Model Number of Lamp)	4 KoneKap Mantles / 2 Chimneys / 1 Mounted Wick	$2.45
No. 2	6 KoneKap Mantles	$2.10	No. 6 (Give Model Number of Lamp)	6 KoneKap Mantles / 2 Chimneys / 1 Mounted Wick	$3.15
No. 3	2 KoneKap Mantles / 2 Chimneys	$1.40	No. 7	3 KoneKap Mantles / 1 Chimney	$1.40
No. 4 (Give Model Number of Lamp)	2 KoneKap Mantles / 2 Chimneys / 1 Mounted Wick	$1.75	No. 8 (Give Model Number of Lamp)	3 KoneKap Mantles / 1 Chimney / 1 Mounted Wick	$1.75

To Aladdin Lamp Users

Naturally we are interested in having every Aladdin Lamp user secure a maximum of service from the Aladdin. We are therefore offering here a few suggestions which if followed will go a long way toward this end. If your Aladdin has not been in use for some time and oil has been allowed to stand in the bowl, the wick may have become hard and clogged so that it will not draw up the oil freely. A new wick will quickly and easily solve this kind of wick trouble. Examine the generator and see that it is free from carbon deposit. If black residue has deposited on the generator, scrape it off with a knife and blow off any little particles that may have gotten into the little holes. The carbon can be thoroughly removed by boiling the generator in a strong solution of lye or Gold Dust, such as is used around the kitchen for cleaning purposes.

CAUTION If the generator is dented—that is if any of the little bridges of metal between the holes are jammed and dented—put in a new generator, as a damaged generator will not give good results. A slight dent in the generator interferes with the introduction of the air, and consequently will not produce a uniform flame. Be sure and see that there are no little particles of residue or dirt in the generator holes; they must be clean and open. If the old mantle is not in good order, use a new one.

Fresh oil—a clean Aladdin Chimney—perfect generator—a new wick with a proper surface will give you your old time soft, white light again.

We will gladly include with your order a direction booklet for your Aladdin if you will request it on your order and mention model of your lamp.

140

Aladdin Supplies and Extra Parts

The many improvements made in the Aladdin from time to time, have necessitated new designs of certain parts that could not always be made interchangeable in all the different models. Therefore, to make it convenient for our customers to order supplies and extra parts, we show herein parts that fit the different models of the Aladdin.

In ordering, it is well to always specify the model of your Aladdin, as well as the finish. The model number appears on the button of wick ratchet of Nos. 5-6-7-8-9-10-11 and 12. For extra parts for Aladdin lamps of models previous to Model 5, send the old part in for duplication, if you cannot determine what to order from information given.

Mantles

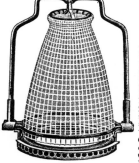

NOTE — Where customers are unable to procure mantles of our distributors or dealers, they will be supplied direct from our office, prepaid by mail or express at price quoted if quantity ordered is not less than 4. Remit by Bank Draft, P. O. or Express Money Order.

Owing to cost of handling, packing, etc., we cannot accept orders for less than $1.40, the amount necessary to cover an order for 4 mantles. Mantles do not spoil with age.

Aladdin Lox-on Mantle
For use on Model 12 Aladdin or on Models 7 to 11 inclusive equipped with Model 12 Instant-Light Burner.
Price 35c

Aladdin KoneKap Mantle—For use on Models No. 3, No. 4, No. 5, No. 6, No. 7, No. 8, No. 9, No. 10 and No. 11.
Price 35c

IMPORTANT: *When ordering Mantles, be sure and state whether you want Lox-on or KoneKap Mantles. It will be easy for you to determine what kind of Mantle you require if you will refer to the illustration above. If you are then in doubt, note gallery used in your Aladdin—under illustration of same shown below you will find the style of Mantle you should order.*

FLAME SPREADERS

Aladdin Flame Spreaders (sometimes called generators) are not interchangeable but must be used on the model Aladdin for which designed with the exception that Model 6 flame spreader can be used on Model 5 as well, and Model 11 flame spreader can be used on Models 7 to 11 incl.

No. 12 Flame Spreader
For Model No. 12 Aladdin only. Used in connection with Aladdin Lox-on Mantle.

Model No. 11
(Same as No. 7,8,9 or 10)
For Model No. 11 Aladdin. Also used on No. 7, 8, 9, 10 and 11. Used in connection with KoneKap Mantle.

Model No. 6
(Same as No. 5)
For Models No. 5 and 6 Aladdin. Used in connection with the KoneKap Mantle.

Price each, any model, 15c

GALLERIES

Gallery for KoneKap Mantle—Used on No. 3, No. 4, No. 5 and No. 6 Model Aladdin with KoneKap Mantle only. Satin and nickel finish.

No. 11 Gallery—Used on No. 11, No. 10, No. 9, No. 8, No. 7 Model Aladdin with KoneKap Mantle. Satin and nickel finish.
In ordering specify Model Number and finish desired.

No. 12 Gallery—Used on Model 12 Aladdin only with Aladdin Lox-on Mantle. Nickel and Bronze finish.

Price each, any style, 70c

ALADDIN BRACKETS

Bracket—6-inch diameter, used with No. 1104, No. 1105, No. 1100 and 1101. Can be used also for Model 10, 9 and No. 6 or earlier models. Satin or nickel finish. (Give Model No. of your lamp and finish desired.)

Price each, either style, 90c

Model 12 Aladdin Bracket, complete with shade arms for holding 10-inch shade and Slotted Basket for attaching lamp to bracket. Can be used with Models 7 to 12 inclusive. Nickel and Bronze finish.

ALADDIN CHIMNEYS

Aladdin Chimneys are all 12½-inches long and nearly 2-inches in diameter at top inside. A high-grade chimney scientifically proportioned especially for Aladdin lamps. To insure best results use only chimneys branded "Aladdin."

Aladdin Lox-on Chimney
For use on Model 12 Aladdin only. Illustrated at left. Special ribs at bottom hold chimney firmly in gallery.
Price, each 35c

Aladdin Old Style Chimney
For use on Models 1 to 11 inclusive. Illustrated at right. Cannot be used on Model 12.
Price, each 35c

Aladdin Chimney Cleaner
Especially designed and constructed so that the 12½-inch Chimney on the Aladdin may be easily and quickly cleaned, dried and polished. Saves time and trouble. It's a convenience the busy housewife will greatly appreciate. **Price, each, 25c**

SPECIAL NOTICE

We aim to establish headquarters for Aladdin Supplies with a reliable merchant at every point where Aladdin Lamps are used. It sometimes happens, however, that a patron is unable to secure Mantles, Chimneys, Wicks or other parts, and in such instances we shall be pleased to fill orders direct from here at prices quoted in this circular. On account of the expense involved in packing, handling, etc., on small orders for supplies we have found it necessary to ask that orders be placed so that the total amount of the order will not be less than $1.40. Order may consist of all mantles, all chimneys, all wicks, or a combination of any of these in such proportion as may be desired. Remittances to be made in advance by P. O. or Express Money Order or Bank Draft. If more convenient to send personal check, add 5c for exchange. On supply orders for $1.40 or over, at prices shown in this circular, we will pay parcel postage—but if you wish shipment insured, send five cents additional. Parcel post shipments are sent at owner's risk unless insured. **See suggested assortments on other side.**

The Mantle Lamp Company of America, Inc.

609-613 W. Lake Street   *Largest Kerosene (Coal Oil) Mantle Lamp House in the World*   **Chicago, Illinois**

-- **TEAR HERE** --

August 15, 1928   If there is no Supply Dealer in your vicinity, you may use this blank, and mail your order to us, with remittance to cover.

The Mantle Lamp Company of America:

P.O. _____ State _____ Date _____

Street and Number _____

Enclosed find _____ *in payment for supplies listed below.*   Ship by _____ to _____
Amount   Parcel Post or Express   Rural Route and Box Number
                                                                Name of Station

How Many	Article	Amount	How Many	Article	Amount
	Aladdin Lox-on Mantles			*Aladdin KoneKap Mantles*	
	Aladdin Lox-on Chimneys			*Aladdin Chimneys (old style)*	
	Aladdin Mounted Wicks *(Be sure to give Model No.....)*				
	Supply Assortment No. . . *(Be sure to give Model No.....)*				
	Total . .			Total . .	

Add 5c to your remittance if you wish to insure parcel post shipment against loss or breakage. All mail shipments sent at owner's risk unless insured.

Sign Your Name Here

Aladdin Supplies and Extra Parts—*Continued*

ALADDIN SHADES

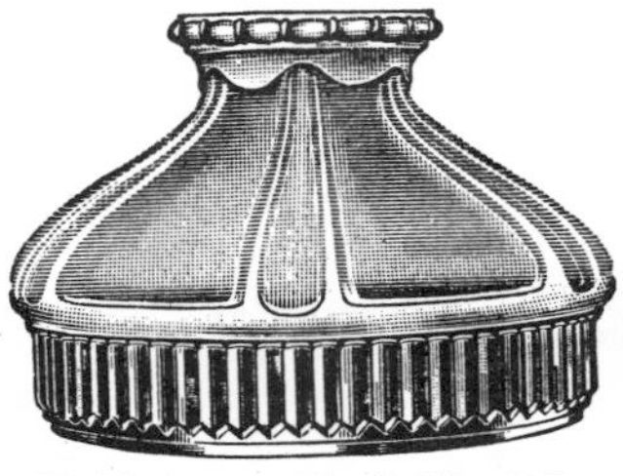

Table Lamp Shade No. 601

A strikingly beautiful exclusive Aladdin design shade. The dome is handsomely ribbed and is satin-white finish and the apron or drop is in clear crystal glass in prismatic form which allows the passage of the maximum amount of light yet diffuses it, preventing glare. Made especially for Model 12 Aladdin table lamp No. 1200 and bracket lamp No. 1204. Can also be used on Aladdins in Models 6, 9, 10 and 11 table and bracket lamp styles. Can also be used on Models 7 and 8 if you purchase a new 10-inch tripod (see tripods). Shade No. 601 is 10-inch diameter at tripod, 11¼-inches at largest diameter and 7⅜-inches high. **Price each, $2.00**

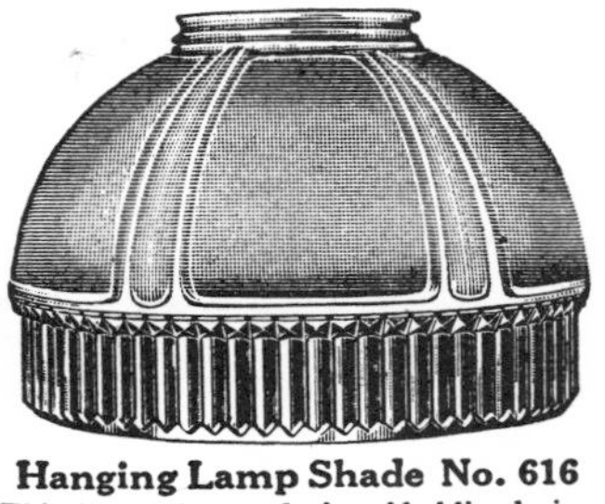

Hanging Lamp Shade No. 616

This is another exclusive Aladdin design shade, rich and handsome in appearance. It is a companion shade to the table lamp shade No. 601 described at left. Dome is very graceful, artistically ribbed and scientifically designed to reflect light downward. Finish of dome is satin-white and the drop or apron is in clear crystal glass in prismatic form allowing maximum passage of light yet softly diffusing it. Size 12¾-inches in diameter by 8½-inches high. For use only on Model 12 Aladdin hanging lamps.

Price each, $2.50

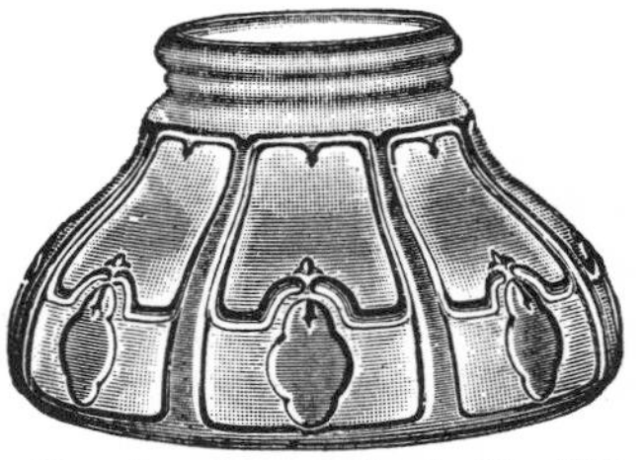

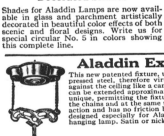

Hanging Lamp Shade No. 516

A beautiful satin-white shade of our own exclusive design. Made especially for Aladdin hanging lamps, Model 11, in styles 1114, 1115, 1116 and 1117. Fits Model 9 and 10 Hanging lamps. (Will not fit model 6 or 12 lamps.)

Price each, $3.00

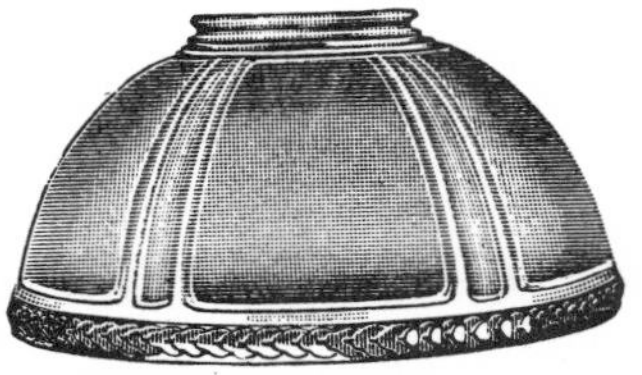

Hanging Lamp Shade No. 620

The exclusive design Aladdin Shade No. 620 shown above may be used on all Aladdin hanging lamps used in home, store, school and church lighting where general illumination is needed. Its wide 14-inch diameter opening at bottom and its scientifically shaped dome reflects the light downward covering a wide area. The dome is artistically ribbed and is finished satin-white. A clear crystal rim 1-inch in width in Grecian design gives the shade a sparkle and crispness much admired. Fits all Aladdin hanging lamps Model 12.

Price each, $2.50

Decorated Shades

Shades for Aladdin Lamps are now available in glass and parchment artistically decorated in beautiful color effects of both scenic and floral designs. Write us for special circular No. 5 in colors showing this complete line.

Aladdin Tripods

Tripod (10-inch) Model 12 for holding shade No. 601. Fits table and bracket lamps, Models 7 to 12. Also furnished 14-inch for parchment shades. Finish: Bronze or nickel. Give model number of your lamp, size and finish desired.

Price each, 20c

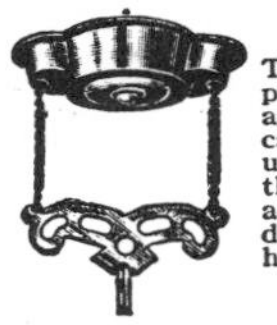

Aladdin Extension Fixture No. 3

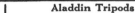

This new patented fixture, unlike any other on the market, is made entirely of pressed steel, therefore virtually indestructible. It is designed to fit snugly against the ceiling like a canopy, which gives it a neat and trim appearance. It can be extended approximately 3 feet and 6 inches. Its locking device is very unique, permitting the fixture to carry any load that can be safely put upon the chains and at the same time will lock at any desired point. It is positive in action and has no friction brake. Very smooth and quiet in operation. While designed especially for Aladdin Hanging Lamps can be used on any style hanging lamp. Satin or nickel finish. State finish desired.

Price $3.00

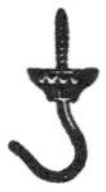

Ceiling Hooks

For Aladdin Hanging Lamps No. 1114 and 1116. Can be used on any Aladdin Hanging Lamp which requires a ceiling hook.

Price 20c

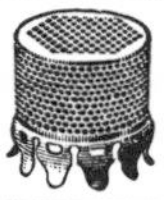

Bug Screens

Made to fit snugly over top of chimney. Will prevent bugs or large flies from falling into chimney and breaking mantle.

Price 40c

Aladdin Mounted Wicks [Be sure to state model desired]

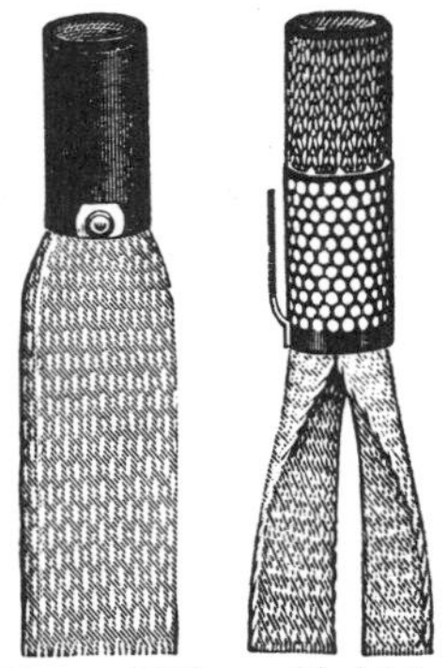

Lox-on Wick Model 12 — Model 6 Wick

Aladdin Mounted Wicks are all reinforced and charred ready for use in model for which they are intended.

Aladdin Lox-on Wick Model 12

Aladdin Lox-on Wick Model 12, reinforced, charred and ready for use. Used on all styles of Aladdins in Models 7, 8, 9, 10, 11 and 12.

Price each, 30c

Aladdin Wick Model 6

Aladdin Wick Model 6 is reinforced, charred and mounted ready for use. Used on all styles of Aladdins in Models 4, 5 and 6.

Price each, 35c

WICK RAISER

For all models No. 8 to 12 incl. Also for Model 7 which have Model 7or later model wicks installed. Give model number of your lamp.

Price 25c

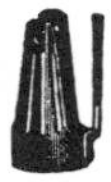

Wick Cleaner

For cleaning wick and wick tube flange; can be used on all Aladdin lamps.

Price 15c

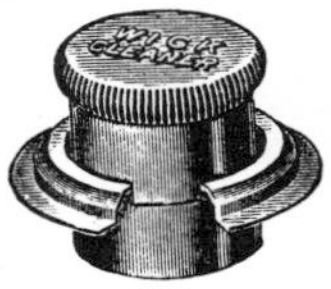

ALADDIN BURNERS

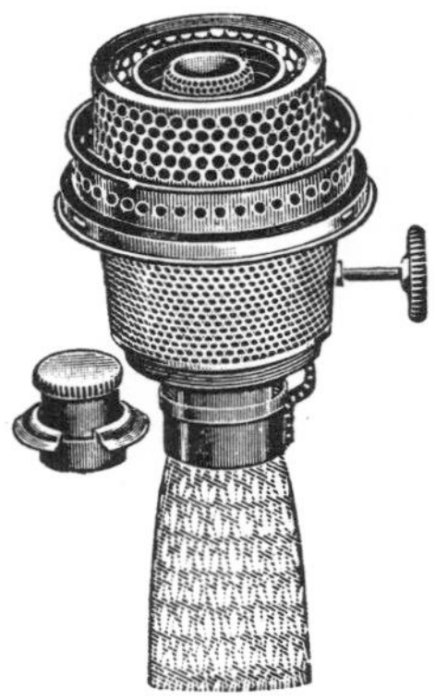

Aladdin Instant-Light Burner, complete for Model 12

Aladdin Instant-Light Burner Complete for Model 12

Complete as illustrated at left, with burner base, outer wick tube, gallery, double swivel wick raiser, wick, flame spreader, and wick cleaner. Nickel and bronze finish. Designed especially for Model 12 Aladdin. This burner complete can be used on all Aladdins, Models 7 to 11 as well if equipped with new Lox-on Mantle and Chimney. This Model 12 Burner makes generating unnecessary and permits the Aladdin to be lighted up instantly—no waiting. Cannot be used on Model 6 or earlier models. Be sure to give model number of your Aladdin, and specify either Satin, Bronze or Nickel finish.

Price $3.50

Aladdin Burner, complete for Model 11

Complete with burner base, outer wick tube, gallery, double swivel wick raiser, wick, generator, and wick cleaner. Satin and nickel finish. Used on Models 7 to 11 inclusive, using KoneKap mantle and old style chimney. Give model number and finish desired.

Price $3.50

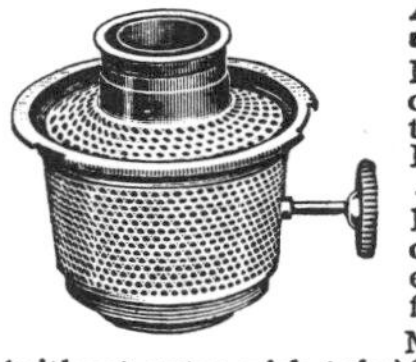

Aladdin Burner Bases *with* Outer Wick Tubes

Model 12 Burner Base with outer wick tube only as illustrated, fits Model 12 only. Bronze or nickel finish, each $1.95

Model 11 Burner Base with outer wick tube only, fits models 7 to 11. Satin or nickel finish, each $1.95

Model 12 Burner Base only (without outer wick tube) fits model 12 only. Bronze or nickel finish, each $1.45

Model 11 Burner Base only (without outer wick tube) fits models 7 to 11. Satin or nickel finish, each $1.45

Model 6 Burner Base (outer wick tube built-in) with air distributor for models 4, 5 and 6. Satin and nickel finish, each $1.50

Outer Wick Tubes only

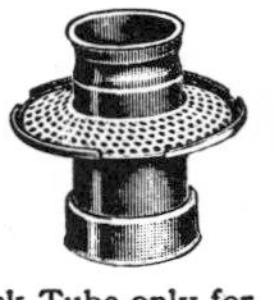

Outer Wick Tube only for Model 11 (illustrated). Fits Models 7 to 11 inclusive. Finished in nickel and bronze. Also outer wick tube only for model 12. Give model number and finish desired.

Price each, 50c

QUICK SERVICE ASSORTMENTS OF SUPPLIES

In order to give Aladdin lamp users the quickest possible service on their supply orders we have made up ready for immediate shipment, several assortments of supplies. You can therefore secure quicker delivery by ordering in the assortments shown below. Small items such as generators or wick cleaners may be added to any assortment, simply add them on the order blank and include additional remittance to cover. Order the assortment wanted by its number in space provided on order blank on opposite side; for instance for 4 KoneKap mantles, you would specify Assortment No. 1K, etc. Prices include postage. You are in no way obligated to order in assortments shown—you may make up your order as best suits your requirements, so long as it amounts to not less than $1.40.

SUPPLIES for use on Models 3 to 11 Inclusive

Order Assortments by Number below	Assortment	Price	Order Assortments by Number below	Assortment	Price
No. 1K	4 KoneKap Mantles	$1.40	No. 5K Give Model Number of Lamp	4 KoneKap Mantles 2 Chimneys, Old Style 1 Mounted Wick	$2.40
No. 2K	6 KoneKap Mantles	$2.10	No. 6K Give Model Number of Lamp	6 KoneKap Mantles 2 Chimneys, Old Style 1 Mounted Wick	$3.10
No. 3K	2 KoneKap Mantles 2 Chimneys, Old Style	$1.40	No. 7K	3 KoneKap Mantles 1 Chimney, Old Style	$1.40
No. 4K Give Model Number of Lamp	2 KoneKap Mantles 2 Chimneys, Old Style 1 Mounted Wick	$1.70	No. 8K Give Model Number of Lamp	3 KoneKap Mantles 1 Chimney, Old Style 1 Mounted Wick	$1.70

SUPPLIES for use on Model 12 only

Order Assortments by Number Below	Assortment	Price	Order Assortments by Number Below	Assortments	Price
No. 1L	4 Lox-on Mantles	$1.40	No. 5L	4 Lox-on Mantles 2 Lox-on Chimneys 1 Lox-on Wick	$2.40
No. 2L	6 Lox-on Mantles	$2.10	No. 6L	6 Lox-on Mantles 2 Lox-on Chimneys 1 Lox-on Wick	$3.10
No. 3L	2 Lox-on Mantles 2 Lox-on Chimneys	$1.40	No. 7L	3 Lox-on Mantles 1 Lox-on Chimney	$1.40
No. 4L	2 Lox-on Mantles 2 Lox-on Chimneys 1 Lox-on Wick	$1.70	No. 8L	3 Lox-on Mantles 1 Lox-on Chimney 1 Lox-on Wick	$1.70

To Aladdin Lamp Users We are interested in having every Aladdin Lamp user secure a maximum of service from the Aladdin. Therefore here are a few suggestions which if followed will go a long way toward this end. If your Aladdin has not been in use for some time and oil has been allowed to stand in the bowl, the wick may have become hard and clogged so that it will not draw up the oil freely. A new wick will quickly and easily solve this kind of wick trouble.

Examine the generator and see that it is free from carbon deposit. If black residue has deposited on the generator, scrape it off with a knife and blow off any little particles that may have gotten into the little holes. The carbon can be thoroughly removed by boiling the generator in a strong solution of lye or Gold Dust, such as is used around the kitchen for cleaning purposes.

CAUTION: If the generator is dented—that is if any of the little bridges of metal between the holes are jammed and dented—put in a new generator, as a damaged generator will not give good results. A slight dent in the generator interferes with the introduction of the air, and consequently will not produce a uniform flame. Be sure and see that there are no little particles of residue or dirt in the generator holes; they must be clean and open. If the old mantle is not in good order, use a new one.

Fresh oil—a clean Aladdin Chimney—perfect generator—a new wick with a proper surface will give you your old time soft, white light again.

We will gladly include with your order a direction booklet for your Aladdin if you will request it on your order and mention model of your lamp.

OUR STANDING REWARD OFFER

WE claim that the Aladdin is the best lamp in the World. In order to prove this to you we have on hand with our bank £5,000 to be paid to any person who shows us an oil burning lamp, not of our manufacture, equal to our new model Aladdin—in the following 26 important points :—

Quality and Whiteness of light, Strength of light, Steadiness of light, Diffusion of light, Absence of smoke, Absence of noise, Simplicity of lighting and cleaning, Simplicity of operation, Economy of oil, Cleanliness, Durability, Reliability, Workmanship, Accuracy, Construction, Durability and Perfection of generator, Durability of mantles, Durability and Perfection of chimneys, Simplicity and Economy in renewal of burner cone, Relief of Eye-strain, Beauty of design and Elegance of finish.

OUR GUARANTEE PROTECTS YOU

YOU take no risk when you buy the Aladdin because every lamp is guaranteed against defect in workmanship or material and is warranted mechanically perfect. The Identification Card which accompanies each Aladdin lamp protects you for years to come. This guarantee card should be filled in and returned to us at time of purchase.

A COMMON INTEREST

IT is in your interest and ours that spare parts supplied for ALADDIN LAMPS are of our manufacture. Accessories for ALADDIN LAMPS like the lamp itself are manufactured with more care and greater accuracy than any other product of a similar nature. The high standard of efficiency set by the lamp itself, can only be maintained by always using an equally high standard of accessory. Any deviation from this practice means a greatly depreciated standard of efficiency; therefore we are compelled, in the interests of all, to withdraw our guarantee in all cases where supplies other than those of our own manufacture are used. We would, however, assure our customers that we shall continue to pursue our practice of dealing with spurious imitations at source wherever possible.

ALADDIN AND SUPER-ALADDIN
MODERN LIGHTING BY PARAFFIN

EVER since its inception, the Aladdin has been the finest lamp in the World, but throughout our years of success, never have we relaxed our efforts to always improve, and many years of tireless research, involving thousands of pounds, have enabled us from time to time to place before the public improved models.

Aladdin Lamps are sold in two models—namely, the Aladdin No. 12 (*centre* draught, instant light) and the Super-Aladdin (*side* draught, instant light). Both models are obtainable in the styles illustrated and the finishes mentioned in this catalogue. Briefly the differences between these two models are as follows :—

ALADDIN No. 12
80 CANDLE POWER

The No. 12 centre draught model embodies the principle on which Aladdin Lamps have become world renowned, and the overwhelming advantages of this model over previous models (Nos. 6, 9, 10 and 11) are due to vast improvements having been made in the burner. The general construction of the lamp, and the appearance, are likewise improved.

SUPER-ALADDIN
125 CANDLE POWER

The Super-Aladdin is a side-draught (draught-controlled) instant light lamp—*the only lamp of this description in the world*—and represents the greatest achievement in modern incandescent lighting. It is also fitted with a patent draught-controlling device making it impervious to draughts. The lamp can be moved about, even shaken, without disturbing the steady flame.

In all other respects the two models are identical and to those who can afford the slightly higher price asked for the Super-Aladdin, *we particularly recommend this model.* To those to whom the price is a definite consideration, the No. 12 model will give all that is required in the way of perfect light, and far better performance than any other lamp of British or foreign make on the market to-day.

Aladdin light is the cheapest form of lighting known (costing less than one farthing an hour) and is the nearest approach to daylight obtainable—far softer and whiter than gas or electricity. A true conception of the amazing qualities of these lamps can only be appreciated by personal examination. *See one therefore and judge for yourself.*

Aladdin Lamps are *better* because they are—INSTANT LIGHTING ; SILENT IN OPERATION ; ODOURLESS AND SMOKELESS ; SIMPLE YET SAFE (they burn paraffin *without pressure*) cannot possibly explode or catch fire. They are cheaper because they give a beautiful light at a cost of *less than one farthing an hour* (compare this with the cost of gas or electricity) and they are covered by our unique guarantee of permanent satisfaction to the user.

Over nine million Aladdin Lamps are in use throughout the World. This, surely, is a certain proof of their sterling qualities, their value, and their outstanding superiority over all other lamps.

FOR ALADDIN HEATING APPLIANCES
See pages 11 and 12

NEW *Super Aladdin* LAMPS

Regd. Trade Mark

THE NEW SUPER ALADDIN is a result of many years of intensive research, and is the most efficient and economical paraffin Lamp in the World. Burning in absolute silence, it gives ONE HUNDRED AND TWENTY-FIVE CANDLE POWER pure white light which will penetrate any corners or alcoves and, at the same time, is restful to the eyes. There is no smoke or smell, and the running cost is less than ONE FARTHING an hour. It can be moved with absolute ease and safety from room to room without even giving a flicker.

OUR GUARANTEE protects you against any defect in workmanship or material.

SUPER ALADDIN TABLE LAMP
STYLE NO. 1400

Complete (less shade), with mechanical wick cleaner, chimney and two Lox-on mantles :—
Price : **42/-** in nickel plate, satin brass, or polished brass,
47/- in chromium plate.
54/- in oxidised copper.
60/- in oxidised silver.
Shade No. 611. Made in our new unshrinkable material, Whip-o-lite, with alternate panels in crackled Rhodoid. Colours :—All white, pink and white, orange and white.
Price **15/-**. Special colours 1/- extra.
For use with Table and Bracket lamps.
Shade No. 625. Similar design but fitted for use with hanging lamps.
Price .. **15/-**

SUPER ALADDIN HANGING LAMP
STYLE NO. 1416

Complete as illustrated (less shade), with automatic extension fixture, mechanical wick cleaner, chimney and two Lox-on mantles :—
Price : **67/-** in nickel plate, satin brass or polished brass.
76/- in chromium plate.
84/6 in oxidised copper.
96/- in oxidised silver.
Style No. 1414. As above, but without extension fixture.
Price : **51/6** in nickel plate, satin brass or polished brass.
58/- in chromium plate.
66/- in oxidised copper.
75/- in oxidised silver.
Shade No. 622. Made in our new unshrinkable material Whip-o-lite with alternate panels in Moire. Colours : All white, pink and white, orange and white.
Price **15/-** Special colours 1/- extra.
Shade No. 608. Same design but fitted for use with table or bracket lamps.

SUPER ALADDIN BRACKET LAMP
STYLE NO. 1404

This lamp is specially suitable for halls, landings, and kitchens. Complete with special Aladdin bracket, mechanical wick cleaner, chimney and two Lox-on mantles :—
Price : **49/-** in nickel plate, satin brass or polished brass.
55/- in chromium plate.
63/- in oxidised copper.
70/- in oxidised silver.
Prices without bracket same as Table Lamp No. 1400.

SUPER ALADDIN CONVERTIBLE LAMP
STYLE NO. 1404 (less bracket)

For use with bracket, hanging fixture, pedestals, floor standards, or as illustrated. Prices same as SUPER-ALADDIN Table Lamp No. 1400.

Hexagonal Stand in solid Oak, 20/- in solid Mahogany 21/6

Shade No. 1142. 14 in. Whip-o-lite with design. (Available in 7 assorted designs, No. 1138 to 1145 inclusive).
Price .. **9/9**

Similar shades in eggshell vellum, trimmed gimp with design (Nos. 1170 to 1175 inclusive).
Price .. **5/6**

(See page 5)

Other finishes, such as Antique Brass, Florentine Bronze, Dutch Brass and Roman Bronze, can be made to order at 5/- extra to price quoted for Oxidised Copper.

Aladdin LAMPS

Regd. Trade Mark

MODEL NO. 12

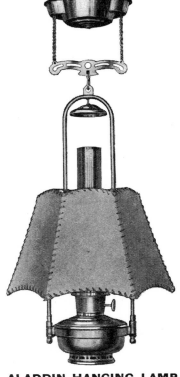

ALADDIN TABLE LAMP

STYLE NO. 1200

Complete (less shade), with one mechanical wick cleaner, chimney and two Lox-on mantles :—

Price : **33/-** in nickel plate, satin brass or polished brass.
38/- in chromium plate.
45/- in oxidised copper.
51/- in oxidised silver.

Shade No. 612. Attractive shade in Whip-o-lite and crackled Rhodoid.

Colours : All white, alternate panels pink and white, orange and white.
Price **11/6**. Special colours **1/-** extra.

For use with Table and Bracket lamps.

Shade No. 626. Same design and colours, but fitted for use with hanging lamps.
Price .. **11/6**

ALADDIN BRACKET LAMP

STYLE NO. 1204

Complete with special Aladdin bracket, mechanical wick-cleaner, chimney and two Lox-on mantles. This lamp is specially suited for the hall, landings and kitchen.

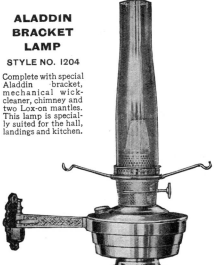

Price : **40/-** in nickel plate, satin brass, or polished brass.
46/- in chromium plate.
54/- in oxidised copper.
61/- in oxidised silver.

Prices without Bracket same as Table Lamp No. 1200.

ALADDIN HALL LANTERN

A modern lamp made to old and picturesque pattern. An extremely novel and very attractive method of lighting the hall, landing or passages. Finished in antique silver. Style No. 6412.

Price **45/-** (without lamp)

ALADDIN CONVERTIBLE LAMP

STYLE NO. 1204 (less bracket).

For use with bracket, hanging fixture, pedestals, floor standards, or as illustrated.

Prices same as the Table Lamp No. 1200

Hexagonal Stand only, in solid Oak .. **20/-**
in solid Mahogany .. **21/6**

Shade No. 1170 14 in. Empire (illustrated) available in six assorted designs in eggshell vellum trimmed gimp (Nos. 1170-5).

Price **5/6**

Also available for table and bracket lamps.

No. 4040 in plain vellum and **No. 4040B** in tinted vellum, 14 in. Empires.

Price **4/6**

For Hanging Lamps.

No. 5050 in plain vellum and **No. 5050B** in tinted vellum, 18 in. Empires.

Price **6/9**

ALADDIN HANGING LAMP

STYLE NO. 1216

Complete as illustrated (less shade), with automatic extension fixture, mechanical wick cleaner, chimney and two Lox-on mantles.

Price : **58/-** in nickel plate, satin brass or polished brass.
67/- in chromium plate.
75/6 in oxidised copper.
87/- in oxidised silver.

Style No. 1214. As above, without extension fixture

Price : **42/6** in nickel plate, satin brass, or polished brass.
49/- in chromium plate.
57/- in oxidised copper.
66/- in oxidised silver.

Shade No. 624 (illustrated). Made in our new unshrinkable material Whip-o-lite. Standard colours : All White, alternate panels red and white, pink and white, orange and white, amber and white.
Price **8/6**. Special colours **1/-** extra.

Shade No. 610. A similar shade for use with table and bracket lamps only. Price **8/6**.

147

IMPORTANT NOTICE
To existing users of old model Aladdin Lamps (Models 6, 9, 10 and 11.)
TWO SPECIAL EXCHANGE OFFERS
NEW LAMPS FOR OLD

To those persons using old model Aladdin Lamps, we make a unique offer to take back their old lamp and replace it with a new Super-Aladdin. This offer enables them to enjoy all the advantages of this remarkable new lamp without having to pay the full price.

Take back your old lamp to any ironmonger or store (your local dealer for preference) and you will be allowed 15/- for your old lamp in exchange for any model Super-Aladdin. This is a definite saving to you of 15/-. *Do not hesitate to take advantage of this offer*—consult your dealer at once or write us for full particulars of the Scheme.

SPEND 10/6 AND SAVE 13/5

Exchange your old Aladdin Burner (models 6, 9, 10 and 11) for a new No. 12 Burner Outfit (instant light model). We realise that in these hard times, some 'Aladdin' users may not be able to afford a new Super-Aladdin *even under our very attractive offer* but these customers are not neglected. They can exchange their old burners for new No. 12 Burners at a cost of 10/6, and a saving of 13/5. Take your present burner, complete with wick, generator, chimney and wick cleaner, to your local dealer—pay 10/6, and you will receive in exchange a new No. 12 Burner, complete with wick, generator, chimney and wick cleaner. This new burner will fit into your existing container and you will have exactly the same advantages as if you had purchased a new No. 12 lamp complete at 33/-, or more. The normal price of the burner outfit complete is 23/11 and so you will be saving 13/5.

This special exchange price applies to burners in standard finishes—Nickel, Satin Brass, or Polished Brass. For Oxidised Copper or Oxidised Silver, the exchange price is 12/-. Broken chimneys are not returnable, and in this event an additional charge of 1/11 is made.

Every customer, rich or poor, can benefit under one or other of our exchange schemes. No person need be deprived of the opportunity of having a better lamp. Ask your ironmonger for all particulars and make up your mind to benefit by one of these two remarkable offers.

A WARNING AND A RECOMMENDATION

The use of inferior grades of paraffin definitely impairs the efficiency and life of any oil burning apparatus. Do not be tempted to buy paraffin merely because it is cheap. There are good brands of paraffin on sale but, unfortunately, you cannot tell the good from the inferior because *they all look alike.*

To protect the public against inferior grades of oil, ALADDIN PARAFFIN is now sold and is coloured PINK as a safeguard. It is distributed on our behalf by Messrs Shell Mex and B.P. Limited, and their Associate Companies in Scotland and the Irish Free State. Always use ALADDIN PARAFFIN—it is the finest burning oil on the market and look for the colour when you buy. No other is genuine. ALADDIN PARAFFIN is sold by most ironmongers.

ALADDIN SHADES FOR ELECTRIC LIGHT, GAS OR PARAFFIN LAMPS

Having the most modern shade factory in the country, we manufacture shades of every description, in any design and in any material, for any type of lighting.

WHIP-O-LITE. This is a remarkable new shade material—*exclusive to ourselves.* It will be noted that the majority of shades illustrated in this catalogue are made of Whip-o-lite. It is more durable than other materials. It gives perfect diffusion of light, is attractive in appearance and is washable. Always buy shades made of Whip-o-lite.

Estimates are given free. Consult us, no matter how large or small your requirements.

Super Aladdin METAL STANDARD LAMPS

Regd. Trade Mark

(ADJUSTABLE IN HEIGHT)

STANDARD FLOOR LAMP →

This is a particularly elegant standard. No trouble has been spared to ensure that every detail of its beautifully balanced lines is exactly right and that its workmanship and finish are the finest obtainable.

Supplied in three metal finishes.

MS26 Polished Brass .. £5 5 6
MS27 Oxidised Copper .. £6 4 0
MS28 Oxidised Silver .. £6 18 9

Fitted and wired for electric lighting—

Polished Brass £3 5 0
Oxidised Copper £3 10 0
Oxidised Silver £3 17 3

Shade No. 709. 20 in.
A handsome shade in Bexoid. Design on white panels. Alternate panels in rose, red, orange, yellow, blue or green, Silk fringe.

Price .. £2 5 0

STANDARD FLOOR LAMP

A metal standard of clean and elegant design. It can be adjusted in height and the "tout ensemble" makes the price extremely attractive. Supplied in three finishes.

MS16 Polished Brass £4 5 6
MS17 Oxidised Copper £5 2 0
MS18 Oxidised Silver £5 11 0

Fitted and wired for electric lighting—

Polished Brass £2 5 0
Oxidised Copper £2 8 0
Oxidised Silver £2 9 6

Shade No. 3658. 20 in.
Vellum. Alternate panels coloured to match fringe.
Price .. £1 11 6

STANDARD FLOOR LAMP ←

This attractive and handsome metal model goes well with most decorative schemes. Its clean slender lines are the result of careful designing and manufacture.

Supplied in three different finishes.

MS20 Polished Brass .. £4 11 6
MS21 Oxidised Copper .. £5 8 0
MS22 Oxidised Silver .. £6 4 6

Fitted and wired for electric lighting—

Polished Brass £2 11 0
Oxidised Copper £2 14 0
Oxidised Silver £3 3 0

Shade No. 556. 20 in.
Taffeta with fringe to match. Colours: Rose, orange, gold and salmon.

Price .. £1 17 6

STANDARD ← FLOOR LAMP

A fine specimen of metal craft with substantial well weighted base designed in perfect harmony with the standard.

Supplied in three different finishes.

MS23 Polished Brass £4 18 0
MS24 Oxidised Copper £5 14 0
MS25 Oxidised Silver £6 6 6

Fitted and wired for electric lighting—

Polished Brass £2 17 6
Oxidised Copper £3 0 0
Oxidised Silver £3 5 0

Shade No. 756. 20 in.
8-panel. Large panels in white parchment, shaded, small panels in green, rose, yellow or orange. Hand painted and fringe to tone.
Price .. £1 19 9

STANDARD FLOOR LAMP →

This standard may be confidently selected for inclusion in any furnishing scheme. It will be noted the lines are bold and yet dignified and in perfect harmony and balance.

Supplied in three finishes.

MS7 Polished Brass £7 16 0
MS8 Oxidised Copper £8 11 0
MS9 Oxidised Silver £9 18 0

Fitted and wired for electric lighting—

Polished Brass £5 15 6
Oxidised Copper £5 17 0
Oxidised Silver £6 16 6

Shade No. 528. 22 in.
Pale gold Taffeta shade gimped velvet.
Price .. £3 7 6

A reduction of 9/- can be made on the above Floor Standards when fitted with No. 12 Aladdin Lamps.

Aladdin Lamps will not give the fine service we claim for them, if spare parts other than those manufactured by Aladdin Industries Ltd., and bearing their trade mark, are used. Aladdin spare parts only should be used, and only under these circumstances can the Aladdin Guarantee hold. All Aladdin Lamps, spare parts and accessories are packed in cartons bearing the trade mark **Aladdin**

SuperAladdin WOOD STANDARD LAMPS

Regd. Trade Mark

STANDARD FLOOR LAMP

A very popular wooden standard on account of its low price. It is nevertheless a very attractive and suitable ornament to any house. Supplied in three finishes.

W41a Stained Oak £3 12 6
W41b Stained Mahogany £3 15 0
W41c Stained Walnut £3 15 0

Fitted and wired for electric lighting—
W41a .. £1 12 0
W41b .. £1 14 6
W41c .. £1 14 6

Shade No. 702. 20 in. Grained Vellum, hand painted design, silk fringe to tone
Price .. £1 6 3

STANDARD FLOOR LAMP

A nicely designed, yet inexpensive, wooden standard. Supplied in three finishes to tone with any style of furnishing.

W42a Stained Oak £4 8 0
W42b Stained Mahogany £4 11 0
W42c Stained Walnut £4 11 0

Fitted and wired for electric lighting—
W42a .. £2 7 6
W42b .. £2 10 6
W42c .. £2 10 6

Shade No. 720. 22 in. Grained Vellum. Small panels, natural; large panels, rose, peach, maize or orange. Gold gimp.

Price .. £1 1 9

STANDARD FLOOR LAMP

A beautiful wooden model for use with certain styles of decoration and furniture where metal standard lamps do not harmonise.

Supplied in Solid Oak or Mahogany
W1 Plain Oak £5 5 0
W2 Plain Mahogany .. £5 15 0
W3 Carved Oak £7 5 0
W4 Carved Mahogany .. £7 15 0
W5 Twisted Oak .. £6 0 0
W6 Twisted Mahogany .. £6 10 0

Shade No. 3606. 22 in. Vellum
Price .. £1 16 9

All standards quoted complete with polished brass lamp and basket—special quotations for any other finish.

STANDARD FLOOR LAMP

A wooden standard of bolder and more massive appearance, yet retaining the same pleasing lines as the other models illustrated.
Supplied in two styles.
W37A Solid Oak £5 14 6
W37B Solid Mahogany £6 3 6

Fitted and wired for electric lighting—
Solid Oak .. £3 14 0
Solid Mahogany £4 3 0

Shade No. 718. 20 in. An attractively designed shade with alternate panels in rose, red, orange, yellow, blue or green. Silk fringe.
Price .. £2 5 0

STANDARD FLOOR LAMP

This wooden standard is of a simple and plain design primarily intended for use in bungalows and cottages.

Supplied in two styles.
W36A Solid Oak .. £4 17 6
W36B Solid Mahogany £5 1 6

Fitted and wired for electric lighting—
W36a £2 17 0
W36b £3 1 0

Shade No. 753. 20 in. Shade in Imitation Vellum. Shaded in old gold, peach, orange, rose, with fringe at base to tone. Decorated with gold line
Price .. £1 4 9

A reduction of 9/- can be made on above Floor Standards when fitted with No. 12 Aladdin Lamps.

Standards when fitted with Aladdin Lamps are 4 ft. 4 in. in height. When supplied fitted and wired for electric light, height, 5 ft.

We accept no responsibility for Aladdin Lamps fitted to Table Pedestals or Floor Standards other than those purchased from or otherwise approved by us. It is in the customer's interest to note this when purchasing.

Super Aladdin PEDESTAL LAMPS

Regd. Trade Mark.

PEDESTAL TABLE LAMP

This beautiful model reveals good taste and dignified restraint in every line. Of substantial yet graceful design it is not too heavy to be moved from room to room.

Complete as illustrated, less shade, together with one mechanical wick cleaner and one extra Lox-on mantle.

CP200	Lacquered Brass	£3 6 9
CP201	Oxidised Copper	£4 1 6
CP202	Oxidised Silver	£4 11 6

Shade No. 719. 20 in. Hexagonal shape in vellum, laced gold leather with Japanese design.

Price .. **£1 7 9**

ALADDINIQUE
(CROWN DEVON WARE)

A beautiful vase made in two original and modernistic colour designs:—Lustre, orange and pastel green. Supplied complete with delightful hand-painted shade in Whip-o-lite at the remarkable low price of **£3 3 0**

Same (supplied with vellum shade, same design).
Price .. **£2 18 0**

If supplied with No. 12 lamp, the price is 9/- less in each case, i.e. **£2 14 0** and **£2 9 0** respectively.

PEDESTAL TABLE LAMP

This Pedestal Lamp, with its handsome wooden stand has been designed to meet the demand for an artistic yet substantial lamp for dining room use. It is beautifully finished and is of the finest quality and workmanship

Supplied in Solid Oak or Mahogany.

WP1	Plain Oak	..	..	£3 6 6
WP2	Plain Mahogany		..	£3 8 0
WP3	Carved Oak	..	..	£4 5 0
WP4	Carved Mahogany		..	£4 6 0
WP5	Twisted Oak	..	..	£3 11 7
WP6	Twisted Mahogany		..	£3 16 6

Shade No. 723. 20 in. Grained vellum, with design on small panels.
Colours : Rose, peach, maize or orange.
Price .. **£1 9 3**

THE *Aladdin*
SAFETY FILLER

Does away with the bother, mess and waste of overfilled lamps.

Standard Finish
One quart size	..	..	3/6
Half-gallon size	..	..	5/-
One gallon size	..	..	6/6

Oxidised Copper Finish
One quart size	..	..	4/6
Half-gallon size	..	..	7/6
One gallon size	..	..	8/6

ALADDIN EXTENSION FIXTURE

Is made of pressed steel, fits snugly against the ceiling like a canopy and can be extended approximately 3ft. By its special locking device it will remain locked in any desired position. Although it is designed specially for Aladdin lamps it can be used universally.

In polished brass, satin brass or nickel .. **15/6 each.**
Oxidised copper **18/6** each. Oxidised silver **21/-** each.

A reduction of 9/- can be made on above Table Pedestals when fitted with No. 12 Aladdin Lamps.

ALADDIN HANGING FIXTURE

A neatly designed and very attractive hanging fixture for all model Aladdin lamps. Folds up flat when packed and lamp can be easily removed for filling. Shade rests on top ring

In nickel plate, polished brass or satin brass.

9/6

In Chromium plate
11/-

In Oxidised copper
12/-

In Oxidised silver
15/-

LARGE BASE ADAPTOR

To take Shades with Duplex fitting. Fits on the tripod fitting of the Aladdin Lamp.

Price .. 1/11

SMALL BASE ADAPTOR

To take Shades with Duplex fitting. Fits on burner of Aladdin Lamp. Price 1/11

WICK CLEANER

For cleaning wick and wick tube flange.

Price .. 1/- each.

GENERATOR

Generator shown is our special baffle Generator No. 12, for use with all styles and numbers of lamps illustrated in this catalogue.

No. 11 Generator. For use with Models Nos. 8, 9, 10 and 11

Price **10d.** each

SUPER ALADDIN MOUNTED WICKS

These special patented wicks, vital to the efficient working of the Super-Aladdin Lamp are charred ready for use and packed in special protective Aladdin cartons.

Price .. **2/-** each
For Super-Aladdin Lamps ONLY.

LOX-ON WICK
For No. 12 Burners ONLY

Price .. **2/-** each

NO. 11 WICK
For Models 8, 9, 10, 11 ONLY

Price .. **2/-** each

ALADDIN CHIMNEY CLEANER

Specially designed for use with Aladdin or any make of chimney. Metal holder, with renewable high grade wash leather pad.

Price .. **9d.**

SUPER ALADDIN BURNER

This is a special instant lighting, draught-controlled burner for use on SUPER-ALADDIN Lamps only.

Price : **25/-** in nickel plate, satin brass or polished brass.

27/- in chromium plate.
29/- in oxidised copper.
32/- in oxidised silver.

ALADDIN BRACKET

Supplied with bracket lamp Nos. 1204 and 1404. Can be purchased separately at prices shown below, and used to convert hanging lamps Nos. 1214 and 1414 to wall lamps.

Price : **7/-** nickel plate, satin brass or polished brass.
8/- chromium plate **9/-** oxidised copper.
10/- oxidised silver

NOTE.—Can be used with any model Aladdin.

INSECT SCREENS

An effective guard against the destruction of the mantle by insects. Strongly made and supplied in brass only. A most useful accessory and one that is particularly necessary in tropical countries.

Price .. **2/6**

ALADDIN LOX-ON CHIMNEYS

Price **1/11** each

The chimney illustrated is our new patented Lox-on type, specially designed for SUPER-ALADDIN lamps, and for Aladdin lamps using the **No. 12 burner.** This chimney locks into the gallery and cannot be tilted or knocked off, and—at the same time—regulates the intake of air. Made of heat-resisting glass and guaranteed.

For Aladdin lamps, models Nos. 8, 9, 10 and 11, the No. 11 Branded Chimney must be used.

Price .. **1/11** each

ALADDIN HEAT GLASS PROTECTOR

For use with Aladdin or similar chimneys.

Price .. **2/–** each

A very useful accessory Prevents discolouration of low ceilings by heat.

STAND FOR CONVERTING A BRACKET LAMP INTO A TABLE LAMP

Enables a Bracket Lamp to be converted into a Table Lamp at an extremely reasonable price. Made in three detachable pieces, it can, if so desired, be packed flat when not in use. Black or walnut finish.

Price .. **3/6** each

ALADDIN KONE KAP MANTLE

The Aladdin Kone Kap mantle is for use with model burners Nos. 8, 9, 10 and 11. Supplied in two qualities.

First quality, pink

Price .. **2/–** each

Second quality, white

Price .. **1/6** each

ALADDIN LOX-ON MANTLE

Price .. **2/–** each

The Aladdin Lox-on Mantle is for use with all SUPER-ALADDIN lamps and with Aladdin lamps using **No. 12 burner.** For models using burners Nos. 8, 9, 10 and 11, the Aladdin Kone Kap mantle, illustrated opposite, must be used.

No. 12 ALADDIN WICK RAISER

For use with No. 12 burners only.
Price .. **1/–**

BASKETS

For adapting electrical or other standards for use with Aladdin Lamps. Can be supplied—

Standard finishes **6/–**
Chromium .. **7/–**
Oxidised copper **7/6**
Oxidised silver **9/–**

SUPER ALADDIN WICK RAISER

This Wick Raiser is for use with SUPER-ALADDIN lamps only.

Price .. **1/–**

We accept no responsibility for Aladdin Lamps fitted to Table Pedestals or Floor Standards other than those purchased from or otherwise approved by us. It is in the customer's interest to note this when purchasing.

10

Decorative Glass Aladdin Electric Table Lamps

Ca. 1935

Shade Design No. 940

Shade Design No. 855

No. E-410
Boudoir
In Colors. Amber, Jade, Peach, Rose, White, and Black and White

Price, Each $2.00

Complete with any design of 8-inch Aladdin Parchment Shade

No. E-340
Table
In Colors: Amber, Jade, Peach, Rose, and White

Price, Each $3.00

Complete with any design of 10-inch Aladdin Parchment Shade

Shade Design No. 910

No. E-380—Table
In Colors: Amber, Jade, Peach, Rose and White
Price, Each $3.50   Complete with any design of 12-inch Aladdin Parchment Shade

No. E-390—Table
In Colors: Amber, Jade, Peach, Rose, White, and Black and White
• Price, Each $6.00 •
Complete with any design of 16-inch Aladdin Parchment Shade
(Illustrated below)

Shade Design No. 905

No. E-360—Table
In Colors: Amber, Jade, Peach, Rose, White, and Black and White
• Price, Each $5.00 •
Complete with any design of 14-inch Aladdin Parchment Shade
(Illustrated below)

Shade Design No. 935

Shade Design No. 920

The Mantle Lamp Company of America, Inc.
609 W. Lake Street, Chicago, Illinois

See Over

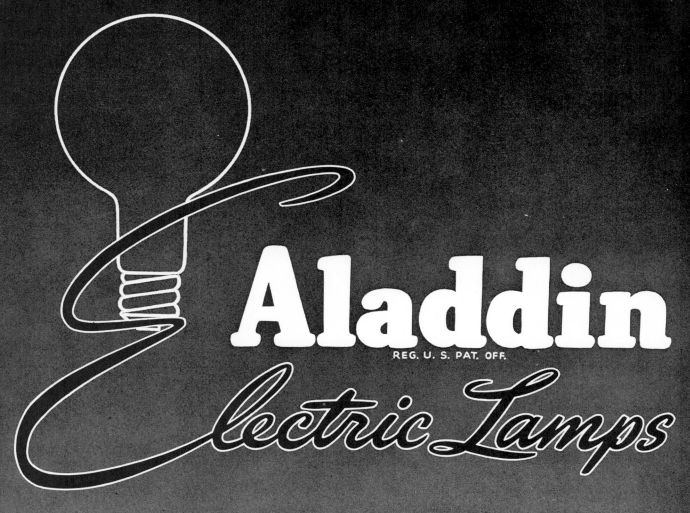

Aladdin
REG. U. S. PAT. OFF.

Electric Lamps

AND WHIP·O·LITE..PARVELOUR
AND FABRIC LAMP SHADES

Foreword

It is with pleasure and pride that we present Aladdin dealers with this graphic representation of our new 1941-42 Fall and Winter line of Aladdin Quality Electric Lamps and Aladdin Quality Whip-o-lite and Fabric Shades. Painstaking effort, exceptional artistry, careful craftsmanship and select materials has made each and every one of these units an exceptional value. Strong irresistible inbuilt eye-appeal assure dealers of a quick and ready consumer acceptance and a surprisingly rapid turnover.

To all our present and prospective Aladdin dealers we dedicate this booklet, solicit their orders for this exceptional-value merchandise in the firm conviction that it will greatly assist in building a most pleasant and profitable lamp business for each and every one of them.

The Mantle Lamp Company of America, Inc.

223 West Jackson Boulevard, Chicago, Ill.　　　721 East Yamhill Street, Portland, Oregon

Form No. 1181 — July 1, 1941 — Printed in U.S.A.

(2)

Aladdin *Electric* Table Lamps

Unusual Creations of Artistic Design, Possessing Outstanding Merit for Value, Eye-Appeal and Craftsmanship Extraordinary

No. M-164

An all-metal, practical modern design, pedestal lamp for homes, offices and hotels. In Satin Silver or Oxidized Bronze Plate, 10½" metal matching shade No. 950. 1-Light socket, Turn-Knob Switch, Swivel Harp and Ball Finial. 21" High.

No. G-201

A small one-piece, hollow arm, desk or radio lamp. Of Ivory Alacite, or decorated Alacite in Blue, Green or Rose. 1-Light Swivel Socket and Turn-Knob switch. Concealed cord. 9" cone bridge fitter Whip-o-lite shade No. 2044.

No. G-213—Illuminated Base

Of a striking and unusual mounted and leaf-armed bottle design. Ornate cast metal base. In Ivory Alacite, or decorated Alacite in Tan or Blue. Blue has silver plated Base—others Gold. Concealed switch for illuminating base. 1-Light Push-Thru Socket, Harp and Finial. Shade, 13" Whip-o-lite No. 2015 shown.

No. G-186—Illuminated Base

In leaf embossed, acorn shape design in one-piece Ivory Alacite, or Alacite decorated Tan or Blue. 22½" high. 1-Light open socket—1-Light Socket in base to illuminate it—3-Way Switch in open socket controls both. Tall Swivel Harp—Alacite Finial. 12" Fluted Whip-o-lite Shade No. 909H shown.

No. G-202 or G-245

A beautiful one-piece armed vase and square base lamp in Ivory Alacite or Alacite decorated in Rose or Blue. 1-Light Push-Thru socket, Swivel Harp and Alacite Finial. Shade shown 12" Whip-o-lite No. 2049. 21¾" high. Also as Indirect type with 6" Plastic Reflector as No. G-245.

No. G-214 or G-248

Of a most popular oriental design with decagon base in one-piece. Hollow blown pedestal conceals cord. In Ivory Alacite, or Alacite decorated Tan or Blue. 22" High. 1-Light Push-Thru socket, Swivel Harp and Alacite Finial. Shade, 12" Whip-o-lite No. 2054. Also as Indirect Type with 6" Plastic Reflector as No. G-248.

No. G-195—Illuminated Base

Of deep fluted, low-urn design, created in Ivory Alacite only with cast metal base in Antique Gold Plate. 1-Light open socket—1-Light socket in base to illuminate it—3-Way Switch in open socket controls both. Swivel Harp and Alacite Finial. 20¼" high. Shown with 13" Fluted Whip-o-lite Shade No. 2300.

No. G-212—Illuminated Base

A segmented or deep fluted vase mounted on a cast metal Gold-Plated base. In Ivory Alacite, or Alacite decorated Tan. 23½" High. 1-Light open socket—1-Light socket in base to illuminate it—3-Way switch in open socket controls both. Swivel Harp and Alacite Finial. Shade, 12" Fluted Whip-o-lite No. 2300-H shown.

No. G-217—Illuminated Base

A graceful, charming vase design with leaf spray in high relief. In Ivory Alacite, or decorated Tan or Green. Gold Plated Base. 1-Light Open Socket—1-Light Socket in Base to illuminate it—3-Way Switch in open socket controls both. 1-Light Push-Thru Socket, Swivel Harp and Alacite Finial. 20¾" High. Shade, 13" Whip-o-lite No. 2018 shown.

(3)

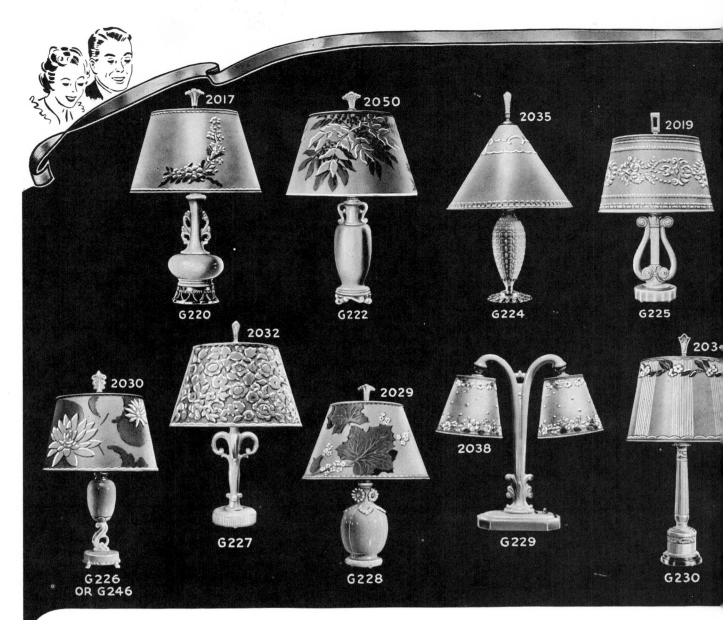

Aladdin *Electric* Table Lamps

• CONTINUED •

No. G-220—Illuminated Base

A charming long necked and winged vase creation, mounted on a gold-plated metal base. In Ivory Alacite or decorated Alacite in Tan or Blue. 1-Light open socket. 1-Light Socket in base 3-way switch controls both. Swivel harp—Alacite finial. 22½" high. Shade, 14" Whip-o-lite, No. 2017.

No. G-225

In the Regency vogue, and created with Lyre and reverse-fluted base in one unit. Hidden cord thru base to 1-Light push-thru socket, with swivel harp and Alacite finial. In all Ivory Alacite, or decorated Rose, Gold or Blue. Shade shown 12" Parvelour decorated Whip-o-lite No. 2019. 20¼" high.

No. G-228

A fascinating medium-sized lamp of fluted urn and pressed flower design, and base in one unit. Cord thru base to 1-Light push-thru socket, swivel harp and Alacite finial. In All Ivory Alacite, Alacite decorated Rose or Blue. 13" Shade —No. 2029 in Parvelour Whip-o-lite shown. 21½" high.

No. G-222

A simple, yet most artistic armed vase with integral base. In Ivory Alacite, or decorated Alacite in Tan, Blue, or Green. 22½" high. 1-Light push-thru socket, Swivel harp and Alacite finial. Shade shown, 14" Whip-o-lite. No. 2050.

No. G-226 or G-246

A most delightful design created in one-piece Alacite, with secreted cord. Graceful scroll unites footed base and ovate urn. Has 1-Light push-thru socket, swivel harp and Alacite finial. In all Ivory Alacite, or decorated in Green or Brown. Shown with 12" Parvelour decorated Whip-o-lite shade No. 2030. 20¾" high. Also as Indirect type with 6" Plastic Reflector as No. G-246.

No. G-229

An ingenious "between bed" lamp of one-piece construction. Oblong base, with 2 graceful and ornate arms which conduct hidden cord to 2 standard sockets from switch in base. In All Ivory Alacite, or decorated Alacite in Rose or Blue. 16½" high. Shown with 2 special 6" reverse clamp fitter Parvelour Whip-o-lite shades No. 2038.

No. G-224

A beautiful combination Alacite and metal lamp with all-over embossed urn, and graceful open-work, cast, gold-plated metal base. Has 1-Light push-thru socket, swivel harp and Alacite finial. In Ivory Alacite, or in Gold or Rose. 13" Special Cone Parvelour decorated Whip-o-lite Shade No. 2035 shown; especially made and fitted to this lamp, 21½" high.

No. G-227

An artistic modern interpretation of the Prince's feathers of Regency era. Hollow blown spindle conceals cord. Created in one-piece Alacite. In All Ivory Alacite or Ivory Alacite decorated in Brown. Has 1-Light push-thru socket, swivel harp and Alacite finial. 14" Parvelour Whip-o-lite shade No. 2032 shown. 22¾" high.

No. G-230

A strictly authentic Regency creation of dignity and refinement, in Alacite with cast Gold-plated metal sub-base. Has 1-Light push-thru socket, swivel harp and Alacite finial. 24" high. In All Ivory Alacite or Alacite decorated in Brown or Blue. Shown with 12" Special Parvelour decorated Shade No. 2034.

(4)

Aladdin *Electric* Table Lamps

• CONTINUED •

No. G-231

An exquisite example of harmony in line and design. Beautiful embossed urn surmounts open-work metal base—gold plated. Has 1-Light push-thru socket, swivel harp and Alacite finial. In All Ivory Alacite, or Alacite decorated in Rose or Gold. 21″ high. Shade 12″ Parvelour decorated Whip-o-lite No. 2034, Special for G-230, G-231 and G-234.

No. G-234

A tall, modern, pedestal design with Golden Crowned Pheasant figure mounted on an oval base. In one-piece Ivory Alacite, or in Alacite decorated in Rose or Blue. Hollow blown spindle secretes cord. Has 1-Light standard push-thru socket. Harp and Alacite finial. Height 22½″ overall. Shown with Special 12″ Parvelour Whip-o-lite Shade No. 2045. Alternate Shade No. 2034.

No. G-237

A combination glass and metal lamp, reminiscent of the Colonial period. In two different combinations:—Alacite Ivory Bowl or Ruby Crystal Bowl, both with Gold Pedestal. 25½″ high. Has 1-Light push-thru socket, bowl-matching Finial, and Harp. Illustrated here with 15″ Bell Shaped Fabric Shade No. B-456.

No. G-232—Illuminated Base

Of delicately winged, long-neck fluted urn design, mounted on Gold-Plated metal base. Has 1-Light standard push-thru open socket and standard socket for 7W bulb, and 3-way switch on open socket to control both. In All Ivory Alacite, or decorated Alacite in Rose or Blue. 14″ Shade—Parvelour fluted Whip-o-lite No. 2304 shown. 22½″ high.

No. G-235

In a very graceful serpentine and floral design with round footed base, of one-piece construction. Available in Ivory Alacite, or decorated Alacite in Rose or Brown. Hollow spindle hides cord. Has 1-Light standard push-thru socket. Harp and Alacite finial. Height 21¼″ overall. Shade shown, 12″ No. 1007, in decorated Whip-o-lite.

No. M-238

A medium sized, all-metal, all purpose inverted type desk or table lamp for hotels or homes; of one piece base and hollow arm construction. In Black and Silver or Oxidized Bronze and Gold. Has 1-Light socket in canopy with turn-knob switch. Fitted with 6″ ornamented Plastic Shade No. P-94 in Tan or White. Height of lamp overall—15½″.

No. G-233—Illuminated Base

A delightful ball-type lamp with deep embossed stone flower design bowl, gold plated open-work metal base. Has 1-Light open socket, and socket in base for illuminating it—3-way switch in shade socket controls both. In All Ivory Alacite or decorated Alacite in Tan. Shown with 17″ Fabric Shade No. B-453, 23¼″ high. 17″ Fabric Shade No. B-457 or 17″ Whip-o-lite Shade No. 2300 as alternates. (B-457 shade shown on G-236.)

No. G-236—Illuminated Base

This outstanding artistic lamp is in urn design with surface highly embossed in stone flowers and leaf spray. Mounted on Gold-Plated base. Has 1-Light open socket, and 1 in base for illumination—a 3-way switch in open socket controls both. In Ivory Alacite, or decorated Alacite in Rose, Blue or Tan. 23″ high. Harp and Alacite finial. Shade shown Fabric No. B-457. (Alternates 17″—Fabric B-453 shown on G-233 or Whip-o-lite Shade No. 2300.)

No. G-239 or G-250

An interesting, intriguing one-piece lamp of much artistic merit and charm. Embossed floral design in bowl. In Ivory Alacite, or decorated Alacite in Tan or Rose. Has 1-Light push-thru socket, swivel harp and Alacite finial. Its height overall is 22″. Shown in illustration above with 14″ Parvelour Whip-o-lite Shade No. 2046. Also available in Indirect type with 6″ Plastic reflector as No. G-250.

(5)

Aladdin *Electric* Table Lamps
• CONTINUED •

No. G-240 or G-249
Base of this lamp simulates a column surmounted with a bowl of flowers. Very subtle and alluring. Of one-piece construction. Available in Ivory Alacite, or decorated Alacite in Green or Brown. Has 1-Light socket, push-thru switch, Alacite Finial and Swivel Harp. Height 22½". Shown with 14" Bell Fabric Shade No. M-384. Also in Indirect Type with 6" Plastic Reflector, as No. G-249.

No. G-243—Illuminated Base
A new Aladdin creation in the ever popular ball type of lamp with 7" diameter embossed bowl. Of one-piece pattern, and supplied in Antiqued Ivory Alacite, or decorated Alacite in Rose or Blue. Has 1-Light open socket in base for illuminating it, and 1 open socket; 3-way switch controls both. Tall Harp and Alacite Finial. Designed for 12" tall shade. No. 2305H in Fluted Parvelour Whip-o-lite shade shown.

No. G-241—Illuminated Base
A graceful ornamented and fluted urn mounted on a footed metal base. Available in 4 colors; Ivory Alacite, or Alacite decorated in Tan, Rose or Blue. Is equipped with 1-Light open socket in base for illuminating it; 3-way switch controls both lights. Harp and Finial. Height 23". Shown here with 14" Bell Fabric Shade No. B-401.

No. G-244
A delicate, dainty, small lamp of unusual charm and beauty. Has wing-like scrolls on opposite sides of slender hollow pedestal on round footed base. In Ivory Alacite, or decorated Alacite in Rose or Blue. 18½" high. 1-Light socket, swivel harp and Alacite finial 10" washer fitter. Parvelour Whip-o-lite Shade No. 2048 shown.

No. G-242 or G-247
A charming, slender, cylindrical, one-piece lamp of the vase type with neck ornamented with scroll arms at sides. Made in Ivory Alacite, or decorated Alacite in Rose and Blue. Fitted with 1-Light push-thru socket, Harp and Finial. Height 20¾" overall. Illustrated with 13" Bell Stretched Fabric Shade No. S-466. Also in Indirect Type with 6" Plastic Reflector, as No. G-247.

Aladdin Electric Hang-Up Lamps
No. G-352
Of one-piece ornate vertical panel and scroll arm design. Has single candle and socket with push-knob switch in wall plate. In Ivory Alacite, or decorated Alacite in Rose, Blue or Tan. 7", 8" or 10" Parvelour Whip-o-lite clamp-fitter shades adaptable. Shown here with 8" Shade No. 2028.

No. G-353
Of a most pleasing and restful design with oval wall plate and semi-circle projecting arm. Has a single candle and socket with push-knob switch in wall plate. In Ivory Alacite, or decorated Alacite in Blue or Rose. 7", 8" or 10" Parvelour Whip-o-lite Clamp-fitter shades are adaptable. Shade shown here is 10" of Design No. 2048.

Aladdin Decorative Illuminated Urns

No. G-213A
This delicate dainty urn with its graceful leaf design arms and open-work Gold-Plated metal base is exceedingly popular as a radio, buffet or mantle-piece ornament. Has 1-Light socket in base for illuminating it, with push switch in base. In Ivory Alacite, or decorated Alacite in Blue or Tan.

No. G-232A
This attractive, two-piece, illuminated unit with its slender necked, fluted and eared urn, and its Gold-Plated metal base makes an ideal ornament for radio, buffet or mantle. Has 1-Light socket in base for illumination, with push-switch in base. In Ivory Alacite, or decorated Alacite in Rose or Blue.

Delightful Aladdin *Electric* Boudoir Lamps of *Charm*

⟦ With the exception of Boudoir Lamp G-16, All Boudoirs shown have hollow blown spindles
to secrete cord, and allows its entrance thru base and spindle;—a most desirable, exclusive
and patented Aladdin feature. All have long Approved cord and Single Push-Thru Socket. ⟧

No. G-16
As illustrated, In Ivory Alacite only with Gold Plated metal spindle. 17" high. Shown with 10" clamp fitter. Parvelour Whip-o-lite Shade No. 2048.

No. G-21
As is shown above in Ivory Alacite or Alacite decorated Rose, Blue or Green. 15" high. Shade shown—7" Parvelour Whip-o-lite No. 964.

No. G-22
Illustrated above, available in Ivory Alacite or Alacite decorated Blue, Rose or Tan. 15⅛" high. Shade shown— 8" Fluted Parvelour Whip-o-lite No. 2305.

No. G-24
As in above illustration, available only in Ivory Alacite. Delicately Antiqued. 14½" high. Shown with 7" Juvenile Whip-o-lite No. 2059 Variegated.

No. G-25
Shown top row right. Available in Ivory Alacite, or Alacite decorated Rose, Blue or Green. 16½" high. 7" Shade Parvelour Whip-o-lite No. 2021.

No. G-27
Illustrated at left center. Supplied in Ivory Alacite or Alacite decorated Rose, Blue or Tan. 14" high. 8" Parvelour Whip-o-lite Shade No. 2033 shown.

No. G-28
Shown at right center. Available in Ivory Alacite or Alacite decorated Rose, Blue or Green. 16½" high. Parvelour Whip-o-lite Shade No. 2036 Shown.

No. G-29
Illustrated lower left. Supplied in Ivory Alacite, or Alacite decorated Rose, Blue or Green. 14½" high. 7" Parvelour Whip-o-Lite Shade No. 2037 shown.

No. G-30
Pictured in lower row left. Available in Ivory Alacite, or Alacite decorated in Rose or Blue. 15¾" high. 8" Parvelour Whip-o-lite Shade No. 2052 shown.

No. G-31
Shown in Picture in lower right. In Ivory Alacite, or Alacite decorated Rose or Blue. 13¾" high. Shade illustrated 7" Parvelour Whip-o-Lite Shade No. 2049 shown.

No. G-33
Illustrated in lower row left. Supplied in Ivory Alacite, or Alacite decorated in Rose or Blue. 8" Juvenile Parvelour Whip-o-Lite Shade No. 2055 shown.

Delicate · Aladdin Bed Lamps · Colorful
IN PARVELOUR DECORATED WHIP-O-LITE

All Aladdin Bed Lamps are equipped with generous Approved Cords 1-Light Chain-pull socket, and rubber covered hooks.

No. 2036SS—(9" high x 9" wide x 6" deep). In Parvelour Decorated Whip-o-lite in White, Rose, Blue or Green. (Matches Shade No. 2036).

No. 2037SS—(9" high x 9" wide x 6" deep). In Parvelour Decorated Whip-o-lite in Variegated colors. (Matches Shade No. 2036.)

No. 2305SS—(6" high x 10½" wide x 7" deep). In Fluted Parvelour Decorated Whip-o-lite in Rose, White, Blue or Tan. (Matches Shade No. 2305.)

(7)

Aladdin *Electric* Floor Lamps

• CONTINUED •

Aladdin Swing Arm Reflector Bridge No. 7073

Fitted with 1-Light Mogul Socket with 3-Way Turn-Knob Switch in Canopy. Canopy arranged for and supplied with 8″ Glass Reflector. 7½″ Offset Double Swing Arm.
57″ High to Top of 8″ Glass Reflector.
Oxidized Bronze or Ivory and Gold Finish
16″ Cone Fabric Shade No. M-387 Shown.

Aladdin Multi-Adjustable Reflector-Bridge No. 7073-A

Fitted with a jointed arm that rotates thru a complete circle, and also permits the raising or lowering of the arm from a horizontal to a vertical position at any point on circle. Has 1-Light Mogul Socket and 3-Way Canopy Switch.
Height to top of 8″ Glass Reflector in low position—53¾″; in top position 63½″.
Oxidized Bronze or Ivory and Gold Finish
18″ Cone Parvelour Whip-o-lite Shade No.2040 Shown.

Aladdin Reflector No. 3674

One-Light Mogul Socket with 3-Way Switch, and 3-Candle Arm Sockets and 3-Way Switch.
61″ High to Top of 10″ Glass Reflector.
In Gold, or Silver and Gold Finish
18″ Parvelour Whip-o-lite Shade No. 2033 Shown.

Aladdin Reflector No. 3675

One-Light Mogul Socket with 3-Way Switch, and 3-Candle Arm Sockets and 3-Way Switch.
60¾″ High to Top of 10″ Glass Reflector.
Oxidized Bronze or Silver and Gold Finish
18″ Parvelour Whip-o-lite Shade No. 2051 Shown.

Aladdin Reflector and Night Light No. 3976

One-Light Mogul Socket and 3-Way Canopy Switch, and 3-Candle Arm Sockets and 3-Way Switch to control Candle Sockets and 7-Watt Bulb installed in Night Light Globe.
60½″ High to Top of 10″ Glass Reflector.
In Ivory and Gold or Silver and Gold Finish.
18″ Parvelour Whip-o-lite Shade No. 2042 Shown.

Aladdin Reflector No. 3577

One-Light Mogul Socket 3-Way Turn-Knob Switch-in-Canopy—8″ Glass Reflector.
Oxidized Bronze or Silver and Gold Finish
18″ Empire Fabric Shade No. R-376 Shown.

Aladdin Torchere No. 4577

Equipped with 1-Light Mogul Socket with 3-Way Turn-Knob Switch located in Flaring Ornamental, Torchere Reflector Holder. Aladdin Torchere Reflector No. T-161 only, Adaptable.
54½″ High to Top of Torchere Reflector Holder.
Oxidized Bronze or Silver and Gold Finish
10″ Ornamental Torchere Reflector No. T-161 Shown.

Aladdin All-Metal Smoking Stand No. 7548

As illustrated above. In Serpentine Design of one-piece cast metal spindle and base. Heavy pressed steel plate and ornate handle. Deep flanged 7″ Ivory Alacite removable tray. Three finishes: Oxidized Bronze, Colonial Brass or Two-Tone Silver and Gold
25½″ High.

(11)

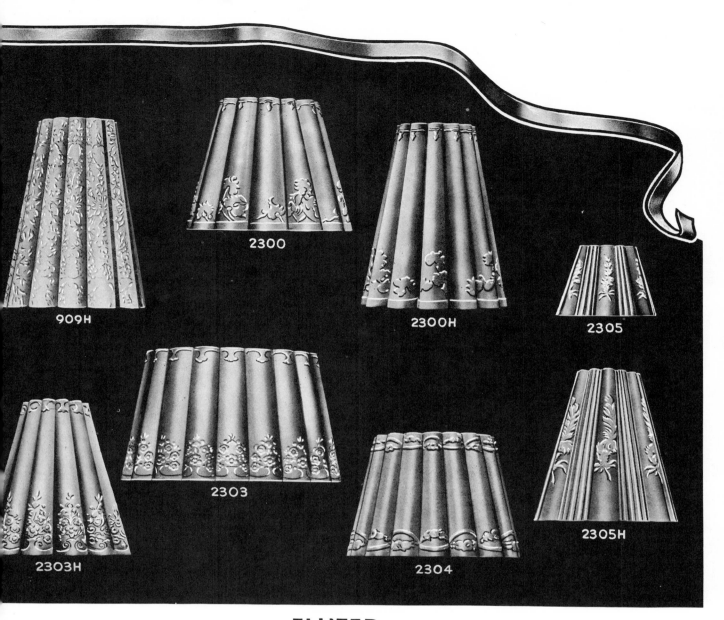

909H

2300

2300H

2305

2303

2303H

2304

2305H

FLUTED
Aladdin *Electric* Lamp Shades
Parvelour Decorated Whip-o-lite

No. 909H

As is shown above. In Parvelour decorated and Fluted Whip-o-lite. In 12″ washer fitter size only (5″x12″x12¾″ high). In 4 colors—Rose, White, Blue or Tan. Especially designed for Table Lamps Nos. G-186, G-212 or G-243.

No. 2300

Pictured in illustration above. In Parvelour Decorated and Fluted Whip-o-lite. In 12″ size, both bridge and washer fitter; 13″, 14″ and 18″ washer fitter only in White or Tan. Also in 17″ size, in White, Rose, Blue or Tan especially for Table Lamp G-236 and G-233.

No. 2300H

Of same design as No. 2300 pictured above, and in Parvelour decorated Whip-o-lite. In 12″ size (5″x12″x12¾″ high) washer fitter only. In White, Blue or Tan. Especially designed for Table Lamps G-186, G-212 or G-243.

No. 2303

Illustrated above, of Fluted Parvelour decorated Whip-o-lite. In one size only—18″ and is available in choice of 3 colors: White, Blue or Tan.

No. 2303H

Of same design as No. 2303 illustrated above, and in Fluted Parvelour decorated Whip-o-lite. In 12″ size (5″x12″x12¾″ high) washer fitter only, in White, Blue or Tan. Especially designed for G-186, G-212 or G-243.

No. 2304

As is illustrated above, of Fluted Parvelour decorated Whip-o-lite. In 12″ regular bridge fitter; also 13″, 14″, 16″ and 18″ in washer fitter. In Variegated colors only.

No. 2304H

Of same design as No. 2304, of Fluted Parvelour decorated Whip-o-lite. In 12″ size, (5″x12″x12¾″ high) in Variegated colors. Especially designed for Table Lamps Nos. G-186, G-212 and G-243.

No. 2305

As is shown in illustration above, of Fluted Parvelour decorated Whip-o-lite. In 8″ size (clamp fitter) and in 12″ washer fitter, and 14″ washer fitter. In 4 colors—Rose, White, Blue or Tan. Also 18″ washer fitter in White or Tan. Also as Bed Lamp No. 2305SS.

No. 2305H

Of same design as No. 2305, of Fluted Parvelour decorated Whip-o-lite. In 12″ size (5″x 12″x12¾″ high) washer fitter, in 4 colors—White, Blue, Rose or Tan. Made especially for Table Lamps Nos. G-186, G-212 and G-243.

(19)

GIVE YOUR HOME A "Lift"

2063
2064
2068
2065
G34
G35
G375
B469
G251
2060
G252
2062
2061
G253
G254
G255
G256
S465
2306H
G257
G258

New 1942 Aladdin Electric Table Lamps
In Characteristic Beauty and Refinement

DESIGN No. G-251
As illustrated, in Genuine Alacite in Ivory or Alacite decorated in Rose or Blue. 1-Light push-thru Socket, harp and finial. 18″ high. 10″ Whip-o-lite Shade No. 2068 shown.

DESIGN No. G-252
Shown above, in Genuine Alacite in Ivory or Alacite decorated in Rose, Blue or Tan. 1-Light push-thru socket, harp and finial. 22″ high. 12″ Whip-o-lite Shade No. 2065 shown.

DESIGN No. G-253
As illustrated, in Genuine Alacite in Ivory or Alacite decorated in Rose or Blue. 1-Light push-thru socket, harp and finial. 20¼″ high. 12″ Whip-o-lite Shade No. 2060 shown.

DESIGN No. G-254
ILLUMINATED BASE
As shown in Genuine Alacite in Ivory, or Alacite decorated Blue or Tan. One 3-way turn-knob switch socket, harp and finial. 23⅜″ high. 16″ Fabric Shade No. B-469 shown.

DESIGN No. G-255
ILLUMINATED BASE
Shown above, in Genuine Ivory Alacite or Alacite decorated Blue or Tan. One 3-way turn-knob switch socket, harp and finial. 20¼″ high. 14″ Whip-o-lite Shade No. 2061 shown.

DESIGN No. G-256
As shown above, in Genuine Alacite in Ivory, or decorated Alacite in Rose or Tan. One Light push-thru socket, harp and finial. 21½″ high. 14″ Shade No. 2062 in Whip-o-lite shown.

DESIGN No. G-257
ILLUMINATED BASE
Illustrated at left, in Genuine Alacite in Ivory, or decorated Alacite in Blue or Tan. One 3-way turn-knob switch socket, harp and finial. 17½″ high. 14″ Fabric Shade No. S-465 shown.

DESIGN No. G-258
ILLUMINATED BASE
As shown at left. Same as G-257 above, except with high harp to accommodate No. 2306H high fluted Whip-o-lite Shade. 22¾″ high.

ALADDIN BOUDOIR LAMPS
DESIGN No. G-34
Illustrated upper left. In one-piece with patented hollow blown pedestal in Genuine Alacite in Ivory, or decorated Alacite in Rose, Blue or Tan. One-Light push-thru socket. 15½″ high. Shown with 8″ Empire Whip-o-lite Shade Design No. 2063.

DESIGN No. G-35
As is shown at upper left. In one-piece, with patented hollow blown pedestal in Genuine Alacite in Ivory or decorated Ivory in Rose or Blue. 15″ high. Illustrated with 7″ Empire Whip-o-lite Shade No. 2064.

Aladdin Decorative Lighted Ur[n]
DESIGN No. G-375
In a most artistic and realis[tic] representation of dancing figure[s] In Genuine Alacite in Ivory o[r] with Gold plated metal ba[se] One Light socket and push[-] switch in base.

INDEX